CW00660795

Origins, Invention, Revision

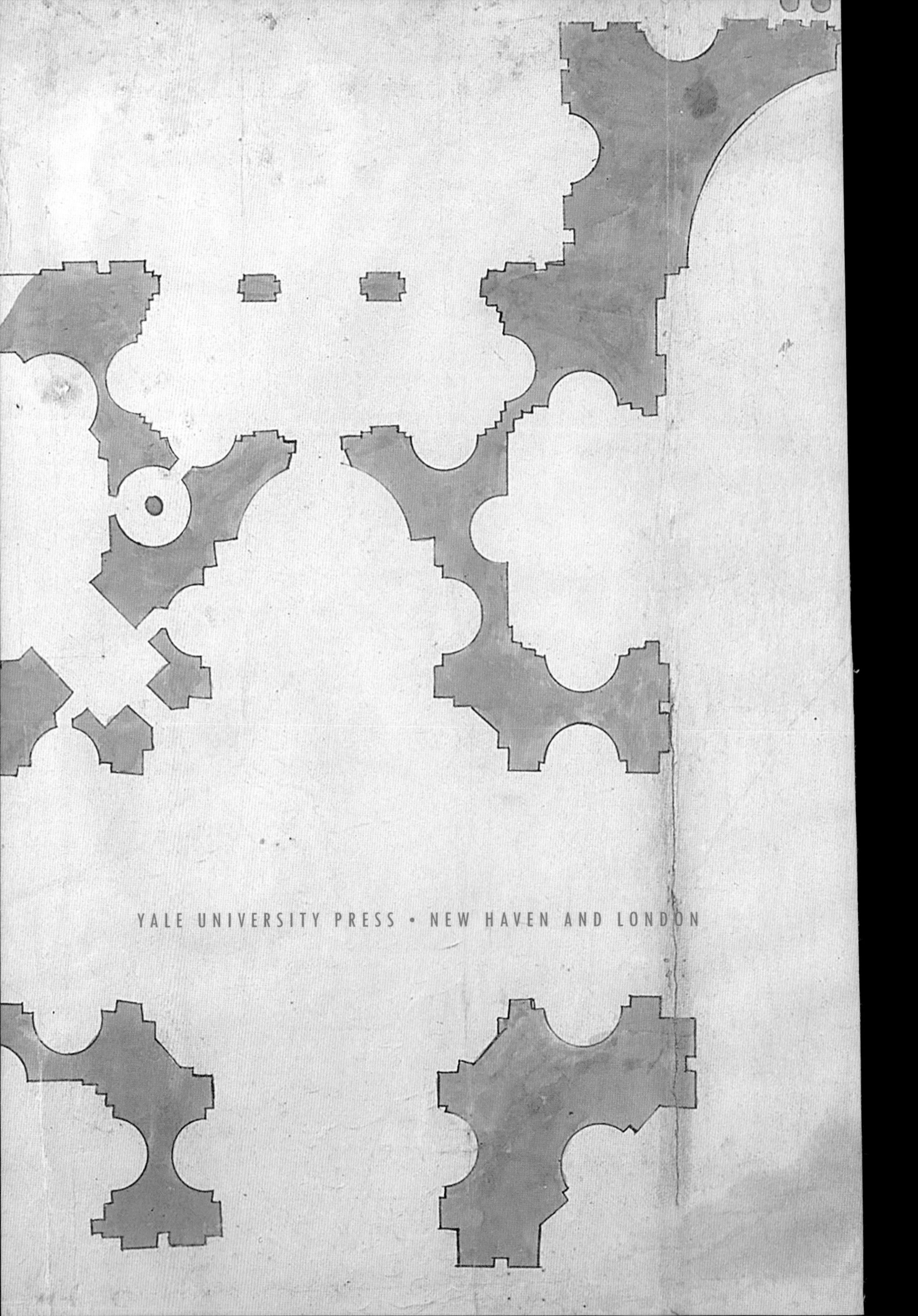

YALE UNIVERSITY PRESS • NEW HAVEN AND LONDON

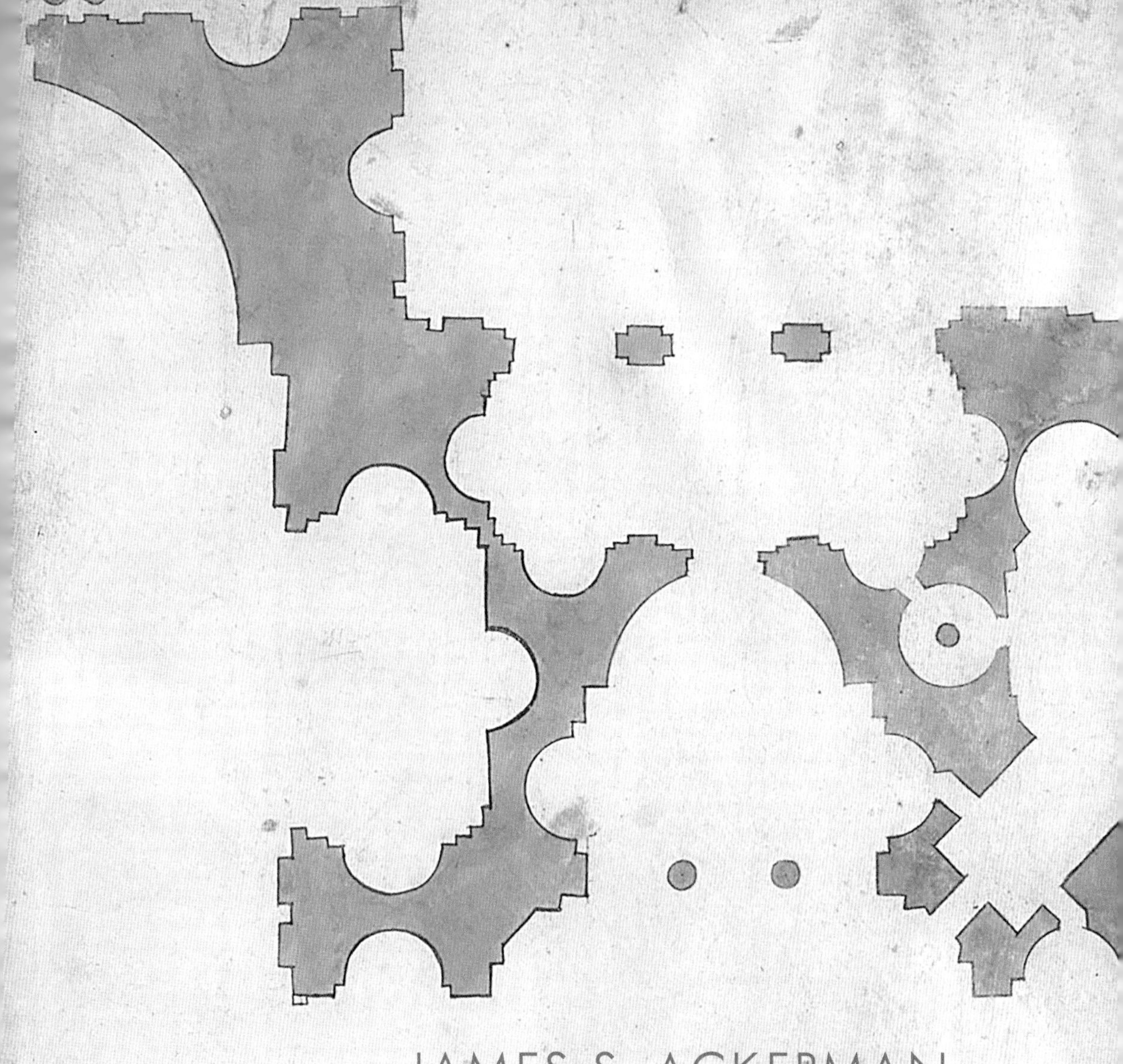

JAMES S. ACKERMAN

Origins, Invention, Revision

STUDYING THE HISTORY OF ART AND ARCHITECTURE

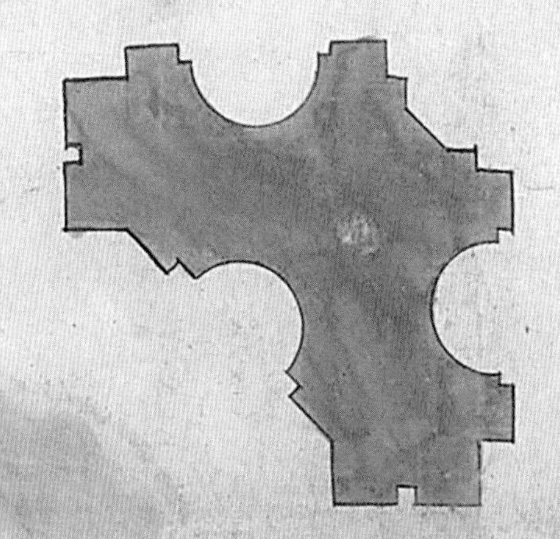

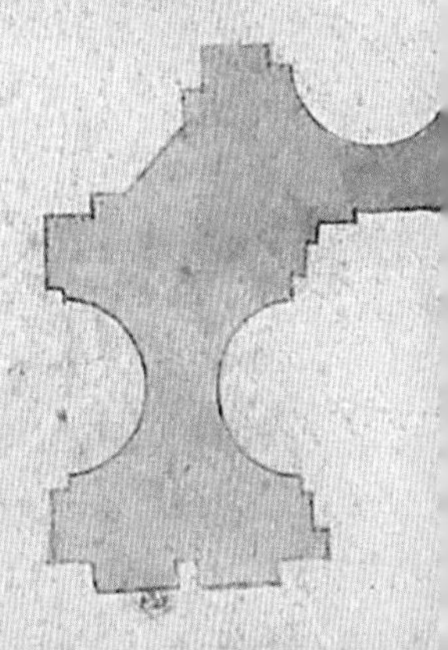

ON THE ORIGINS OF ART HISTORY
Originally published in *Studi in onore di Guilio Carlo Argan*, Florence, 1994

LA FONDATION LOUIS VUITTON
Originally published in *Frank Gehry: The Foundation Louis Vuitton*, Orléans, France, 2014

THE PHOTOGRAPHIC PICTURESQUE
Originally published in *Artibus et Historiae*, no, 48, 2003
Republished in *Composite Landscapes: Photomontage and Landscape Architecture*, Ostfildern, Germany, 2013

ART AND EVOLUTION
Originally published in *The Nature and Art of Motion*, ed. G. Kepes, New York, 1965

Printed in China

Library of Congress Cataloging-in-Publication Data

Names: Ackerman, James S., author.
Title: Origins, invention, revision : studying the history of art and architecture / James S. Ackerman.
Description: New Haven : Yale University Press, 2016. | Includes bibliographical references and index.
Identifiers: LCCN 2016013701 | ISBN 9780300218718 (hardback)
Subjects: LCSH: Ackerman, James S. | Art. | Architecture. | BISAC: ART / Criticism & Theory. | ARCHITECTURE / Criticism. | HISTORY / Historiography. | HISTORY / Social History.
Classification: LCC N7483.A29 A29 2016 | DDC 700 – dc23
LC record available at http://lccn.loc.gov/2016013701

A catalogue record for this book is available from the British Library

Frontispiece Bramante, plan for the new basilica of St. Peter (detail of pl. 7)
Image on p. vi Proposal for San Petronio (detail of pl. 73)
Image on p. viii Sabhamandaraka ceiling of Dharanvihara, Ranakpur, Rajasthan, India. Reproduced courtesy of the American Institute of Indian Studies

For Jill

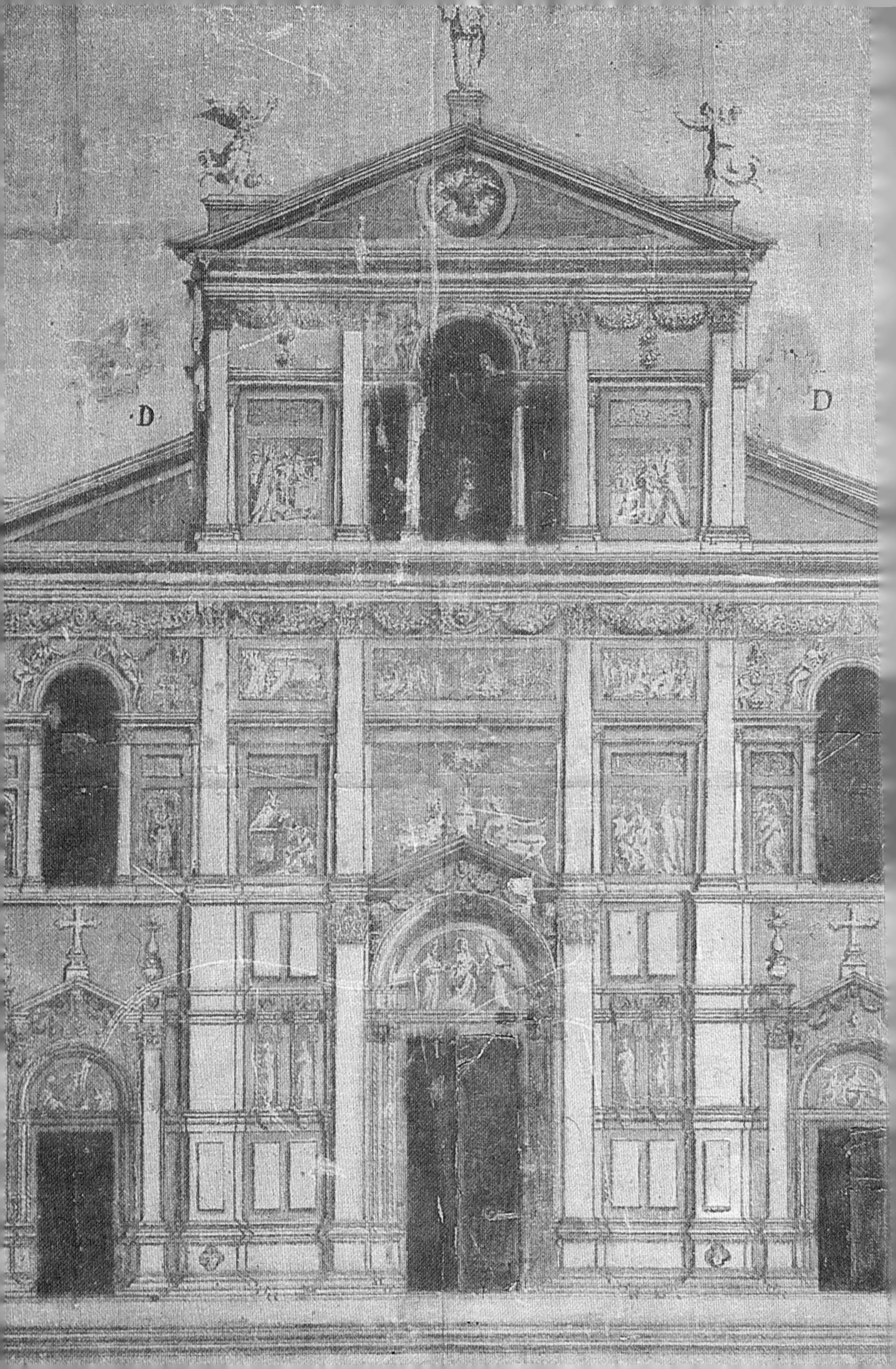
D
D

CONTENTS

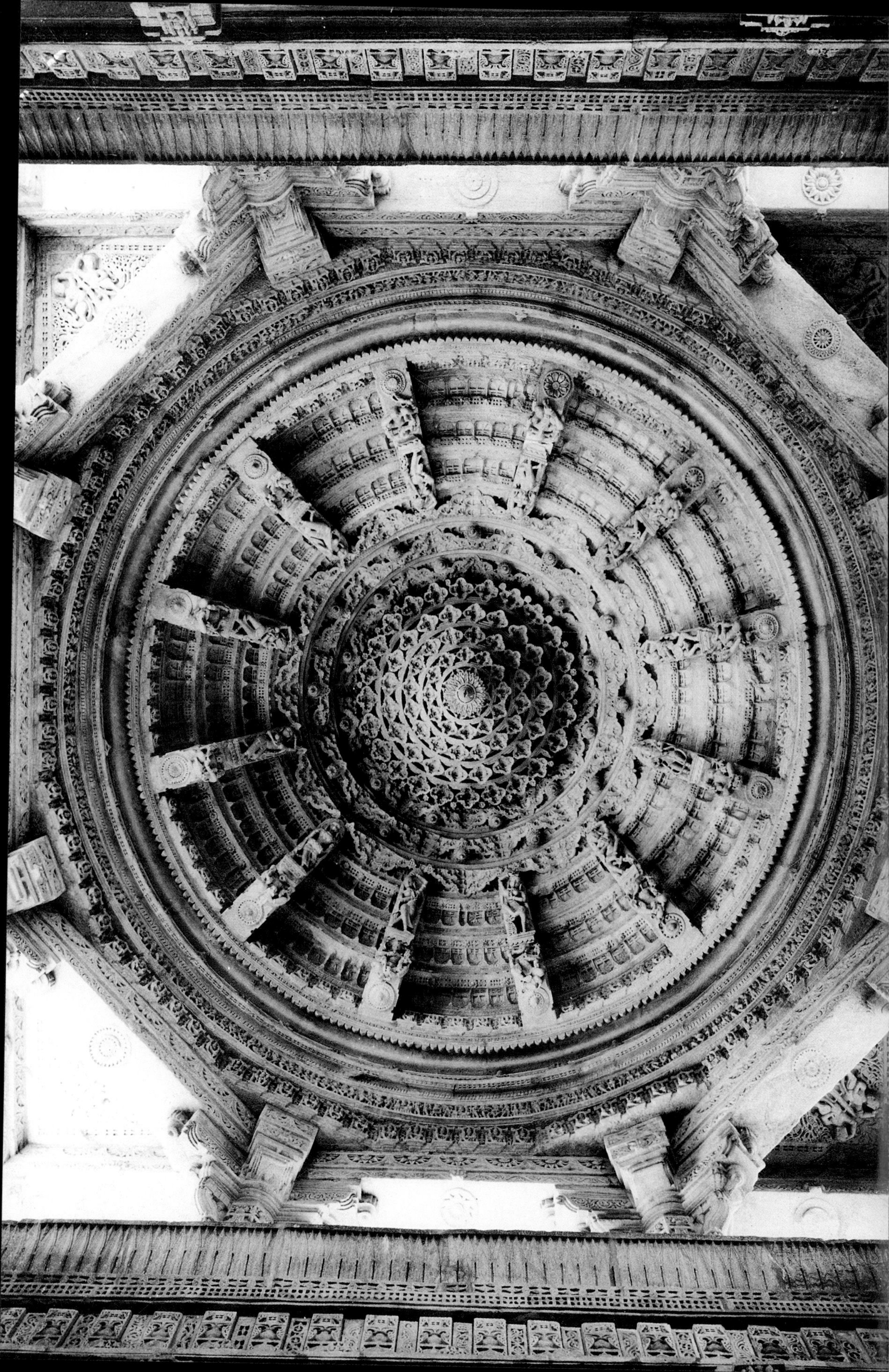

ACKNOWLEDGMENTS

My approach to art history was first influenced by a one-page study in the *Architectural Review* of a villa by Palladio by Georgina Masson (the nom-de-plume of Marion Johnson), and most importantly by the method of my Italian colleagues Michelangelo Muraro and Manfredo Tafuri, pioneers in the analysis of buildings in terms of their social, political, and economical impact.

I am indebted to friends and colleagues for rich exchanges that have informed my thinking and work, among them Gordon Baldwin, Guido Beltramini, Joseph Connors, David Friedman, Ralph Lieberman, Alina Payne, Edward Rothfarb, Scott Schiamberg, and Natasha Staller. And I am especially indebted to my editor, Gillian Malpass, at Yale University Press for her wisdom regarding the contents. A fellowship from the John Simon Guggenheim Memorial Foundation supported some of this work.

Without Somers Killian, my steady, thoughtful, organized assistant, these essays could not have been brought together.

I am thankful to my physicians Drs. Dale Adler and Tammy Hshieh and their staffs, whose expert devoted care made it possible for me to continue my work in the last few years. I am grateful also for my children, Anne, Tony, Sarah, and Jesse, whose presence in my life keeps me from being carried away by my work. And finally, I want to thank my wife, Jill Slosburg-Ackerman, for her insightful editing, but more importantly for the essential conversations that helped to clarify and refine the ideas in these studies.

JANUARY 2016

ILLUSTRATIONS

8 MY PASSAGE TO INDIA

el cielo e la terra

e l dì e la nocte parlano e dichono noi abiano chol nostro veloce
[corso] chondocto alla morte el ducha giuliano e ben giusto che e ne facci vendecta
e la uendecta e questa che auendo noi morto lui lui chosi morto
[a tol]ta la luce a noi e chogli ochi chiusi a serrato e nostri che non ris[plendon]
[piu so]pra la terra che arebbe di noi dunche fatto mentre vive[a]

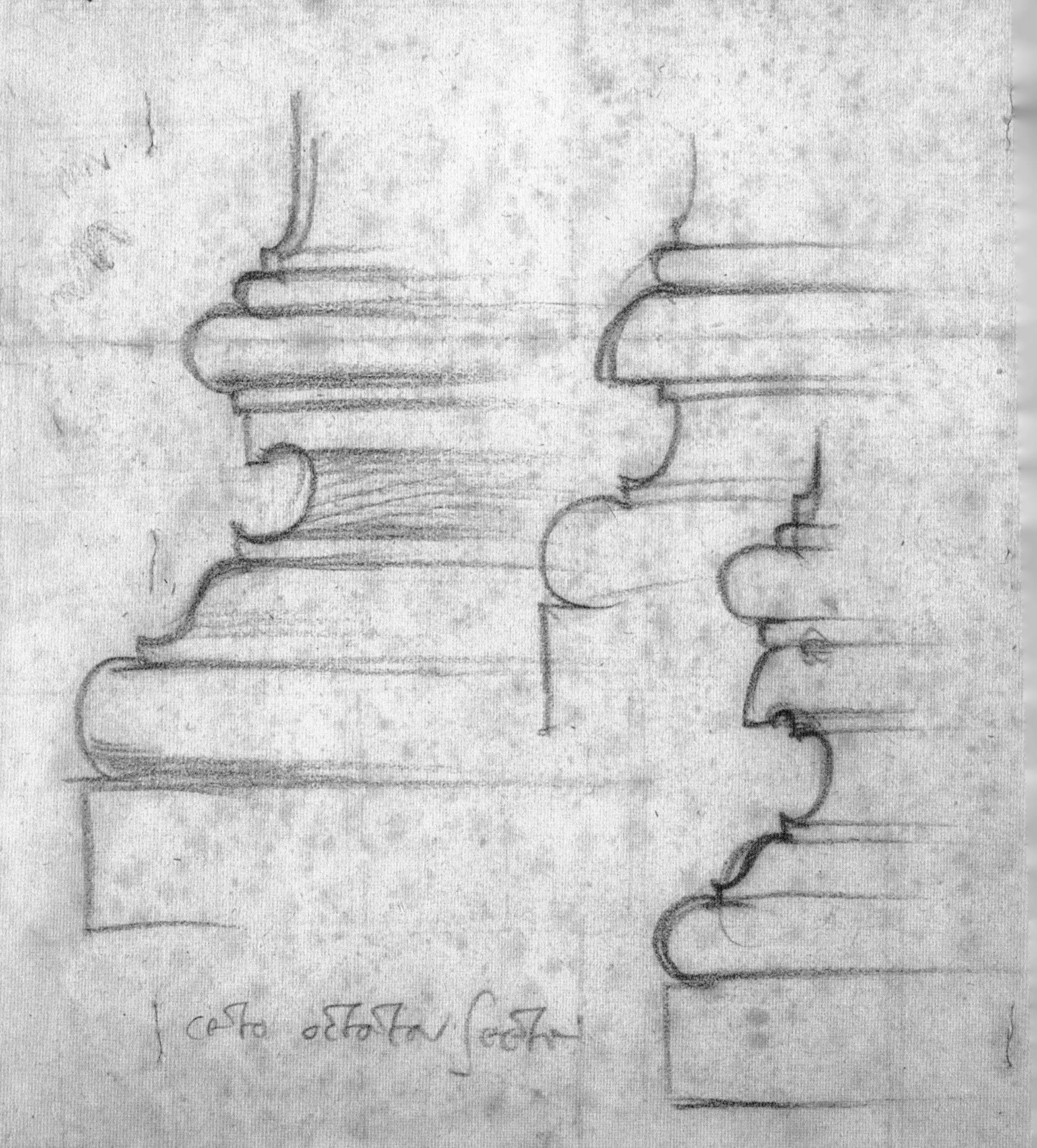

I

The Origins of Sketching

ALTHOUGH FIGURAL ARTISTS BEGAN TO SKETCH in the fourteenth century, the first descriptions of sketching appeared in print only in the mid-1500s, in Giorgio Vasari's *Le vite dei più eccellenti pittori, scultori e architettori* (1550, revised edition 1568) and Lodovico Dolce's *Dialogo di pittura* (1557).

> [Vasari] We call sketches a first sort of drawing made to find the kind of poses desired and the first composition of the work: they are made in the form of a blot (*macchia*) and are put down by us as a rough draft of the whole. Because they are executed hastily, with the passion (*furor*) of the maker, in a short time, with a pen or other tool or charcoal, only to test the spirit of what is intended, they are called sketches.

> [Dolce] I would also like to warn the painter not to be satisfied with a single invention when it comes to trying out in his preliminary sketches the imaginative ideas inspired in his mind by the subject matter. I still want to warn you, to choose several of these and then pick out the one which succeeds best, taking into account both the collective and whole and the individual parts.

These statements highlight the initial approach to defining figural elements for use in pictorial composition. Rapid execution and creative intensity distinguish the sketch from more deliberate preparatory drawings. Its function

Detail of pl. 14

for sculpture and architecture is not discussed. The inference that the purpose of sketching is to prepare for a fully realized work deflects attention from the aspect that Vasari calls *furor*, a loosening of control that allows the unpremeditated action of the hand.

I want to examine a variety of impulses that led artists to sketch. This essay itself is a sketch in the form of statements about the origins of sketching. The statement mode may appear arbitrary, but the lack of nuance is often, as in other sketches, an advantage of liberation from convention. I shall discuss three principal kinds of sketches: one that explores, as in Vasari's definition, possible solutions for a particular work; one without a specific goal – an open pursuit of potentialities that may not even represent anything; and one that records an object or occurrence in the external world – a building, a person, landscape, an existing work of art, an event, or something else, with some degree of reliability.

Medieval draftsmen, with certain exceptions, did not sketch freely but made studies for a particular work, or for inclusion in model books intended for use in preparation for future works. Such images are sometimes unfinished: they rarely exhibit the freedom and exploration that modern usage associates with the sketch. There is evidence that medieval architects engraved or scratched architectural or structural elements on the walls or floors (e.g., the north porch of Wells cathedral) of a building while it was being built. The difficulty of incising architectural plans and elevations in stone understandably reduced the spontaneity associated with sketching. While not appearing spontaneous, the incision illustrates a kind of on-site thinking or problem solving.

The rarity of medieval sketches is attributable primarily to the unavailability of inexpensive materials on which to draw. Parchment, the most common material used by medieval draftsmen, was too resistant to the free movement of the hand for painters and architects to engage in experimental imagery. The cost of parchment – as illustrated in some of the pages in the handbook of Villard de Honnecourt from the thirteenth-century workshop of Reims cathedral, presumably after the master architect (pl. 1) – led draftsmen and scribes to attempt to scrub away preexisting designs or texts, not always entirely successfully, as this image shows. In one instance, an architectural detail incised in the wall of the Gothic basilica of St. Quentin in northern France illustrates the practice of turning the stones of the building into a drawing surface.

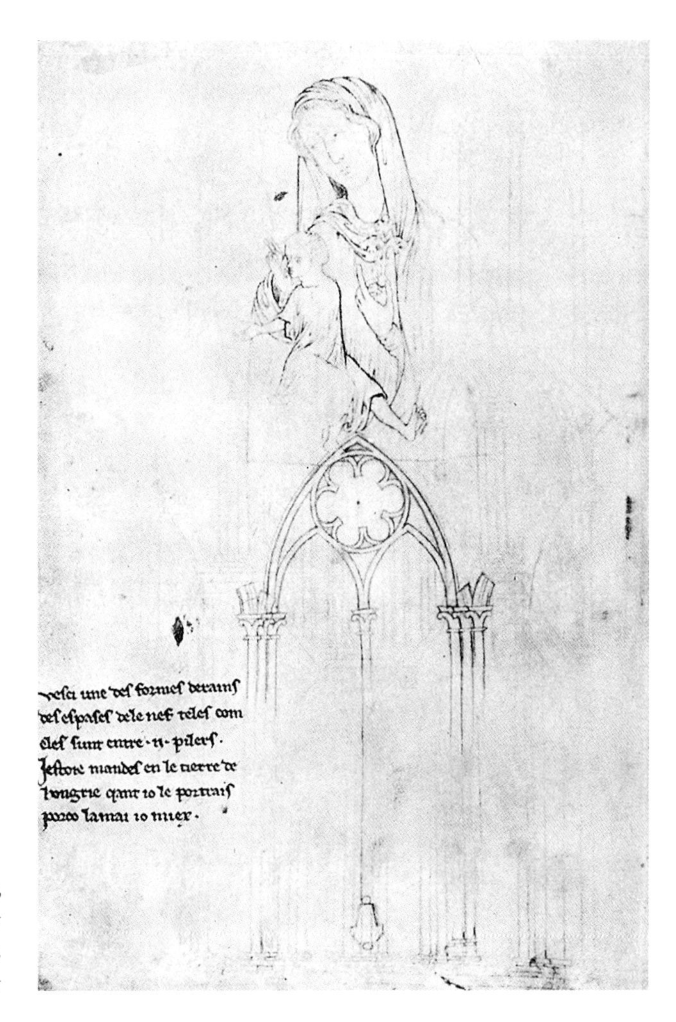

1 Villard de Honnecourt, drawing of a clerestory window from Reims cathedral, thirteenth century

Prior to the widespread availability of rag paper, which was first manufactured in the western world at the close of the fourteenth century, artists occasionally found surfaces upon which to sketch experimentally without predetermined aims. While fresco painters often drew at full scale the composition of a large mural using a monochrome medium on the smooth plaster *intonaco* applied to the wall, they or their apprentices sometimes used the rough surface on which this was laid for experimental freehand sketches. An example was discovered when a fresco by the Veronese painter Altichiero (1369–d. before 1393) was peeled from the wall for restoration (pl. 2),

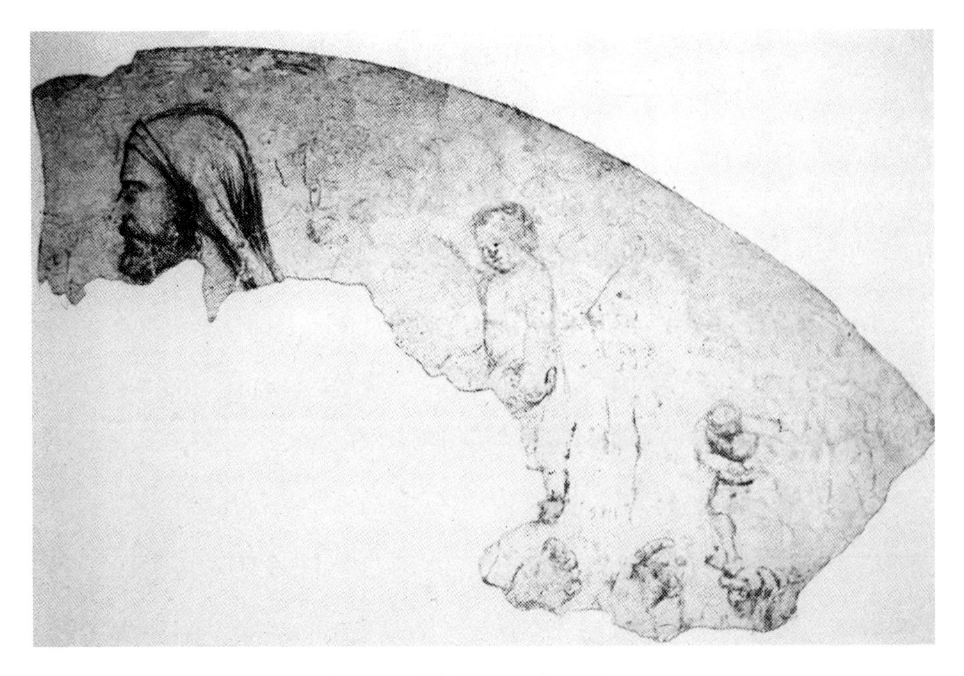

2 Altichiero, fresco fragment, Castelvecchio, Verona, late 1380s

revealing sketches on the plaster base behind. They represent, without intended order, the relatively finished profile of a man and – less finished – a three-quarters view of the head of a man and a profile of a lion, the full-length figure of a child, a foot, two hands, two men wrestling with a man behind them, and a (?)rope curled in a spiral. This example gives the impression of being executed more for recreation than for exploration, probably by apprentices.

But material explanations of the origins of sketching are insufficient. Mural surfaces would have been available to early medieval painters but were not used because at that time the concept of what it meant to make a work of art differed from that of later periods. Art in the medieval west meant craft, and concepts of self-expression, artistic experiment, and recording visual experiences did not yet exist.

The painter Pisanello (1395–1455), who, like Altichiero, was a citizen of Verona, could qualify as the inventor of modern sketching. He continued the tradition of the pattern book composed of nature studies, but his vital inter-

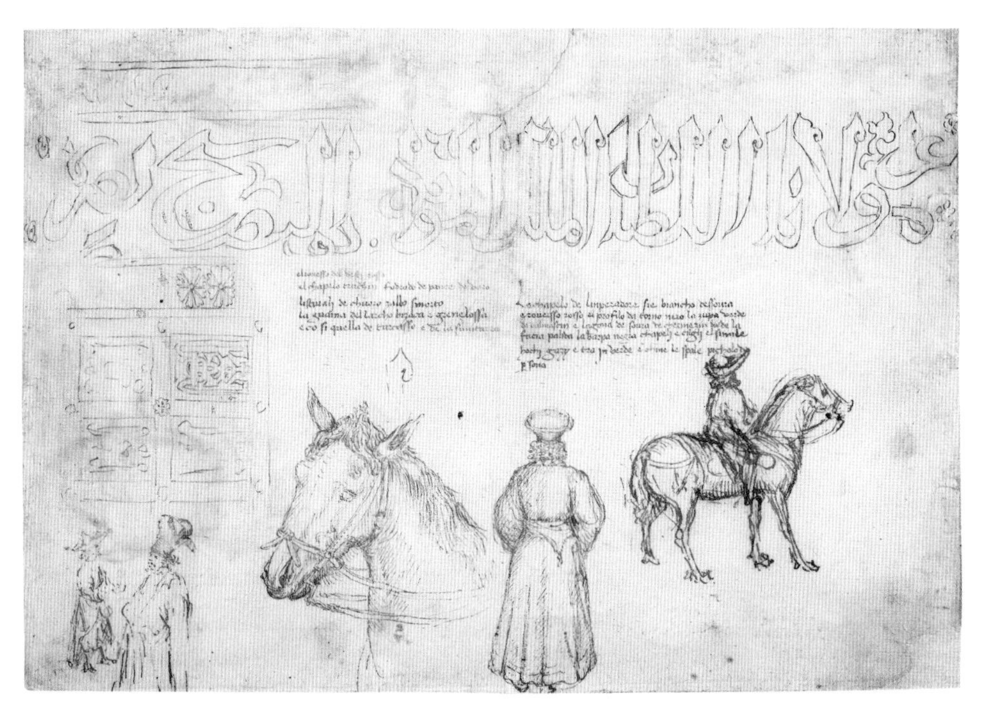

3 Pisanello, sketches of the costumes of the riders and harnesses of the horses of the Patriarch of Constantinople attending the council of Ferrara, 1438

est in the world about him led him to new subjects, new observations, and new means of recording them.

Pisanello was the author of the first drawn, on-site description of a current event in history (pl. 3), documenting the visit of the Patriarch of Constantinople and the Byzantine emperor, John VIII Paleologus, to the Council of Ferrara at its inauguration in 1438. It is the closest Renaissance artists ever came to what is now called photo-journalism, which is to say that its principal purpose was to produce a record of an event – primarily for the artist's use in future paintings. Pisanello was intrigued by the dress of the visitors, the horses' harnesses, and the exotic Arabic inscriptions. Since he drew with a pen, he could not record the vivid color or the texture of the costumes, and had to resort to words, which he jotted in the empty space: "The hat of the emperor should be white on top and red underneath, the profile black all around, the doublet of green damask, and the mantle on top crim-

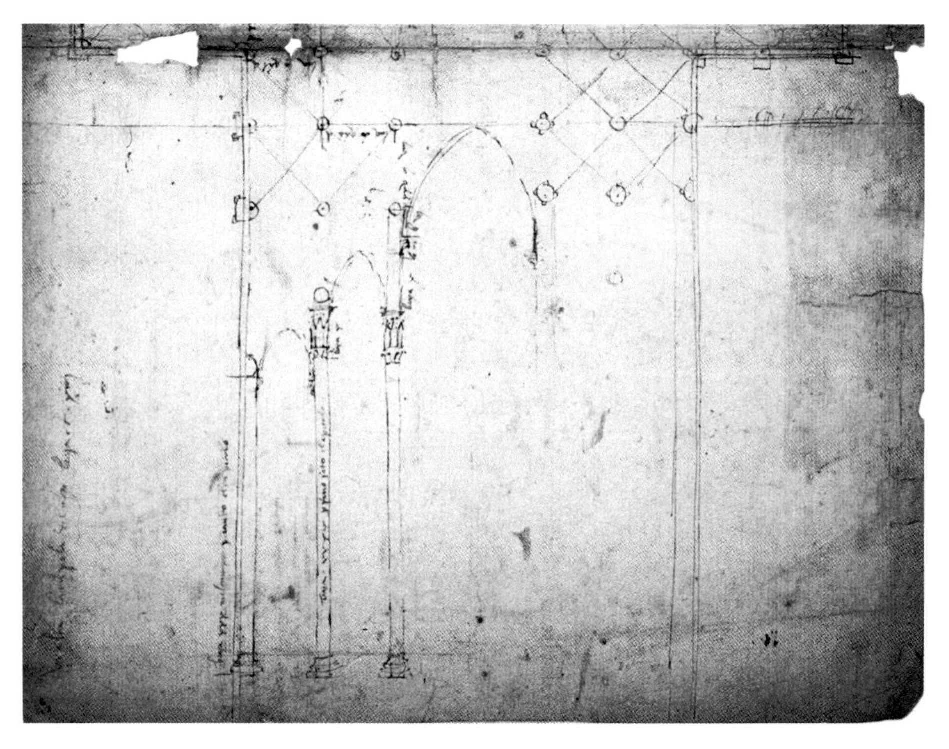

4 Antonio di Vincenzo, plan of Milan cathedral, *c.*1390

son. A black beard on a pale face, hair and eyebrows alike." He did make a medal with the bust of the emperor in the following year, but these drawings were not directed toward its design. The sheet illustrates the importance of paper; the artist could hardly have made his notes in the street on parchment, which was not suited to binding into sketchpads. This ancestor of modern pictorial recording of current events bore no fruit in Italy. The classical bias of Renaissance culture scorned topical mimesis of the sort, which was revisited only a century and a half later.

Many Renaissance and later architectural sketches represent existing buildings, primarily Roman ones that gave authority and inspiration to new projects. But a sheet from about 1390 by Antonio di Vincenzo, recording the plan and section of the cathedral of Milan (pl. 4), is one of the few examples of a medieval representation of a building still in the early stages of construction. Antonio recorded the project for use in the construction of the church of

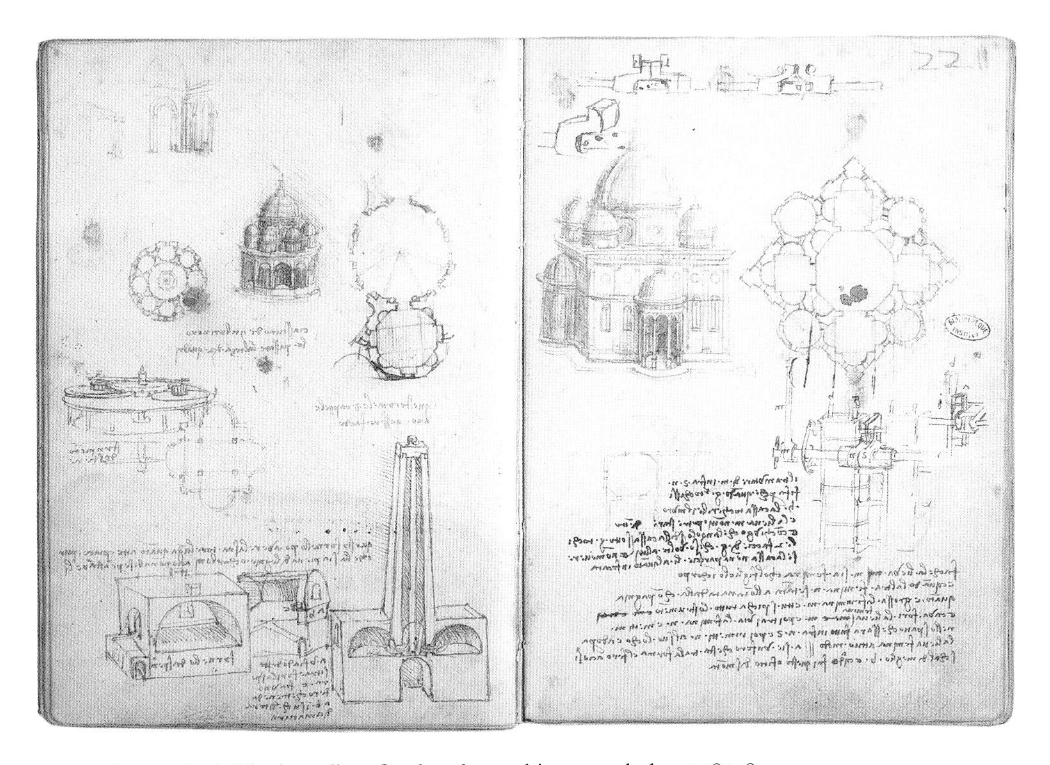

5 Leonardo da Vinci, studies of a church, machinery, and plan, 1485–8

San Petronio in Bologna, where he served as the head of the Fabbrica. This drawing, though done by an accomplished architect, foreshadows the practice in Renaissance studios of requiring apprentices to copy drawings and paintings of the masters of the past, exemplified in Michelangelo's copies of figures from frescos by Giotto and Masaccio.

There was hardly a moment in the centuries that followed when architects did not make sketches of the Roman buildings that they found most relevant to their own interests. The invention of photography did not much diminish this activity. Apart from the architect's capacity to interpret a building with an idiosyncratic emphasis, or distortion, he/she can record much more than the photograph: for example, showing in the same drawing both the interior and exterior, or the plan and elevation, of a building.

Leonardo da Vinci was the quintessential master of the sketch (pl. 5). He was, moreover, the first person known to have used the verb "to sketch" when

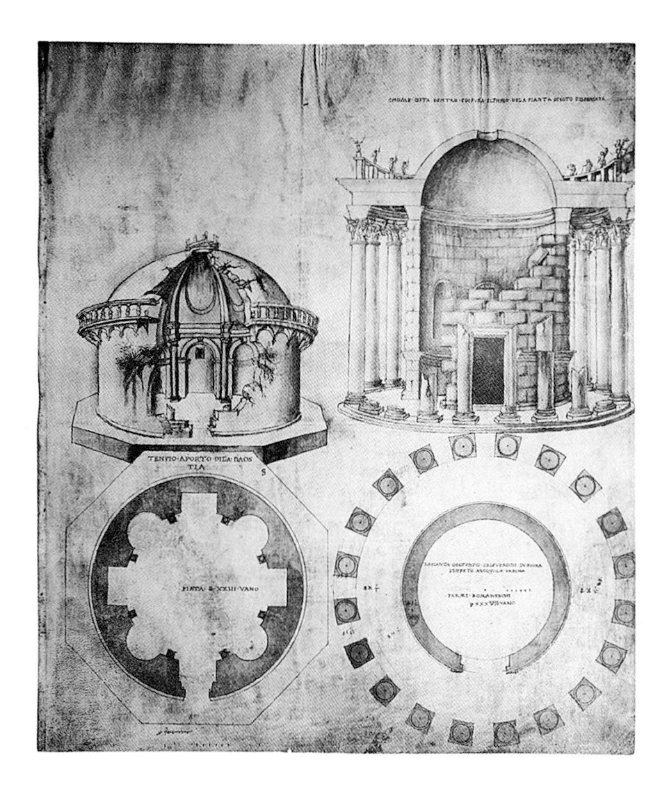

6 Giuliano da Sangallo, the temples of Portunus and Vesta, Rome, 1541

he referred to a notebook of studies for the cartoon of the *Battle of Anghiari* as a "libro di chavalli sc[h]izati pel cartone." Like Vasari, he defined sketching, in his *Treatise on Painting*, as the initial step in preparing paintings: "The sketching (*bozzar*) out of the narratives should be rapid, and the arrangement of the limbs not too defined but merely confined to a suggestion of their disposition. Later, at your leisure, you can finish them to your liking."

In practice, Leonardo's sketching was the way he studied nature, solved problems, developed compositions, and fantasized. He rarely meant his sketches to be seen by others, though some were developed into intended illustrations of treatises, particularly the ones on anatomy and mechanics.

Round buildings seen in perspective first appeared toward the end of the fifteenth century. A drawing from an album by Giuliano da Sangallo, the architect of Lorenzo de' Medici, ruler of Florence (pl. 6), was still on parchment, but it contained representations – in part imaginary – of Roman temples in a way that reveals both the exterior and the interior.

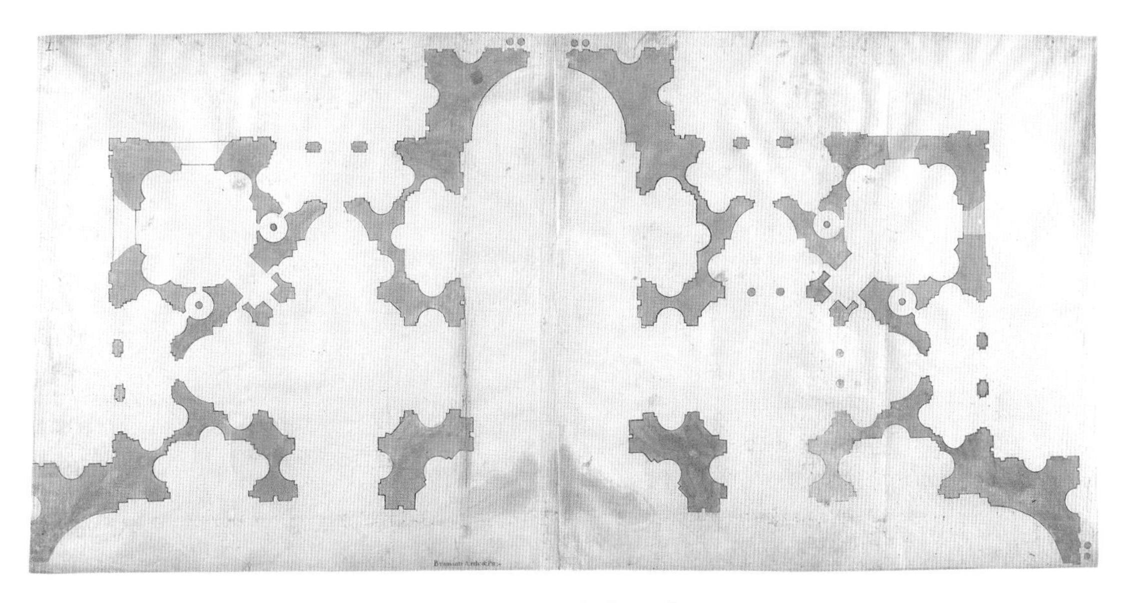

7 Donato Bramante, plan for the new basilica of St. Peter, Rome, 1505

Leonardo and the Sienese architect Francesco di Giorgio were the first to use paper extensively for architectural drawings. Most of the churches drawn by Leonardo in his Manuscript B have centralized plans. None of these was built, indeed none was developed beyond a preliminary phase that could not have been built, lacking scale and measurements. While he received one unrealized commission to design a villa, he was never asked to design a church, although he seriously pursued possible forms for one. In his perspective views, he never adopted the classical vocabulary used by all of his contemporaries; yet this plan in MS B introduced a prophetic vision of a new architecture with cupolas supported by molded piers, one that was realized only a few years later in Bramante's project for St. Peter in the Vatican (pl. 7).

Bramante had been in contact with Leonardo in Milan at the close of the fifteenth century, and Bramante's initial thoughts about St. Peter's reveal a similarly innovative modeling of mass and space. It was in the Fabbrica of St. Peter that modern architectural drawing was developed. The documentation of his thinking process in the sketches on this sheet is of a kind that remained the same throughout the centuries, despite radical shifts in style and material.

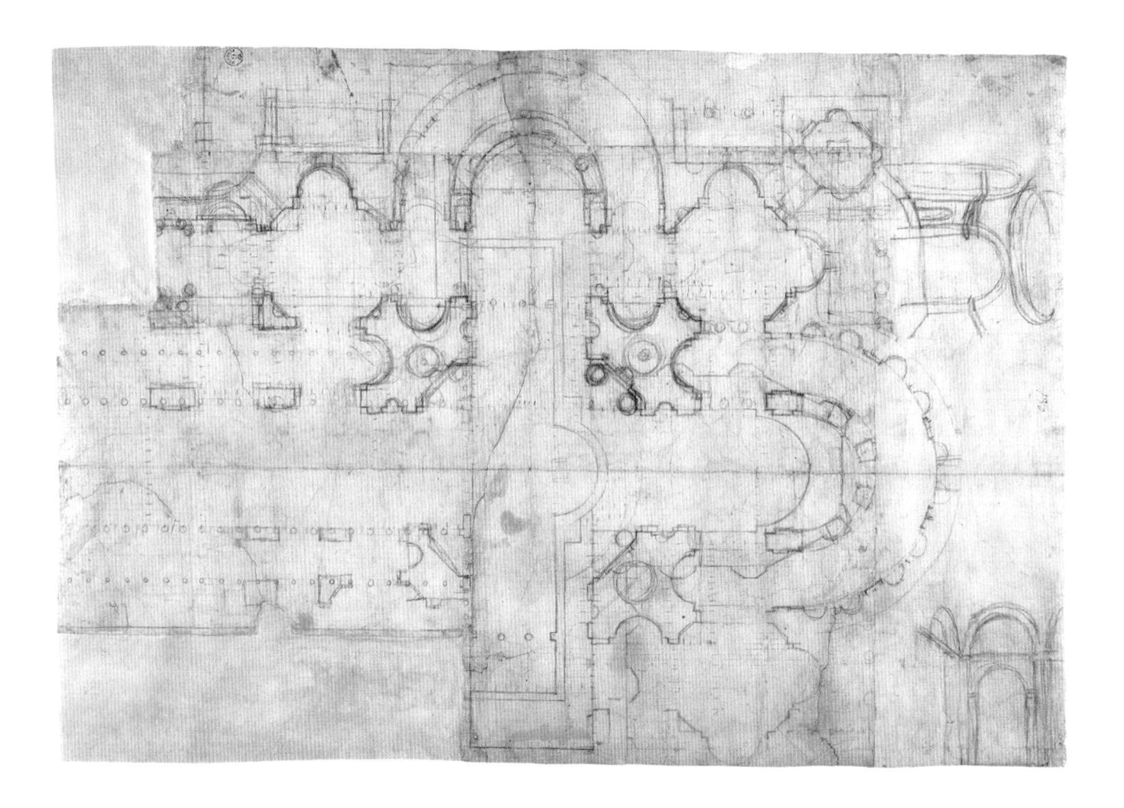

These drawings exemplify the fundamental contrast between architectural and figural sketches: buildings are almost always conceived initially in plan, a convention that determines the way in which the disposition of spaces fulfills the requirements of the program. Plans are abstract representations; they indicate the footprint of a building on the ground. But they cannot reflect irregularities of terrain, responses to which are most often worked out in section drawings that are rarely preserved. Other variations of level, for example in a staircase of the raised choir of a church, have to be indicated all on the same plane. Plans of vaulted buildings normally represent the arches and ribs of the vault in the bays of the floor; with this exception, what is represented in plans is invisible to viewers of actual buildings.

Bramante's fascinating folio (pl. 8) represents the many alternatives that came to his mind in the course of designing the support system for the heaviest dome in the world at St. Peter's. In this drawing each of the piers of the crossing is of a different form.

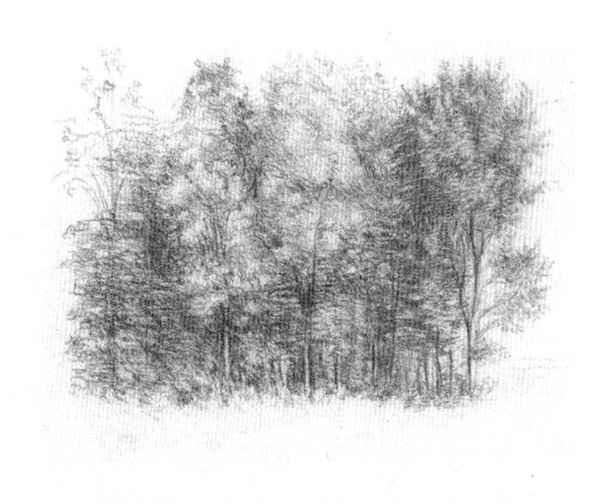

8 (*facing page*) Bramante, plan for the new basilica of St. Peter, 1520

9 Leonardo, sketch of a copse of trees, *c.*1500–10

The type of instrument chosen strongly influenced the vitality of the sketch. Pen and ink, and even more the metal tip of the stylus, produce a fine line, not naturally suited to modulate light and shade. Pencils were not available in the Renaissance; the privileged instrument in the sixteenth century was black chalk (made, as Vasari tells us, from stones found in the hills of France), a kind of pastel, the ancestor of the Conté crayon, which was pressed into sticks and could be sharpened to a point but was capable of producing a broader variety of texture than charcoal.

Shortly after the turn of the fifteenth century a softer alternative, red chalk (made from a German stone which was easily ground and could be sharpened to a fine point) became available and was used with unprecedented effectiveness in certain drawings by Leonardo. A small sketch of a copse of trees (pl. 9) placed in the upper corner on the verso of a sheet with a conventional composition on the recto marks one of the important changes in the history of western art. The trees drawn and painted in the Middles Ages

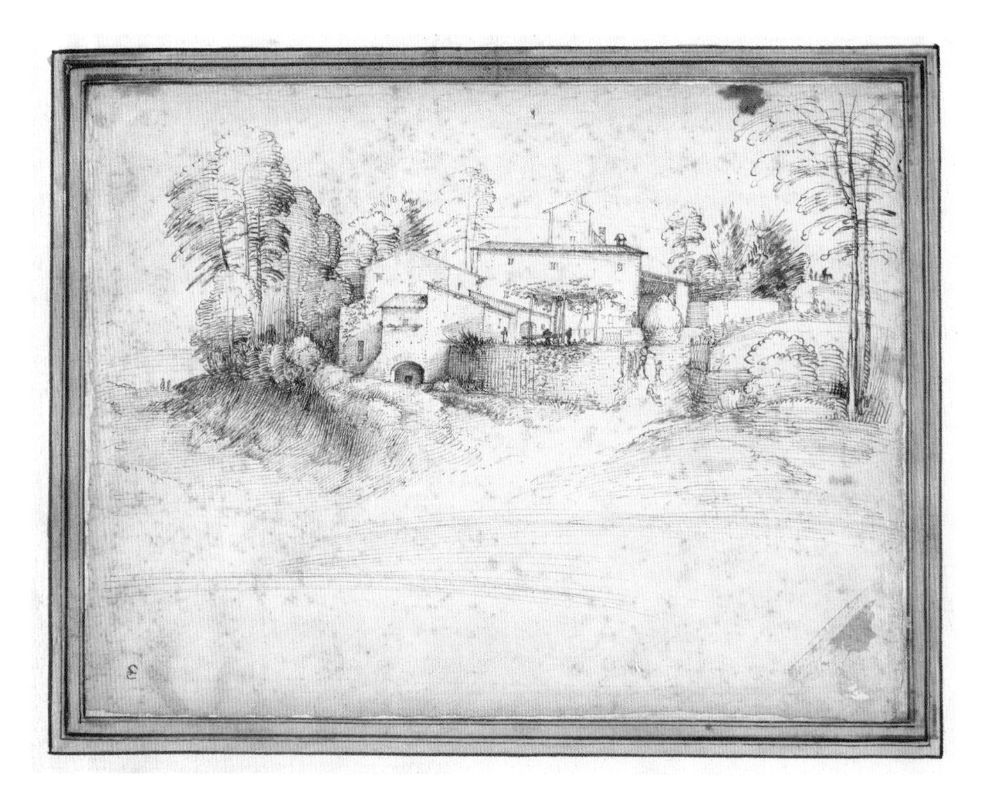

10 Fra Bartolomeo, sketch of a farmhouse on the slope of a hill, *c.*1508

and in the fifteenth century, like those of Fra Angelico and Botticelli – but also those present in an early *Annunciation* by Leonardo – are depicted as individual objects solid enough to be counted. But here Leonardo approached the clump of trees seeking to grasp the visual continuum at a particular time of day, as Monet did 400 years later. The trees are not individual units but are receptors of light and atmosphere. This could not have been achieved without the new license to sketch liberally, which encouraged both the artist and the viewer (who previously might not have been able to observe such qualities in the environment) to seek new visual experiences.

The landscape sketches of Fra Bartolommeo, many of which include rustic buildings and monastic retreats (pl. 10), carried out between the end of the fifteenth century and the beginning of the sixteenth, were unique in the history of the Italian Renaissance. They do not seem to have had a specific

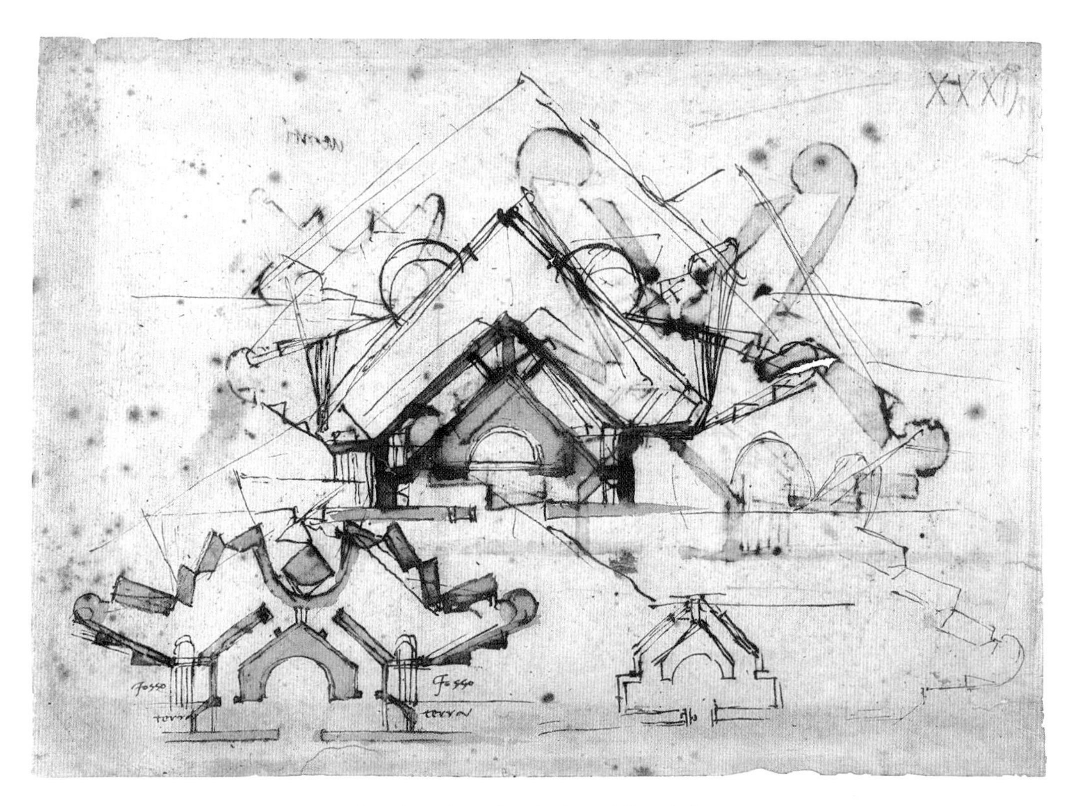

11 Michelangelo, drawing of fortifications for the Republic of Florence, 1529

function. While they could have been planned for use in painting backgrounds of devotional pictures, the fact that only one out of some hundred of his surviving landscape sketches can be recognized in these paintings suggests that they were mainly a record of the pleasure he felt while wandering in the tranquil Tuscan countryside. The landscapes, obviously made on the spot, are more mimetic than those the artist employed in his paintings. During the Renaissance, mimesis, as noted in the discussion of Pisanello's sketches (see pl. 3), had a bad reputation in sixteenth-century art theory; portraits and landscapes were ranked at the lowest levels in the evaluation of genres, and this affected approaches to sketching.

The fortification drawings done by Michelangelo, commissioned by the besieged republic of Florence in 1529 (pl. 11), are unique in the history of architecture. They show open-ended experimentation. The lines representing

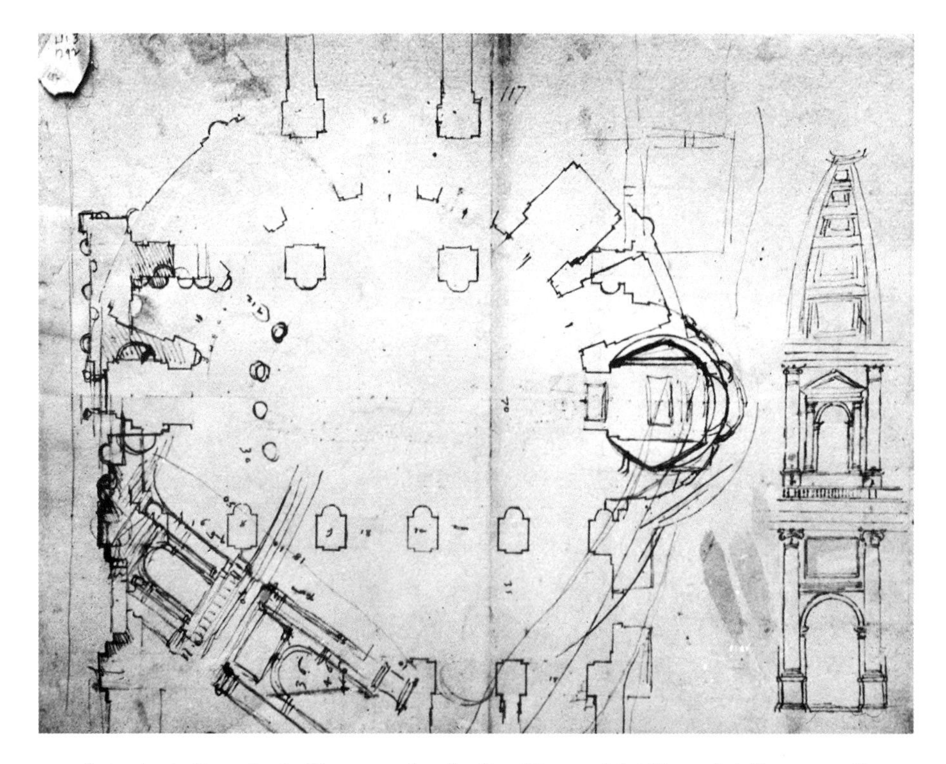

12 Antonio da Sangallo the Younger, plan for San Giovanni dei Fiorentini, Rome, 1518–19

gunfire bursting from the walls reflect the urgency of the situation. Fantastic, prophetic, combining extraordinary vitality with a degree of control, despite the fact that the city was already under fire and in no position to construct masonry bastions that would have taken years and a huge expenditure to build.

The two sketches for a proposed church of San Giovanni de' Fiorentini in Rome by Antonio da Sangallo the Younger and Michelangelo are inventive in very different ways (pls. 12 and 13). The first, made in preparation for a competition submission in 1518–19, reveals Antonio's debt to his mentor Bramante. It ingeniously combines on one sheet a proposal for a longitudinal church with side chapels and a centralized one with a ring of chapels; he later made finished versions of each on separate sheets. He also drew the elevation of a bay of the central-plan versions. Michelangelo's drawing proposes only one solution, but with the aid of ink wash over pen and ink, black chalk and areas of sanguine it employs the variety of techniques and materi-

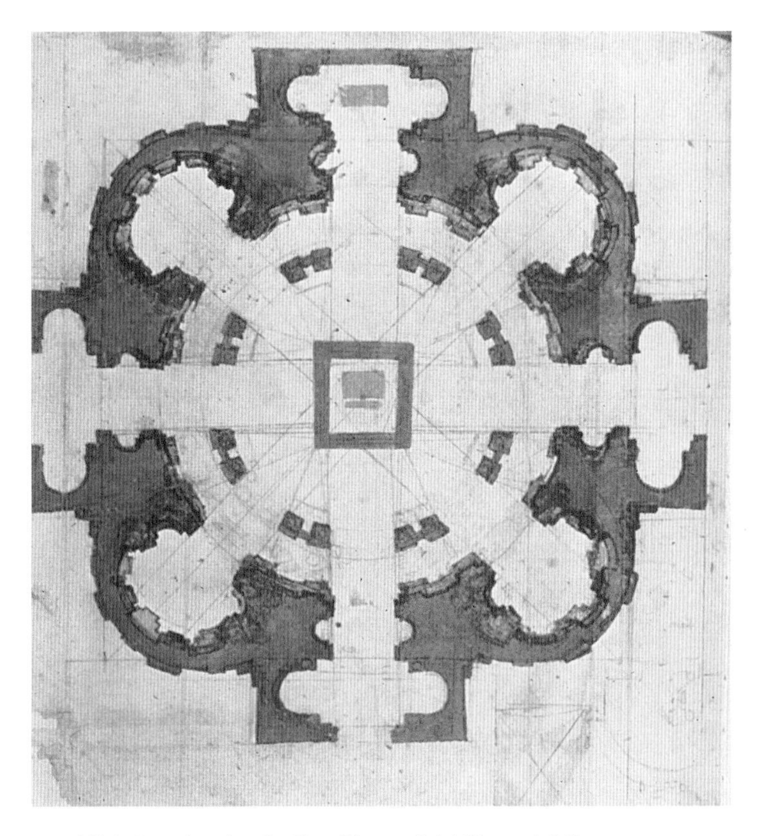

13 Michelangelo, plan for San Giovanni dei Fiorentini, Rome, 1539

als to achieve ends that had not been available before. It eloquently expresses process: the walls seem to pulsate, to be in a state of becoming. In designing architecture, he thinks like a sculptor. As in the fortification of drawings, there are lines that have nothing to with structure, representing in this case visual and conceptual axes.

Michelangelo's approach to architecture was extended to human analogies. In a letter of unknown date and recipient he wrote that the human body is emulated in the symmetry of architecture (nose and mouth centered, and eyes, ears, and limbs duplicated on either side, etc.). In a sketch of the base of a pillar (pl. 14), the addition of an eye draws attention to the similarity of the superimposed molding to the human profile. Eyes also appear on each of the cross-axes of an alternative drawing for San Giovanni dei Fiorentini.

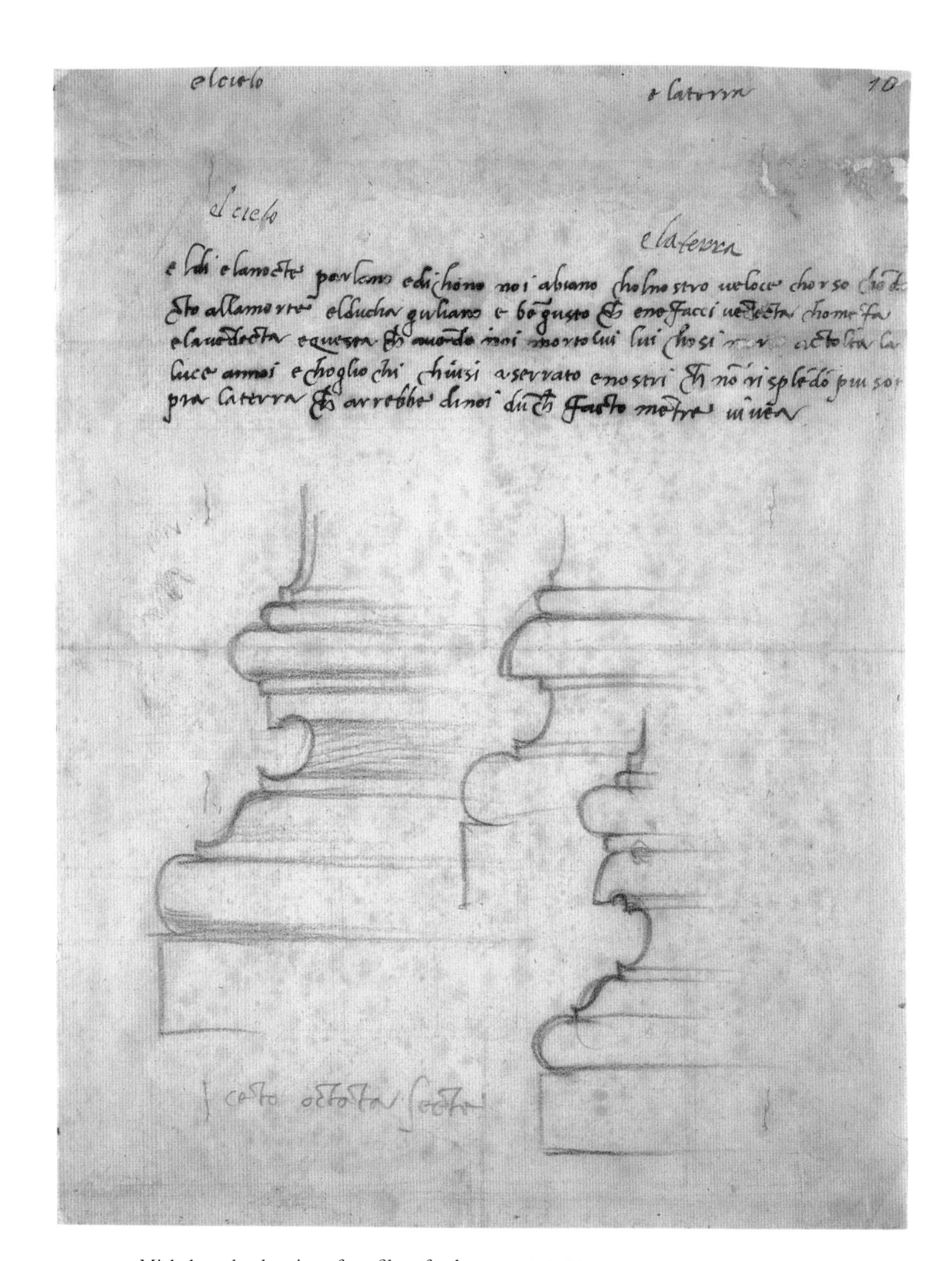

14 Michelangelo, drawing of profiles of columns, 1519–20

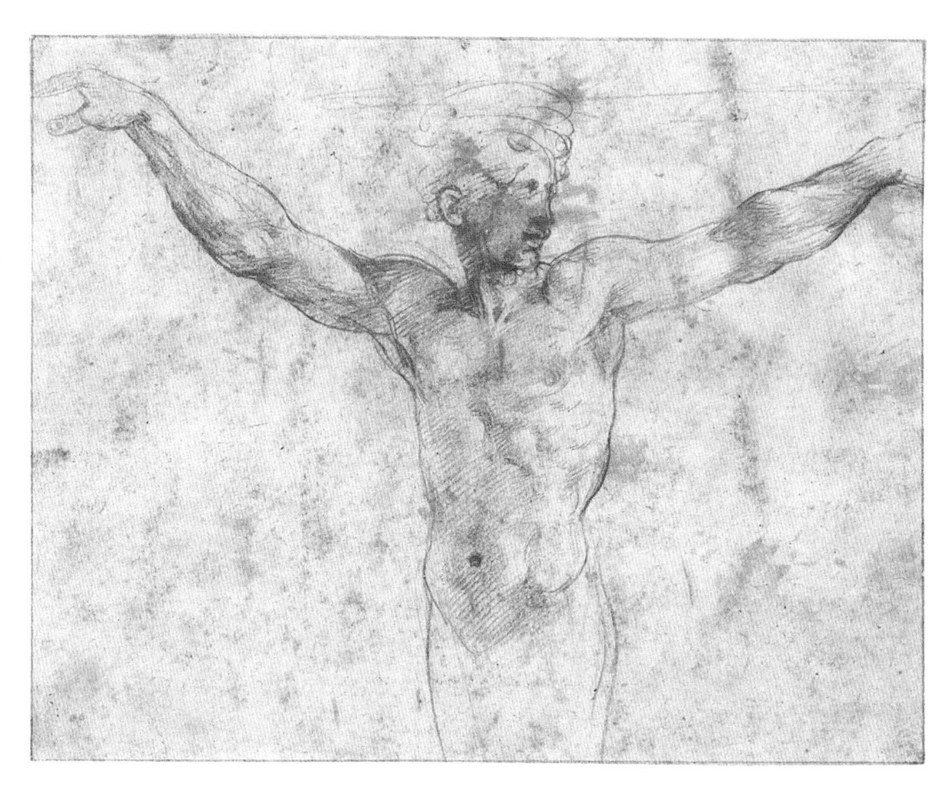

15 Giulio Romano, figure study for the Stanza dell'Incendio, *c.*1516–17

Most painters in the sixteenth century did not draw to explore and experiment freely as Leonardo did. Giulio Romano's study of a figure in the Stanza dell'Incendio (pl. 15) is characteristic in employing sketching primarily to block out compositions or to refine details of composition already organized in his mind. Vasari, in his biography of the artist, emphasized the vivacity of his drawings:

> [One sees] on a sheet of St. Sylvester, which was very well drawn by him and is much more graceful than the painting of the same subject, that Giulio always expressed his ideas better in drawing than in finished work or in paintings, because the former displays more vivacity, spirit and feeling; and that might perhaps occur because one makes a drawing in an hour, full of spirit and immediacy in working, whereas the paintings consumed months and years, so that the latter came to annoy him; and lacking that

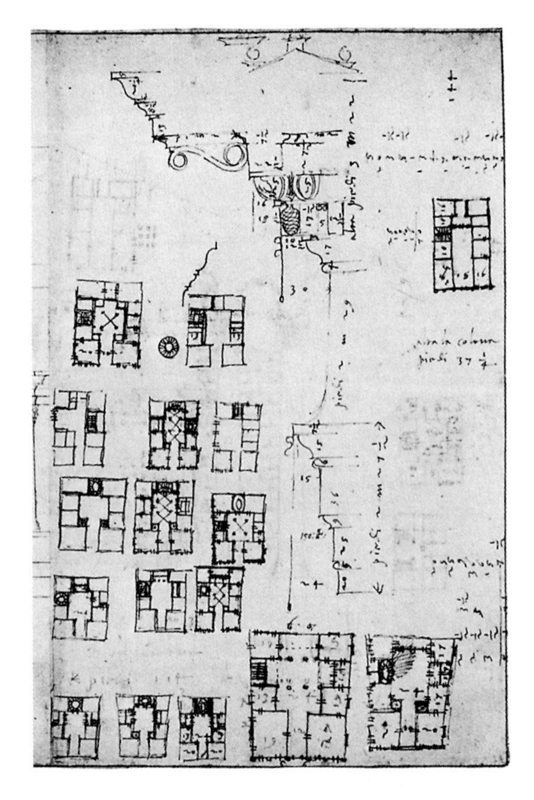

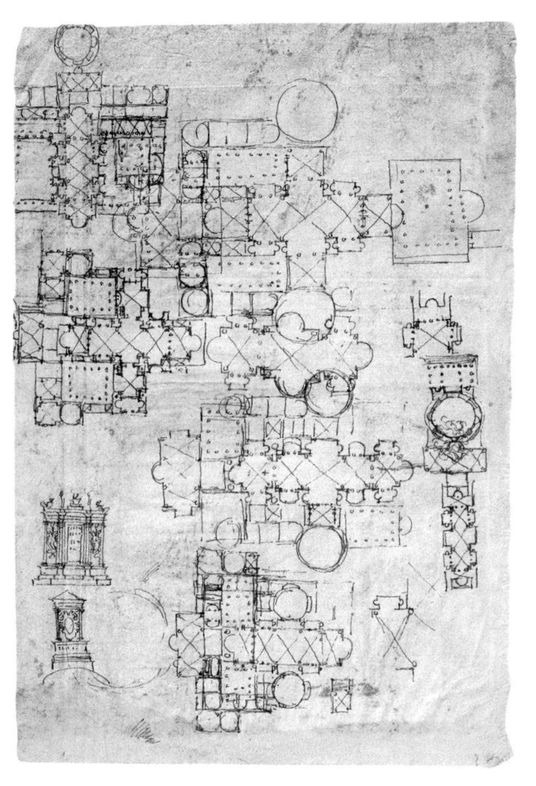

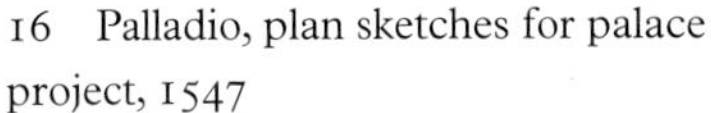

16 Palladio, plan sketches for palace project, 1547

17 Palladio, sketches of a reconstructed plan of the Baths of Agrippa, Rome, 1550

lively and ardent love that one has in beginning anything, it is no wonder that he did not give that complete perfection that one sees in his drawings.

Andrea Palladio, thirty-three years younger then Michelangelo, was the only architect of the period who prepared for his career in a workshop of stonecutters where drawing was not regarded as the foundation of art. His early drawings are rather stiff. But two sheets of sketches represent his acquisition of the skills of freehand sketching in his later years. On the right of a sheet folded in half (pl. 16), a conventional section at scale reconstructs a Roman temple that ingeniously combines longitudinal sections of the porch and nave drawn with a ruler and, distinguished by a darker wash, the beams of the porch roof. On the right of the same sheet he used pen and ink for

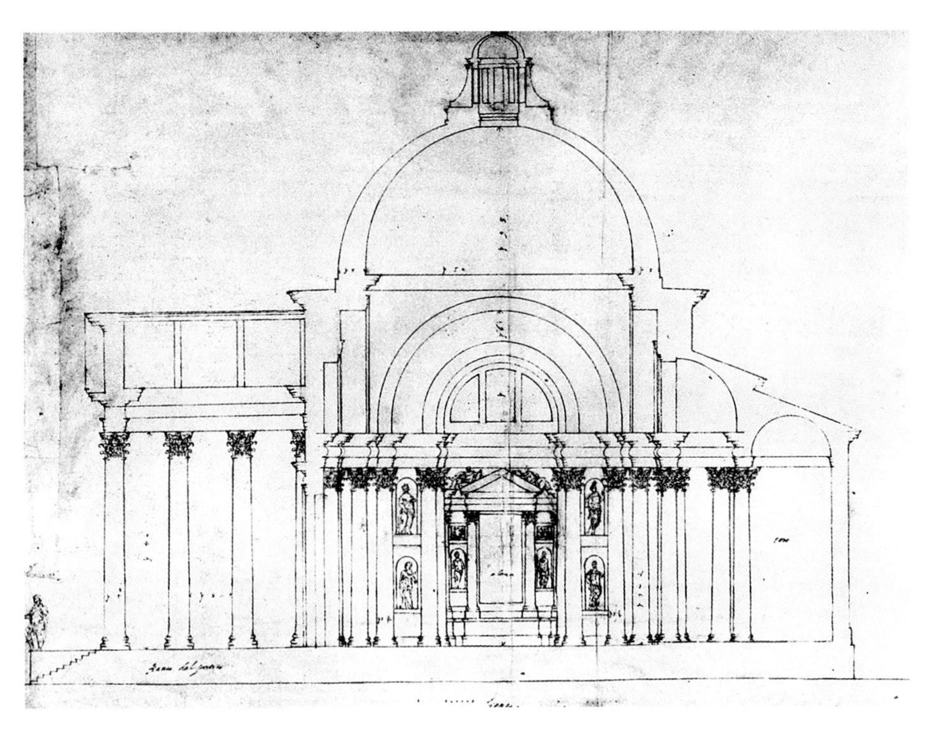

18 Palladio, longitudinal section of a rejected project for a church for the members of the Venetian Senate, 1575–6

freehand fantasies, studying various types of *palazzetti* of a more modest size than those he actually built. Most Renaissance clients wealthy enough to consider building a residence would not have been satisfied by the small size. Palladio was just exercising his imagination. At the bottom of the sheet he penned plans of small row houses – a feature of late medieval planning in Venice. Rapidly penned pairs of parallel lines indicate apertures, a shorthand symbol that became common in the later Renaissance. One half of the sheet is scrupulously accurate, the other open and experimental.

A Palladio sketch identifiable with the Baths of Agrippa (pl. 17) behind the Pantheon in Rome – like many of Palladio's designs of ancient monuments – has virtually no relationship with the remains, which in this case were scattered and difficult to interpret. These studies, however, may have helped him to develop the project for one of his most important buildings, the church of the Redentore in Venice (1575–6; pl. 18). Like many architects who had recorded images of ancient buildings, he combined the architecture of the past with his own creations. For the architects of the Renaissance, this form of imitation was considered essential.

In sum, Renaissance writers defined the sketch in terms of its rapidity of execution, lack of formal structure, and impassioned engagement. While they typically described sketching as an initial path to the composition of works of art, in practice artists used the sketch for a variety of functions, not all of which involved creativity. The examples I have discussed include preparation for a work (Bramante, Michelangelo, Antonio da Sangallo), free invention without a goal (apprentices of Altichiero, Leonardo, Palladio), representation of existing buildings or the natural environment (Antonio di Vincenzo, Fra Bartolommeo), a current event (Pisanello), and fantasy (Leonardo, Michelangelo in his fortifications).

Renaissance art theory enjoined the artist to seek an equilibrium between decorum or propriety (*decorum*, a Vitruvian term, that also covered decoration) and *licenza* (license). The sketch exemplified license, unrestrained by tradition, loose and indeterminate in structure, and issuing straight from the artist's inspiration and vision, and the hand. Sketching both revealed and furthered the expression of a new individuality and freedom realized by the artists of the Renaissance and later times.

2

On the Origins of Art History

FOR THERE TO BE A HISTORY OF ART, art-making must be perceived as an activity distinct from other human activities and the sequence of past products of that activity as potentially exhibiting some describable pattern of change. These preconditions did not effectively exist in the Middle Ages, when art in the modern sense was rarely distinguished from other functional productions by shop artisans such as stained glass windows and ornamental iron work, and when there were not even names to differentiate classes or periods of artifacts of the past.

The history of modern art history begins in the Italian Renaissance, though with far-reaching dependence on ancient antecedents. But the achievement of a historical consciousness liberated from the unsophisticated mentality of the chronicler was a much more difficult task than has been realized. It remained undeveloped in antiquity, and it was inchoate in the mind of the Renaissance writer who is accepted as the father of modern art history, Giorgio Vasari. The problem was that the most obvious aspect of works of art that could be represented as evolving or at least changing with time was their likeness to nature. History could be the account of the progressive conquering of obstacles – in Renaissance terminology, "difficulties" – to mimesis. The difficulties were overcome by inventions, of which an obvious example would be the painter's perspective; that meant that the history of art could be constructed on the kind of model later adopted for the history of science or of technology. This was consistent with the definition of *ars* in antiquity and the Middle Ages as "technique" or "craft." That satisfied the ancient and pre-Vasarian writers, even though it must have been obvious to them that the works of art themselves were pursuing other, less mechanical and more resonant goals. But those goals were embodied in the artist's imaginative reconstruction of nature, and in order that these first be recognized and described and second become the motivator of change required a new critical consciousness.[1] In one sense, this essay concerns the role of art criticism as the motivator of history.

A historical consciousness more subtle than the recognition of progress in mimesis or in the imitation of the antique first emerged in Giorgio Vasari's *Lives of the Most Excellent Painters, Sculptors and Architects* of 1550, and more fully in the enlarged edition of 1568. It was manifested in a nascent sense of individual and regional style that became the foundation of an exceptional hypothesis, that of a period style. These represent two distinct levels of ambition. Vasari's predecessors could grasp the individuality of an artist by induction, without caring to formulate the style of a period. The concept of a period – apart from the gross distinctions of antiquity, darkness, and rebirth – was a historian's invention, an artifact, and an abstraction of certain features selected from individual instances.

Vasari's style-determined period and sequence of period has been the motivator of modern art history, and has been established as the only plausible way to define what has occurred over time in the production of what is now called art. But while it is legitimate to see the invention of period style as historically important in the formation of modern historical practice, its relevance and utility ended around 1900. Since then, it has been no longer relevant or possible.

The earliest Renaissance commentaries on art have been keenly examined by Michael Baxandall in his book *Giotto and the Orators* (1971), a fundamental study of humanist views on art and their relation to the classical rhetorical tradition. He begins with a fourteenth-century text, Filippo Villani's *De origine civitatis Florentiae et eiusdem famosis civibus*, of 1381–82, which celebrates the distinguished citizens of his city and reviews the painting of the preceding century in terms already suggested by Dante and Boccaccio.[2]

> And so let it be permitted to me, said with all due respect to those who ridicule, to introduce at this point the exceptional Florentine painters, who have resuscitated a lifeless and nearly destroyed art. Foremost among whom Giovanni, whose surname was Cimabue, revived with skill and natural talent the antiquated art of painting that was wantonly straying, as it were, rather far from the resemblance of nature. . . . After Giovanni, with the road to new things now paved. Giotto, a distinguished man of glorious repute who must not only be compared to the ancient painters, but also preferred to them because of his skill and natural talent, restored the art of painting to its former excellence and great renown. For the images fashioned with his brush are consistent with the features of nature, so that they seem to those gazing upon them to live and breath the air. . . . In the opinions of many, and indeed not foolishly, painters are of no lesser talent than those whom the liberal arts have regarded as masters. . . . From this exceedingly praiseworthy man, just as from a spring of purity and great abundance, flowed the brightest rivulets of painting, which would produce in renewed rivalry of nature an art of painting both valuable and favorable.

Villani's passage continues with accounts of a number of more recent painters influenced by Giotto, who initiated the revival of Florentine art. The whole sequence is presented in what Baxandall calls the Prophet–Savior–Apostle mode; it is not quite a historical method. But also it is not simply a medieval chronicle: the metaphors – the road to new things that lies open, the brooklets issuing from a spring – suggest a new ambition, to give the sequence of events a common purpose, which is to explore all aspects of the imitation of nature, an undertaking so demanding that those who succeed in it must be regarded as the equal to university graduates in the liberal arts. From the start, the new effort to endow art with its own history was linked with the identification of a category of craftsmen as fine artists, and with their social empowerment – their escape from the guild and the stigma of belonging to the artisan class. What is notable in this passage is not only that painters are represented as equivalent to scholars, but also that they appear in an account of contemporary events, which implies that their works are historical events.

The most ample model for this proto-art history and for the motivating mechanism of mimesis is found in the accounts of Pliny the Elder, written in the first century BCE, where one artist after another surpasses his predecessors in achievement measured by the attainment of verisimilitude. Pliny's lengthy chronicle was conveniently collapsed into a paragraph by Cicero, who contributed perhaps more than any other ancient writer to the formation of Renaissance art historical consciousness. Ernest Gombrich has called attention to this in Cicero's *Brutus* an essay on oratorical style, which was lifted essentially verbatim by Vasari in the preface to the second section of his *Lives*.[3]

> For who among those who devote their attention to these lesser things does not perceive that the statues of Canachus are too stiff to represent reality? Those statues of Calamis are also hard, but nevertheless are more like real flesh than those of Canachus. Those of Myron have not yet been brought close enough to reality, though now you would not hesitate to call them beautiful. Even more beautiful and indeed quite perfect, as they usually seem to me at least, are those of Polyclitus. There is a similar pattern in painting. . . . And I am inclined to think the same thing occurs in all other things: for nothing is invented and perfected at the same time.

An important difference between the antique historical models and Villani, and subsequently Vasari, is that the ancients represented only a steady forward progress (according to Pliny, writing centuries after the perfection of Polycleitus: "Art has made extraordinary progress, in technique first and afterwards in audacity"),[4] while Villani and Vasari recognized that something had happened after the moment of perfection which, while it was not exactly a decline, was primarily an exploitation of the achievements of the great master or masters.

There are numerous texts in Pliny and other writers on ancient art intended to illustrate the achievement of perfect mimesis. In one, horses led past a series of horse paintings submitted to a competition neighed only at that of Apelles; in a competition between Zeuxis and Parrhasios, the former exhibited a picture of grapes so convincing that birds flew onto the stage to peck at them; elated by this verdict, he turned to his rival and asked him to remove the curtain that covered his work, and was told that the curtain was the painting; he forthwith acknowledged defeat, saying that it was far more prestigious to deceive a painter than a bird.[5]

Stories of this kind, which are mythical in character, must have lingered on from an earlier time, when artists were simply craftsmen, either more or less skilled. It seems odd that a culture that pursued discriminations of the subtlest kind in discussing the nuances of rhetorical and poetic style could be so literally bird-brained about the potentialities of visual art.

This unsophisticated representation of the purpose of painting and sculpture sufficed for most early Renaissance commentaries on the visual arts. This was not only because the formula had the prestige of anything ancient, but also because it fitted the sense of pride felt at having overcome the imagined deficiencies of Gothic art, particularly with respect to the command of verisimilitude. Gothic art was referred to either as German, which was the most disapproving term Renaissance Italians could devise, or modern, which implied not-antique.

In a letter in verse form of around 1427, Guarino of Verona writes of the painter Pisanello, for example:[6]

> When painting a portrait of the night you depict winged creatures flying around at night and never appearing by day: one can see the stars, the sphere of the moon, shadows without sunlight. If you fashion the occurrences of winter, everything shivers in the icy cold, the leafless tree gnashes its teeth. Or if you depict what happens during the season of spring, the multicolored flowers smile throughout verdant meadows, the old light returns to the trees and the hills begin to shine, and then the birds' sweet songs caress the air.

Although Guarino may have written the same kind of thing about other artists, what he says is particularly apt for Pisanello, who made the most advanced nature studies of his time. Among these, birds figure significantly, and it seems that Guarino might have had a sense of individual style.

A notable extension of the Plinian scheme appears in a volume of 1456 called *De viris illustribus*, by Bartolomeo Fazio, which included a section on four famous painters and three sculptors, preceded by an introduction, which reads in part:[7]

> For the care taken by one or the other [i.e. by painters or poets] in the invention and arrangement of their work is almost equal, nor has any painter been considered exceptional, except he who has excelled at representing the qualities of things as they actually are. . . . And hardly does another among those handicrafts demand greater proficiency [than painting], in as much as it requires not only that the face, that the appearance and the features of the whole body be portrayed, but also much more internal sensations and motions, so that that painting seems to live and feel and move expressively in some way.

Baxandall, who introduced art historians to Fazio, has shown how the addition of a significant psychological and affective element to his predecessors' more simple-minded prescriptions for naturalism was the result of reading the Prologue to the *Imagines* of the Greco-Roman third-century writer Philostratus the Younger, a book of detailed descriptions, called *ekphrases*, of individual works of art that emphasize the interrelation of motion and emotion.[8] But Fazio lacked the ability to exercise critical judgment about the visual arts; he was a literary man who does not appear to have looked hard enough at actual works of art to see much besides their subject matter.[9]

Fazio wrote twenty years after the publication of the most important theoretical work on the visual arts of the early Renaissance, Leon Battista Alberti's *De pictura*, released in Florence in 1435 (followed by his Italian translation in 1436). The naturalistic tradition of the ancients is treated in the second book, in which Alberti examines another of the mimesis anecdotes that had been repeated *ad nauseum* in the Middle Ages and Renaissance, because it represented a marginally higher level of subtlety than the norm. In this story, Zeuxis of the grapes, commissioned by the town of Croton to make an image of Helen of Troy, asked to see the most beautiful young women in town; but rather than selecting the most beautiful one as his model, he chose five, and took from each her most attractive feature. Alberti retells the story, which he may have had from Cicero's *De inventione* but introduces it with these words:[10]

> A Demetrio, antiquo pittore, manco ad acquistare l'ultima lode che fu curioso di fare cose assimigliate al naturale molto più che vaghe. Per questo gioverà pigliare da tutti i belli corpi ciascuna lodata parte. E sempre ad imparare molta vaghezza si contenda con istudio e con industria.

> The ancient painter Demetrius failed to achieve the highest praise because he had the desire to make things more naturalistic than ideal. For that it would require combining the most beautiful parts of each woman – always showing great charm, working from study and with industry.

This helped to distinguish the work of art from a mirror and to propose the concept that the artist has something more to offer than his manual skill at reproduction. But unless the perception of beauty is innate, which Alberti expressly excludes by saying that effort is required to attain it, it remains a mystery how one identifies either the most beautiful bodies or their excellent parts.

Alberti himself resolved that mystery in his treatise on architecture, completed around 1450, where he proposes that a man might prefer a thinner or a fuller woman:[11]

> Nonetheless, preferring one or another of the preceding beauties, it doesn't imply that one classify all the remaining as rare or irrelevant; actuality indicates that the choice comes out of the presence of something, the characteristics of which I won't get involved. As for judgments relative to the beauty, it depends on individual opinion from the innate gifts of the mind. Judgments in relation to beauty support not only individual opinion but rather a consciousness innate in the mind.

This probably is related to the passage in Cicero's *Orator*:[12]

> And yet we can picture things more beautiful than both those statues of Phidias, compared to which we see nothing more perfect of that kind, and those paintings that I have mentioned. And surely that famous sculptor, while making a figure of Jupiter or Minerva, did not study some person in order to model the likeness after them, but some extraordinary image of beauty was present in his mind. Contemplating this and focused on it, he directed his skill and hand to the likeness of that god.

Alberti's later characterization of judgment in the arts was surely influenced by the Byzantine scholar Manuel Chrysalorus, who came to Italy in about 1395 and taught Greek to many of the humanists. In a letter cited by Baxandall, written to an Italian colleague during Alberti's early childhood, he wrote:[13]

> . . . we admire not so much the beauties of the bodies in statues and paintings as the beauty of the mind of their maker. This, like well-molded wax, has reproduced in the stone, wood, bronze or pigments an image which it grasped through the eyes to the soul's imagination.

These opinions may seem to resemble the crucial theme of Neo-Platonic art theory, which Marsilio Ficino and peers were developing in the mid-fifteenth century, that ideal images are reflected in the mind of the maker. But whereas for Chrysalorus this is by virtue of a personal gift or genius, and for Alberti it is by virtue of the rational faculty of an educated man; for a Neo-Platonist it has to be the reflection of a transcendental idea that merely travels through the artist and is reflected in the base material of the physical work of art.

Alberti's discussion is restricted to beautiful figures and does not extend to the whole composition in which they appear, which Alberti calls the *historia.* But in one passage, separate from this one, he wrote that something more is involved than choosing the best of what nature offers, saying:[14]

> Parte della istoria sono i corpi, parte de' corpi i membri, parte de' membri la superficie. Le prime adunque parti del dipingere sono le superficie. Nasce della composizione delle superficie quella grazia ne' corpi [elegans in corporibus concinnitas] quale dicono bellezza.

> The parts of history are parts of the body, limbs, parts of the limbs, the skin. The highest aspect of painting is reproducing the surfaces. Out of the composition of the surfaces, one arrives at a level that we call beauty.

So the artist, in putting together the surfaces of bodies, controls, independently of the model, whether the result will or will not be beautiful. That is a foot in the door to criticism, but not one that influenced anyone. In Alberti's construction, the *historia* as a whole would be judged not in the formal terms implied by the references to female beauty, and thus be translatable into a concept of individual style, but rather by how effectively and appropriately it is dramatized through the expressiveness of its action. That is probably the source of Fazio's identification of beauty with the representation of "interior feelings and emotions." In this respect, Giotto's imagery was incomparable in Alberti's time, so the only aspects of Alberti's innovations that could lend themselves to treatment in terms of historical evolution are those in the first book: light, color, and perspective; they were inventions and concepts that could be treated like innovations in science and technology, which in Renaissance terms could responsibly be seen as progressing regularly from darkness to light. It stems from Alberti's propositions that as a result of the selection process and harmonic construction of surfaces, a work of art can be more perfect than nature. Jan Bialostocki has pointed out that this did not bring an end to the rule that the work of art must imitate nature; it merely gave impetus to the distinction between *natura naturata*, nature as it appears to us, and *natura naturans*, nature as an active force that rules the universe and creates.[15]

The path to the recognition of individual style leads to Cristoforo Landino, a Florentine humanist who wrote the first major commentary on Dante's *Divine Comedy*, in 1480.[16] Landino did not devote much of his time to art, but in the brief paragraph in the introduction to his commentary he showed for the first time a willingness to reach beyond the formulas of Pliny and Cicero, and he emerged as the earliest writer capable of transferring a rhetorician's sensitivity to nuances of style to the visual arts.

> Fu Masaccio optimo imitatore di natura, di gran rilievo universale, buono componitore e puro sanza ornato, perche solo si decte all'imitatione del vero, et al rilievo delle figure: fu certo buono et prospectivo qualto altro di quegli tempi, et di gran facilità nel fare, essendo ben giovane, che morì d'anni ventisei. Fu fra' Philippo [Lippi] gratioso et ornato et artificioso sopra modo: valse molto nelle compositioni et varietà, nel colorire, nel rilievo, negl'ornamenti d'ogno sorte, maxime o imitati dal vero o finti. Andreino [del Castagno] fu grande disegnatore et di gran rilievo, amatore delle difficultà dell'arte et di scorci vivo et prompto molto, et assai facile nel fare . . . Fra' Giovanni Angelico et vezozo et divoto et ornato molto con grandissima faciltà.

> Massaccio was exceptional at the imitation of nature. He gave all parts of his painting full three-dimensional relief and composed very well. His paintings were pure and without ornament because he took his models only from life and focused on the three-dimensionality of bodies. He was as good a perspective artist as any of his contemporaries. He had great technical facility for someone so young. He died when he was only twenty-

six years old. Fra Filippo (Lippi's) paintings are graceful, richly ornamented, and imaginative beyond those of anyone else. He composed well and with great variety. His colors, the relief of his figures, and the ornaments of his paintings, both those taken from life and those he invented, were excellent. Andreino (del Castagno) was a great draughtsman and modeled beautifully. He was fascinated by the most difficult challenges of painting and was adept at solving problems of foreshortening. Fra Giovanni Angelico, too, had a great facility as a painter. He was very devout. His work had great charm and was richly ornamented.

Given the problem of characterizing individual style without reference to any work, this is not radically different from what someone might have said in recent times. There is not yet an attempt to define the sixty-odd years in which these artists were working as a period distinct from that of the Giotto followers, but if one added all the adjectives together they would fit the fifteenth century better than the early sixteenth, especially Angelico's *vezzoso*, *divoto*, and *ornato*. The list of artists mentioned does not overlap at all with Fazio's; Landino's were all indebted to antique precedents to a greater degree than Pisanello and Gentile da Fabriano. This is at least in part due to the fact that Fazio was writing in a court setting and Landino in mercantile Florence.[17] The so-called classic age of Italian art that followed, identified since Vasari as beginning with the work of Leonardo da Vinci and encompassing Raphael and Michelangelo, fostered almost no theoretical activity – Leonardo's extensive writings were still based on medieval Aristotelianism and prescribed an effort to reproduce inductively *natura naturans*, nature in the active sense, though some of his precepts sound like those of the ancient writers, for example, "Quella pittura è più laudabile la quale ha più conformi con la cosa imitata, questo propongo à confusione di quelli pittori li quali vogliano raconciare le cose di natura" ("The most praiseworthy work is that which is most like the object imitated").[18]

Imitation, especially the imitation of ancient writers, pervades discussions of literature and of history writing in the early years of the sixteenth century: in particular, which ancients to imitate, and whether to choose one model or several. The question is extended to all the arts in a passage in Castiglione's dialogue *The Courtier*, published in 1528.[19] His major protagonist, Count

Lodovico di Canossa, raises the question what part imitation might have played in the work of great writers like Homer, Petrarch, and Boccaccio, who initiated an art that, if not entirely new, was far superior to that of their predecessors. Their master, he says, was *ingegno* (ingenious) combined with their own *giudizio naturale* (innate judgment). Further, there are many routes to excellence that are dissimilar one from another, as in the various modes of music (and here he unexpectedly compares the styles of two singers, one who inflames the spirit and the other whose soft harmony arouses a delightful passion). The same is true of visual art where the work of Leonardo, Mantegna, Raphael, Michelangelo, and Giorgione is dissimilar in facture but all are excellent to the point that certain of them seem not to lack anything in the manner because one realizes that each is most perfect in his style (*suo stile*). The extension of "style" from the discussion of literature to that of painting is unprecedented. Speaking later of amateur literary critics, he dismisses those who aspire to judge *i stili* and to speak of numbers and of imitation but know nothing of them. Unfortunately, *stili* did not gain currency in sixteenth-century art criticism; the burden of supporting references to the character of the work of an individual, group, region, or period is carried by the vaguer term *maniera*, which could mean facture, or formal style – or it could designate the particular style later called Mannerist.

Maybe in ages of supreme self-confidence art serves as its own theory. In any case, it was Giorgio Vasari, writing long after the passing of the period he represented as having achieved perfection, who first drew together the scattered perceptions of the fifteenth century.

Vasari, himself an architect and painter, defined a historical pattern in the sequence of artists from Giotto to his own time.[20] He divided the Renaissance (he called it *rinascità*) into three "parti, o vogliamole chiamare èta" ("we call them ages"), on the grounds of what he called "per quella manifestissima differenza chi in chiascuna di loro si conosce" ("because of the obvious differences that there are among them"). In the first, the three arts were "Molto lontane dalla lor perfezione; e come che abbiano avuto qualcosa di buono" ("Very far from perfection and yet each has something good about it"); while in the second: "si veggono manifesto esser le cose migliorate assai e nell'invenzioni, e nel condurle con più disegno e con miglior maniera e con maggior diligenza; e così tolto via quella ruggini della vecchiaia" ("One sees clearly that improvement in invention and execution together with better drawing and with greater style and diligence results in removing the awkwardness of the past").

The artists of the third *età*:[21]

> Veramente grande augumento fecero alle arti della architettura, pittura e scultura, quelli eccellenti maestri che noi abbiamo descritti sin qui nella Seconda Parte di queste Vite, aggiungnendo alle cose de' primi regola, ordine [these two refer to architecture], misura, disegno e maniera, se non in tutto perfettamente, tanto almanco vicino al vero, che i terzi, di chi noi ragioneremo da qui avanti, poterono mediante quel lume sollevarsi e condursi alla somma perfezione . . .
>
> Ma chi ardirà dire[22] in quel tempo [second *età*] essersi trovato uno in ogni cosa perfetto, e che abbia ridotto le cose al termine di oggi e d'invenzione e di disegno e di colorito? e che abbia osservato lo sfuggire dolcemente delle figure con la scurità del colore, che i lumi siano rimasti solamente in su i rilievi . . . Questa lode certo è tocca alla terza età; nella quale mi par potere dir sicuramente, che l'arte abbia fatto quello che ad una imitatrice della nature lecito poter fare; e che elle sia salita tanto alto, che più presto si abbia a temere del calare a basso, che sperare oggimai più augmento.

The excellent masters that we have described in the second period of these lives made truly great contributions to the arts of architecture, painting and sculpture. They added rule, order, measure, design and style to the achievements of their predecessors and even if they did not understand these things perfectly they approached the truth closely enough that the artists of the third period, about whom we will speak from here on in, were able, because of the light that they had shed, to arrive at the highest perfection.

But who would dare to say that they had found an artist in the second period perfect in every way, one who had brought the invention, design, and color of their art to the levels of today, or who had seen the way that the darkening of colors softly diminishes figures in the distance or observed the way that light strikes only the forms that project forward. This virtue belongs to the third period alone. I believe I can say with confidence that here art has accomplished all that which a medium that aims to imitate nature may properly achieve. Indeed, art has now risen to so high a level that soon it will be more likely to decline than to make further progress.

Although the evolution is defined in terms of the familiar imitation of nature, this is seen in the sense anticipated by Alberti, as is clear from Vasari's definition of the three rules of figural art: *disegno*, which I shall define in a moment; *misura*, which concerns primarily proportion with its connection to ideal harmonies; *maniera*, which has to do with tirelessly developing one's skill at drawing beautiful parts and combining them into beautiful figures (notice that the composition of the whole is not emphasized). *Disegno*, apart from being drawing, is what Vasari calls[23]

> . . . padre delle tre arti nostre . . . cava di molte cose un giudizio universale; simile a una forma ovvero idea di tutte le cose della natura, la quale è singolarissima nelle sue misure . . . E perché da questa cognizione nasce un certo concetto e giudizio, che si forma nella mente quella tal cosa che poi espressa con le mani se chiama disegno; Si può conchiudere che esso disegno altro non sia, che una apparente expressione e dichiarazione del concetto che si ha nell'animo, è di quello che altri si nella mente immaginato e fabbricato nell'idea.

> . . . the father of our three arts . . . shapes a universal rule from many individual phenomena, that is like a form or an idea of all the things of nature, with one set of proportions that apply to all . . . and because a concept and rule is born from this awareness, the mind then forms that thing that is expressed with the hands and that is called drawing. *Disegno* is nothing other than a visible expression of an inner concept that is given form in the mind.

As Svetlana Alpers has shown in her incisive study of Vasari's descriptions and critical standards, *disegno* is what drives his historical system.[24] Though Vasari often implies that artistic progress is equivalent to the increasing capacity to reproduce nature, it is clear that it is *disegno* that progresses – the capacity to form beautiful elements for the work of art in the mind, and then to execute them. This resembles Platonic idealism to the same degree as Alberti's precept, but it similarly avoids attributing the idea to any power other than the artist's skill and talent: for example, Raphael,[25] studiando le fatiche de' maestri vecchi e quelle de' moderni, prese da tutti il meglio; e fattone raccolta . . . Laonde la natura restò vinta dai suoi colori; e l'invenzione era in lui . . . facile e propria.

studying the work of older masters and that of the moderns, he took the best from each and made a collection of them . . . so that nature was surpassed by his paint, and his invention was . . . effortless and fitting.

This, incidentally, is a far cry from mimesis. At the same time, progress is measured by the overcoming of what Vasari calls *difficoltà*, as it would do in the history of technology. As Alpers pointed out, every artist has the obligation to contribute the solution of some problem to the flow of art, and, although Vasari is sensitive to individual style, as suggested in the statement that Raphael's invention was his alone, and to the development of style within the career of an individual, Vasarian history is not, like modernist history has been, an evolution of style. There is a strange disjunction between Vasari's general characterizations of artists and periods and his approach to individual works. These he bases on the formulas of antique *ekphrasis*, focusing exclusively on narrative expression (which incidentally does not figure in his five basic rules), and do not suggest progress in time.[26]

The dramatic action comes to the fore more than the accuracy of representing the model, as in this description of Raphael's *Transfiguration*:[27]

. . . dove si vede condotto un giovanetto spiritato, acciocché Cristo sceso del monte lo liberi; il quale giovanetto, mentre che con attitudine scontorta si prostende gridando e stralunando gli occhi, mostra il suo patire dentro nella carne, nelle vene, e ne' polsi contaminati dalla malignità dello spirto, e con pallida incarnazione fa quel gesto forzato e pauroso. Questa figura sostiene un vecchio, che . . . mostra, con lo alza re le ciglia ed increspar la fronte, in un tempo medesimo e forza e paura; pure mirando gli Apostoli fiso, pare che, sperando in loro, faccia animo a se stesso. Evvi una femina, fra molte, la quale è principale figura di quella tavola, che inginocchiata dinanzi a quelli voltando la testa loro e coll'atto delle braccia verso lo spiritato, mostra la miseria di colui . . . E nel vero, egli vi fece figure e teste, oltra la bellezza straordinaria, tanto nuove, varie e bello, che si fa giudizio

> commune degli artefici che questa opera, fra tante quant'egli ne fece, sia la più celebrata, la più bella e la più divina.
>
> . . . where you see a youth led before Christ, who has descended from [Mount Tabor] so that he may be freed of an evil spirit. The pose of the youth is contorted; he twists and calls out and rolls his eyes. He reveals his suffering in his flesh, in his veins, and in his extremeties, all infected by the malignancy of the spirit. With a pale complexion he makes that extreme and fearful gesture. The boy is supported by an old man . . . who, with raised eyebrows and wrinkled brow, expresses both strength and fear. The old man looks directly at the Apostles and seems, through his faith in them, to take courage. There is a woman who is the principle figure of the painting. She kneels before the Apostles, turns her head to them and, gesturing with her arm toward the possessed boy, directs their attention to his suffering . . . beyond their extraordinary beauty, Raphael made the figures and the heads so new, varied, and handsome, that it is the common opinion of all artists that this work, of all that he has done, is the most celebrated, the most beautiful, and the most divine.

This is not unlike an account of a good theater performance, and, if one reads this passage without knowing the author of the painting, one could not identify him other than as an artist that Vasari thinks is particularly good. But he could easily have worked in the first or second period of the Renaissance as in the third. Vasari gives no comfort to the modern representation of the history of what is called High Renaissance art as classical. He is not interested in the structure of paintings. His account of some of the features of the third style as offering: "copia de' belli abiti, la varietà di tante bizzarrie, la vagbezza de' colori" ("a wealth of beautiful costumes, a great variety of strange things, and delicacy of colors")[28] might as well be a description of Pisanello's work – no emphasis on the classical requisites of grandeur, equilibrium, or gravity.

The concept of a classical art was not formed by those who made it. It could be seen as an invention of more recent art history calculated to get beyond the imitation of nature and to get out of the corner into which Vasari had painted himself by having his history terminate, or rather apotheose like the resurrected Savior, with Michelangelo.[29] Following writers of the previous generation, Vasari referred to Michelangelo as divine, even *divinissimo.* In a passage cited above, he entertained the possibility that after the age of perfection the whole enterprise could collapse or, one might say, stagnate (as it threatened to do with Vasari's Mannerist contemporaries), and he must have seen that his conception of history had encountered an insurmountable difficulty. But he could not condemn his colleagues to inferiority, because it would diminish them, and equally his Medici patrons, so he left this considerable problem unresolved. Later historians, however, could not escape their responsibility to incorporate Baroque and ultimately modern art into some framework, and the invention of classicism proved useful in this task. A biological model for the writing of political and literary history existed already in ancient Rome, as Erwin Panofsky pointed out in discussing Vasari's historical method. He chose as an example one out of a number of possible sources, L. Annaeus Florus:[30]

> If one were to consider the Roman people as something like a human being and to survey their entire lifetime, how they began, how they grew up, how they attained, as it were, to the flower of maturity, and how they subsequently, in a manner of speaking, grew old, one may discover therein four stages or phases. The first age was under the kings, lasting about two hundred and fifty years, when they fought with their neighbors about their own mother; this would be their childhood. The next age extends for another two hundred and fifty years . . . during which they conquered Italy; this was the period most intensely lived with men and arms, wherefore it may be called their adolescence. Then follow the two hundred years up to Augustus during which they subjected the whole world; this is the youth of the Empire and, as it were, its vigorous maturity. From Augustus up to our own day a little less than two hundred years have passed. During this time the Romans aged and boiled away because of the Emperors' lack of energy unless they put forth their strength under the leadership of Trajan, so that the old age of the Empire, against all hopes, revives as though it had regained its youth.

The biological model of history was taken up by early Renaissance historians, among them Leonardo Bruni, from the mid-fifteenth century on. However, already in the generation prior to Vasari, Machiavelli and Guiccardini had already made it obsolete. Wazbinski has shown that their "historic realism," particularly in incorporating archival research, documentation, and interviews of individuals who recalled events of the past, influenced Vasari's rewriting of the *Vite* between 1550 and 1568.[31] But the new history did not alter his evolutionary scheme.

Vasari's construction of the history of art, then, was not so much a significant innovation as a masterpiece of adaptation, by virtue of its capacity to turn a growing art-critical sophistication into an articulated historical evolution. It was derived more demonstrably from classical sources than most of the art of his time. Traces of Vasari's system survived into modern art history, centuries after it was abandoned in political and cultural history, because the concept of style evolution has remained as central to criticism. I hope in retrospect to have proven my claim that the first history of art could not have been conceived without certain steps in critical sophistication, the goal of which was primarily to make a more complex definition of what it meant to imitate nature. There were four preparatory steps: that of Fazio, who added interior feelings and emotions to the external appearances that had to be emulated; second, that of Chrysalorus and Alberti, who suggested that the most important ingredient of a work of art was a beautiful idea or harmony originating in the mind of the artist; third, the postulation of *natura naturans*, which validated the inventiveness of artists on the grounds that it imitated nature in making things that did not previously exist; and last, that of Landino, who found terms for differences in style among artists of the same period. It remained for Vasari to posit that styles evolved through periods each of which had its own general character. Further, in accepting and emphasizing the potential divinity of an artist Vasari also left a formidable legacy: the concept of creativity, a power previously conceded only to God, and one that could be used to glorify artists and to justify a history devised, like his own, in terms of the succession of works of great artists.[32]

We are indebted to Vasari, not for the specifics of the historical system but, first, for conceiving that art could have a history of a different kind from that of the ancient chroniclers and of technology and descriptive science, and second, for suggesting that stages in this history manifested a period style. What Vasari may have known but did not say was that the "difficulties" that artist after artist resolved on their ways to the perfection of a Raphael or

Michelangelo were not immanent, but had to be reformulated every time one of them was realised, so that history could not come to a halt; Jackson Pollock could be as much the heir to Raphael as Morandi. The greatest challenge to the Vasarian tradition occurred when antique art no longer was accepted as a paradigm; but it survived anyhow, at least through the middle years of the twentieth century.

NOTES

This study was supported by a grant from the John Simon Guggenheim Foundation.

1 On the stages in the development of a concept of individual style in the early Renaissance, see Michael Baxandall, *Giotto and the Orators*, Oxford, 1971; N. Ivanoff, *Il concetto dello stile nella letteratura artistica del '500* (Quaderni dell'Istituto di Storia dell'Arte dell'Università degli Studi di Trieste, IV), Trieste, 1955, p. 545; Martin Warnke, "Praxisfelder der Kunsttheorie," *Idea: Jahrbuch der Hamburger Kunsthalle*, I (1982), pp. 54–71; Martin Kemp, "Equal Excellence: Lomazzo and the Explanation of Individual Style in the Visual Arts," *Renaissance Studies*, I (1987), pp. 1–26.

2 Baxandall, *Giotto*, pp. 70ff. (translation), pp. 146ff. (Latin text).

3 Cicero, *Brutus*, XVII, 70; cited by E. H. Gombrich in "Vasari's 'Lives' and Cicero's 'Brutus'," *Journal of the Warburg and Courtauld Institutes*, XXIII (1960), pp. 309ff.

4 Pliny the Elder, *Historia Naturalis*, XXXIV, p. 38.

5 Pliny the Elder, *Historia Naturalis*, XXXV, p. 65.

6 Baxandall, *Giotto*, pp. 93, 156, 103ff., 163ff.

7 Ibid., pp. 103ff., 163.

8 See the definition of the term by Hermogenes of Tarsus (2nd century CE) in ibid., p. 85.

9 An instance of a subtler evaluation is Leonello d'Este's discrimination of contrasts between portraits of him by Pisanello and Bellini published by Michael Baxandall in "A Dialogue on Art from the Court of Leonello d'Este," *Journal of the Warburg and Courtauld Institutes*, XXVI (1973), pp. 325ff.

10 Alberti, *Della pittura* III. 5; from *Opere volgari*, vol. III, Bari, 1973, p. 96.

11 Ibid.

12 Cicero, *Orator* II, p. 8.

13 Baxandall, *Giotto*, pp. LXXXII, 82, 151ff.; Christine Smith (*Architecture in the Culture of Early Humanism*, Cambridge, MA, 1992) has detailed how extensive was the influence of Chrysalorus

on humanist thought, especially through his having introduced the later Greek rhetorical tradition into Italy.

14 *De pictura* II; from *Opere volgari*, vol. III, p. 35.

15 Jan Bialostocki, "The Renaissance Conception of Nature and Antiquity," in *Acts of the Twentieth International Congress of Art History*, Princeton, 1963, pp. 19–30. He cites (p. 20) Plotinus (*Enneads* 5.8,1): "If somebody does not esteem the arts because they imitate nature, it should be said first that nature herself imitates. Then it should be borne in mind that the arts do not simply copy the visible things but draw from the principles that constitute the source of nature."

16 O. Morisani, "Art Historians and Art Critics, III: Cristoforo Landino," *Burlington Magazine*, XCV (1953), pp. 267–70; the passage is extensively discussed by Michael Baxandall, *Painting and Experience in Fifteenth Century Italy*, Oxford, 1972, pp. 118ff.

17 Landino's critical approach, and some of his vocabulary, was adopted by the author of the much more extensive text *Il libro di Antonio Billi*, most recently edited by F. Benedutticci, Anzio, 1991, who dates the MS 1506–30. The definition of individual style was not exclusively the achievement of intellectuals. Martin Warnke ("Praxisfelder der Kunsttheorie") discusses a number of instances from legal documents, contracts, and letters of the fifteenth and sixteenth centuries in which awareness by fellow practitioners of the unique style of an artist is discussed as a matter of course, as equivalent to writing, with no reference to antique precedent or philosophical positions. A crucial instance is the inquiry of 1457 mandated to determine which portions of the Ovetari chapel in Padua had been executed by Mantegna, as opposed to his deceased partner Pizzolo. The clerk records the testimony of an expert witness, a little-known artist called Pietro da Milano: "Et pro ut Ipse testis percepit ex dictis picturis, dicte hystorie et picture sunt manu dicti magistri Andree. Et dixit se scire eo qua ipse testis bent cognoscit picturas manu dicti magistri Andree, non tamen vidit ipse testis illas depingere, sed tamen ex longa pratica, quam habet in ea arte pingendi cognosict, quod dicte pictores sunt manu dicti magistri Andree, et quia inter pictores semper cognoscitur manu cuius sit aliqua pictura, maxime quando est manu alicui nis magistri" ("according to this testimony these paintings are by the hand of the master Andree. His hand is recognizable in his pictures. Not only does one see the subject in the paintings, but also from his long practice in the art of painting, his expertise"). (The text is transcribed in Creighton E. Gilbert, *L'arte del Quattrocento nelle testimonianze coeve*, Florence, 1988, p. 58). Warnke ingeniously suggests that the humanist theorists did not want to make much of the distinctiveness of an artist's "hand" because they associated it with merely physical workshop activity as against the more elevated achievement of conceiving a *historia*.

For an incisive investigation of fifteenth-century critical terminology, see Martin Kemp, "From 'Mimesis' to 'Fantasia': The Quattrocento Vocabulary of Creation, Inspiration, and Genius in the Visual Arts," *Viator*, VIII (1977), pp. 347–98. Had I sufficient space, this account would include at least two other Quattrocento critics, Lorenzo Ghiberti, in the *Commentarii* (ed. J. Schlosser, *Lorenzo Ghibertis Denkwürdigkeiten: I Commentarii*, 2 vols., Berlin, 1912) and Giovanni Santi (Gilbert, *L'arte del Quattrocento*, pp. 118ff.); Gilbert also cites (pp. 161f.) a letter assessing Florentine artists by the agent of the duke of Milan that shows an awareness of individual style comparable to that of Landino.

18 Leonardo da Vinci, *Trattato* (Vatican, Cod. Urb. Lat 1270), fol. 133r (ed. Heinrich Ludwig, *Das Buch von der Malerei*, Vienna, 1882, p. 411). The brief biographies of Leonardo, Raphael, Michelangelo, and other artists by Paolo Giovio (*circa* 1523–27) (Paola Barocchi, *Scritti d'arte del '500*, 3 vols., Milan and Naples, 1973, vol. I, pp. 3ff.) do not represent a significant advance in critical capacity over Landino's. A brief in a letter purportedly from Raphael to Castiglione would, because of its presumed author, carry great weight in this account if one could be sure of its authenticity: "In order to paint a beautiful woman I should have to see many beautiful women, and this under the condition that you were to help me with making a choice; but since there are so few beautiful women and so few sound judges, I make use of a certain idea that comes into my head. Whether it has any artistic value I am unable to say. I try very hard just to have it." The authenticity has been questioned by a number of scholars, among them, Wilhelm Wanscher, *Rafaello Santi da Urbino: His Life and Works*, London, 1926, p. 148; David Brown and Konrad Oberhuber, "Leonardo and Raphael in Rome," in *Essays Presented to Myron P. Gilmore*, ed. S. Bertelli and G. Rama, 2 vols., Florence, 1978, vol. II, p. 84 n.; and more recently, by John Shearman (see John Shearman, *Raphael in Early Modern Sources: 1483–1602*, 2 vols., New Haven and London, 2003, vol. I, p. 17 and n. 29).

19 *Il cortegiano*, I. xxxvii, xxxviii. See David Summers, *The Judgment of Taste*, Cambridge, 1987, pp. 317–20.

20 This and the following quotations are from Giorgio Vasari, *Le Opere di Giorgio Vasari*, ed. Gaetano Milanesi, Florence: G.C. Sansoni S.p.A., 1973, which is a reprint of the 1906 edition. This quotation: vol. II, p. 95: *Proemio* to Part II.

21 Ibid., vol. IV, p. 7: *Proemio* to Part III.

22 Ibid., vol. II, pp. 95–6: *Proemio* to Part II.

23 Ibid., vol. I, pp. 168–9; Introduction, "Della pittura."

24 Svetlana Leontief Alpers, "Ekphrasis and Aesthetic Attitudes in Vasari's Lives," *Journal of the Warburg and Courtauld Institues*, XXIII (July-December 1960), pp. 190-215.

25 Giorgio Vasari, *Le Opere di Giorgio Vasari*, ed. Gaetano Milanesi, Florence: G.C. Sansoni S.p.A., 1973, vol. IV, p. 11: *Proemio* to Part III.

26 *Ekphrasis* is a genre that comes to the fore in imperial late antique rhetoric; it is defined by Hermogenes of Tarsus in the *Photogymnastica* (See Baxandall, *Giotto*, p. 85). For other references, see *Reallexikon für Antike und Christentum*, vol. IV (Stuttgart, 1959), pp. 922f.; its use to describe works of art is exemplified in the *Imagines* ascribed to Philostratus.

27 Giorgio Vasari, *Le Opere di Giorgio Vasari*, ed. Gaetano Milanesi, Florence: G.C. Sansoni S.p.A., 1973, vol. IV, p. 371: on Raffaello da Urbino.

28 Ibid., vol. IV, p. 9: *Proemio* to Part III.

29 On this issue, see Hans Belting, *Das Ende der Kunstgeschichte?*, 2nd. edn., Munich, 1984, part II (English edn.: *The End of the History of Art?*, Chicago, 1987).

30 *Epitome rerum Romanorum*, Preface; published in Italian in 1546. Cf. E. Panofsky, "The First Page of Giorgio Vasari's 'Libro'," in *Meaning in the Visual Arts*, New York, 1955, pp.

216–18. The essay was first published as "Das erste Blatt aus dem 'Libro' Giorgio Vasaris," *Städel-Jahrbuch*, VI (1930), pp. 25–72.

31 Z. Wazbinski, "L'idée d'histoire dans la première et la seconde édition des Vies de Vasari," in *Vasari storiografo e artista*, Florence, 1976, pp. 1–26. The essay demonstrates the role of Vincenzo Borghini in influencing Vasari's method of documenting the past; it is based on *Vasari i dzieji "Sztuk Rysunk" Uwagi nad Geneza Nowozytnej Biografiki Artystycznej / Vasari et son histoire des arts de dessin: à la source de la biographie moderne*, Torun, 1972; and a work I have not found, also in Polish but cited by the author as *Vasari et l'istoriographie artistigue moderne*, Warsaw, 1975.

32 The divinity of the artist already was claimed in Marsuppini's epitaph for Brunelleschi (1446), and the concept of creativity was extensively discussed by Leonardo da Vinci, whose writings, however, were not published during the Renaissance; see Kemp, "From 'Mimesis' to 'Fantasia'," pp. 376ff.

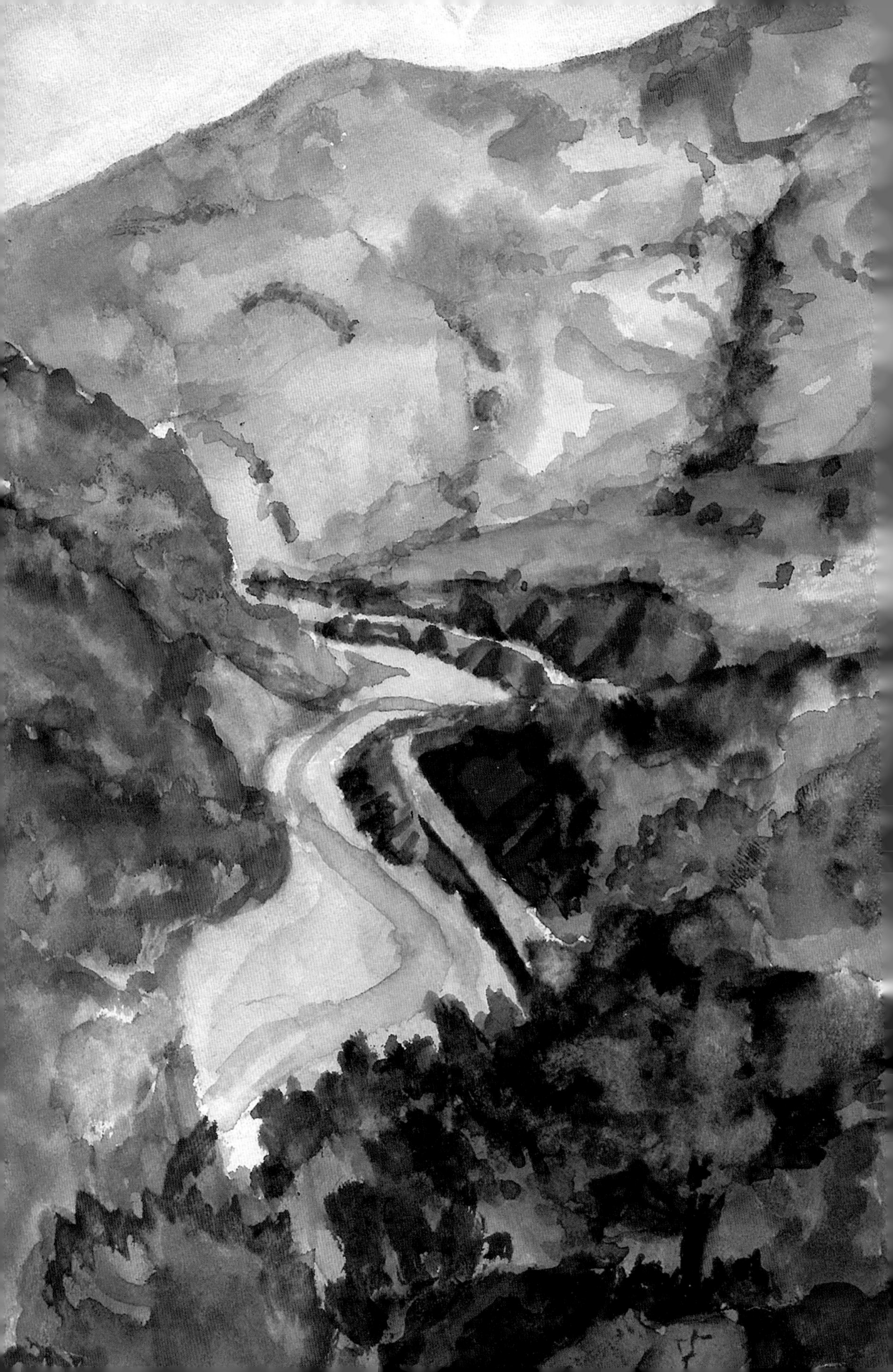

3

The Liberation of Mantua and Other Unintended Consequences of My Military Service during World War II

IN THE SUMMER OF 1942, AFTER BEING REJECTED by the armed services because of my nearsightedness, I attempted to qualify for a job at the Offices of Strategic Services (OSS), the precursor of the CIA, by learning to type. I signed up for a summer course at the Katie Gibbs Secretarial School in my home town, San Francisco. The OSS rejected my application, so I returned to New York University for a second year of graduate studies in art history. But at that very moment I learned that the Draft had run out of candidates with 20/20 vision and was told to report for induction. A classmate in the same situation suggested that we enroll in a program at Columbia University sponsored by the US Army to study languages in preparation for service in Signal Intelligence. We chose Russian, and at the end of one term of daily eight-hour classes, we were reading Tolstoy and conversing hesitantly. After returning home to San Francisco for induction, I was sent to a secret camp in Virginia for training in cryptanalysis.

Initially, the training was primarily boot camp, for which my classmates and I – mostly graduate students – were poorly prepared. Most of them were vociferous in their opposition to being treated like incompetent eggheads, but

19 James S. Ackerman, *Road in the Tuscan Apennines* (detail), 1944

I was so relieved at having an extended respite from the stress and responsibilities of graduate school that not being expected to make any decisions for myself seemed a balm.

When cryptography classes started, we were asked whether we intended to work in German or Japanese (Russian be damned!), and I chose German because we had had to learn it for our art-history research. Then we began the study of an already obsolete approach to cryptography called Playfair, which had been used by the British in the First World War.

After a very short time our group was shipped out to Scotland and immediately boarded trains to London, where we were housed in a semi-destroyed mansion on one of the beautiful West End garden squares. I slept in a bathtub. Shortly, we were sent to the village of Stoke Fleming on the Devon coast, where there was a station in the ring of Royal Air Force posts along the southern and eastern shores of England intercepting communications from the Luftwaffe squadrons that were bombing London. Since each station could determine the direction of the signal, together they could locate the exact position of the planes by triangulation and alert the anti-aircraft teams. We stayed there for a couple of weeks learning the procedures and then in October 1943 returned to London, where we were comfortably housed and could go to the theater and concerts. In December, shortly before our departure from England, I attempted to transfer to the Monuments and Fine Arts division of AMGOT (Allied Military Government for Occupied Territories), but we were suddenly told to prepare for departure. We were taken to a port on the south coast to embark on an old merchant ship equipped with huge machine guns (I was assigned to night duty on one of these, with inadequate instructions about how to operate it – where was the trigger?).

The destination was Algiers, but there were no Luftwaffe planes in Africa. We were billeted a couple of miles to the west of the city in an abandoned Arab spa. We spent time studying messages from the remains of General Rommel's army, whose code books had been captured recently (the German cryptographic methods were as obsolete as ours), but their army in Africa had already been decimated and were not worth listening to.

Though I am Jewish, I decided to prepare for conversion to Christianity at a nearby Anglican church. My motives were mixed. I felt the need for

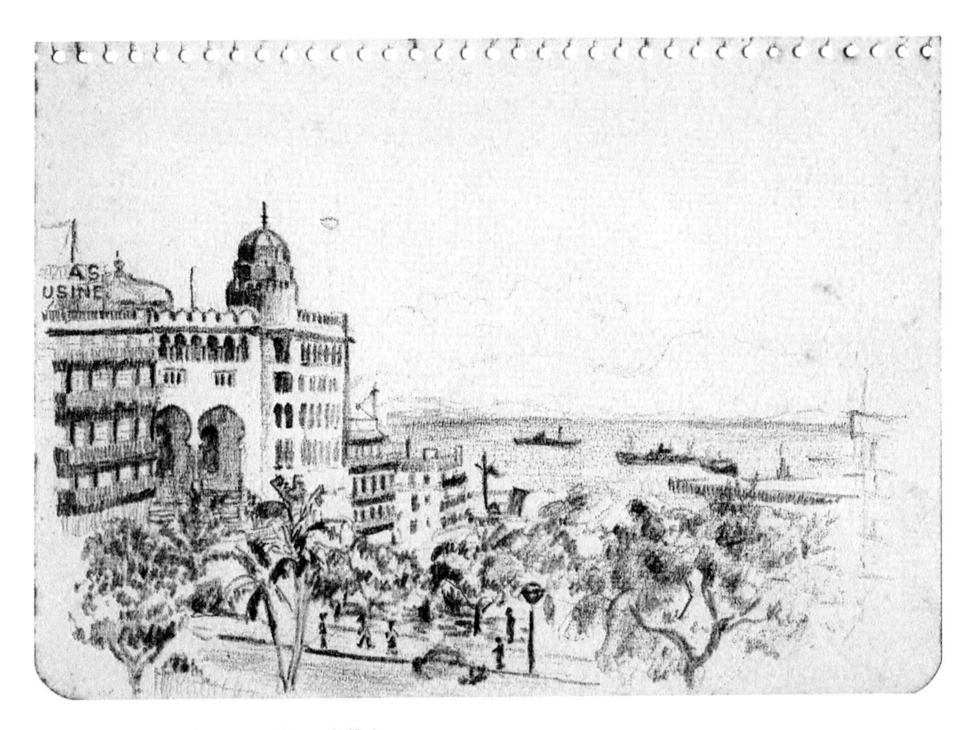

20 James S. Ackerman, *Port of Algiers*, 1944

some kind of spiritual support, and the only religious training I had was at the Episcopalian prep school I attended in California. I was baptized in Algiers, but I deferred confirmation because I feared that my choice was motivated by the urge to escape anti-Semitism. By the time I returned to civilian life, I was embarrassed by the episode.

I was reminded of the details of my service in Algiers and Italy by letters home which my mother had saved, and which had been stored untouched for decades in my basement. They included many drawings and watercolors, including a seaside hotel and ruins at nearby Tipasa.

After our stay in Algiers we were transferred to Caserta, outside Naples, where the Army had established a huge staging center. We were there from July to December 1944. I read *War and Peace* in one of the paperback books given out to GIs (the ancestor of the modern ones), appeared in a performance of *The Pirates of Penzance*, joined a barbershop quartet and met Thornton Wilder, who had come to direct a performance of *Our Town* to

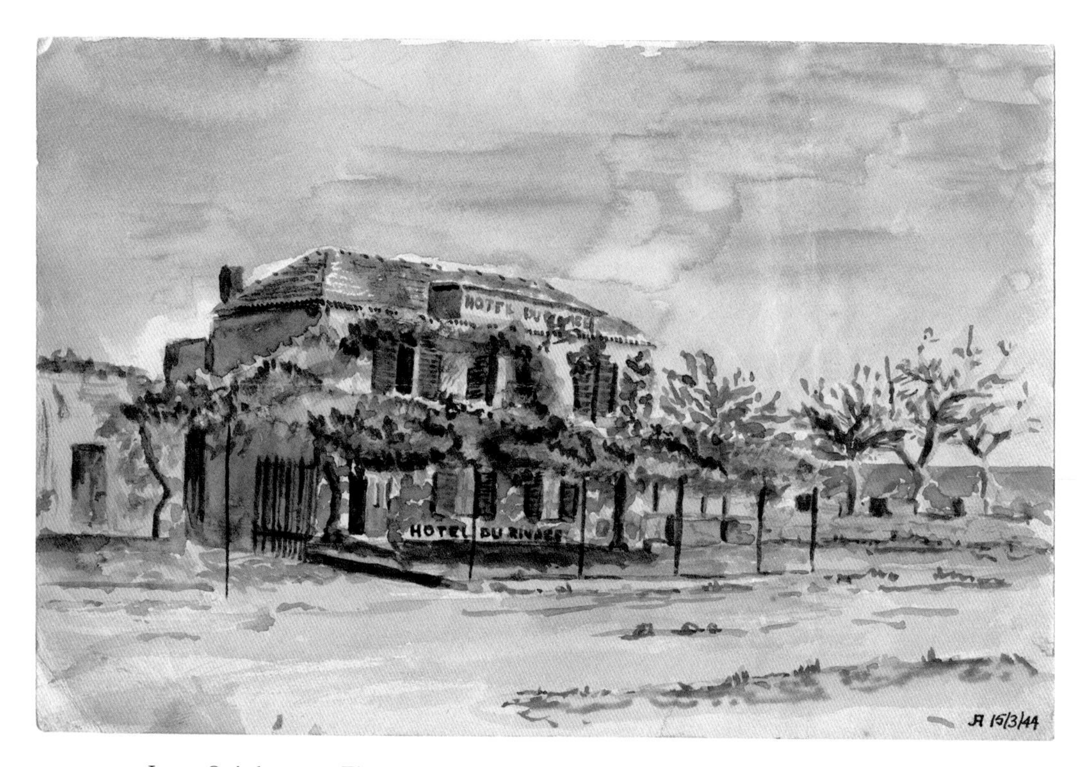

21 James S. Ackerman, *Tipasa*, 1944

provide some non-military culture (as T. S. Eliot had during the brief London stay), and produced more pictures.

By this time our team had been commissioned and equipped as the 849th Signal Intelligence Unit. It was composed of a captain, one second lieutenant, one sergeant, and twenty-six Tech-5s (corporals), roughly half of these radio operators and half cryptographers.

Almost everything arranged during my time in the military was done with a high level of efficiency honed by the Army's two centuries of practice. We were supplied not only with the necessities of transportation, shelter, medical care, and nourishment when required, but also winter clothing, books and magazines, rapidly distributed mail to and from home, eyeglasses, cigarettes, candy rations, shaving equipment, and contraceptives. The frustrations of our mission were not the fault of the Army but of the planners in Washington, probably in the Office of Strategic Services.

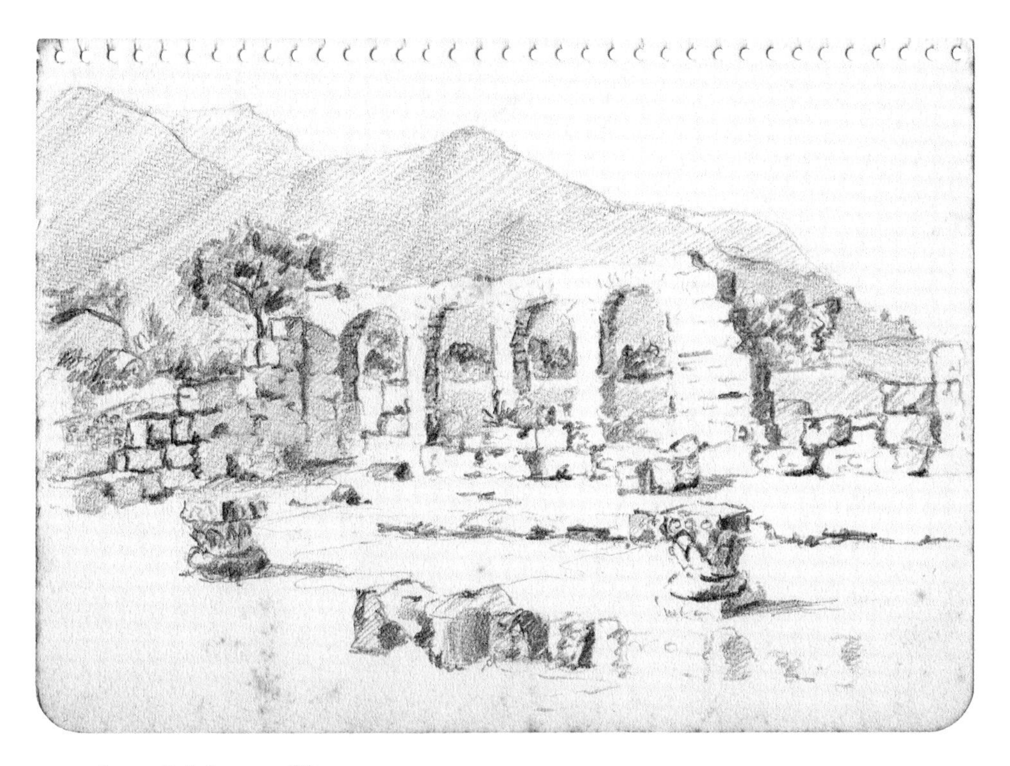

22 James S. Ackerman, *Tipasa*, 1944

During this time I had an extended visit to Rome (which had been an "Open City" spared of bombings and military action). I was an energetic tourist, walking from monument to monument like a medieval and Renaissance pilgrim, with the added pleasure of going to the opera. I wrote of the desperate economy and life-threatening shortages of food and other necessities, which still survived for the poor and elderly when I returned as a Rome Prize Fellow at the American Academy in 1949 to write my dissertation on the Renaissance extension of the Vatican Palace, which I later revised for publication by the Vatican press.

Ultimately, we received an assignment; we were equipped with several two-ton trucks to transport our "offices," those of the radio operators, tents and other equipment, and kitchen, so that we could quickly move about at will to find the best area for reception.

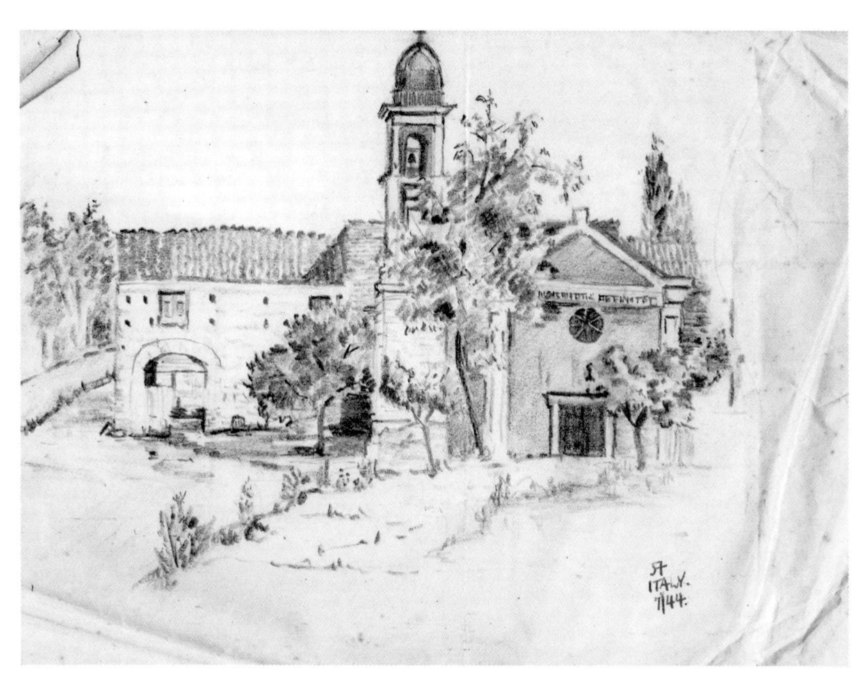

23 James S. Ackerman, *Caserta*, 1944

24 James S. Ackerman, *Caserta Camp*, 1944

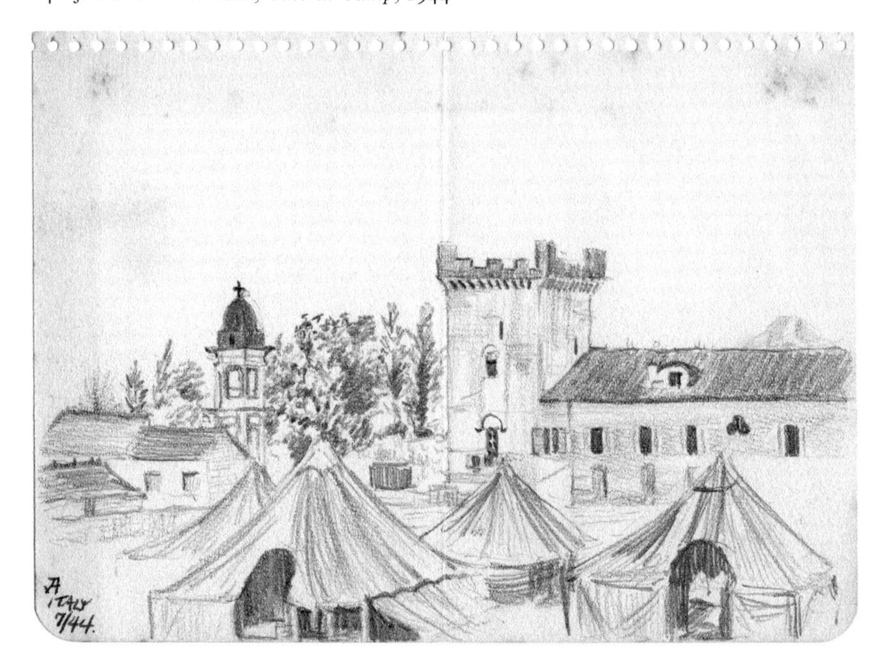

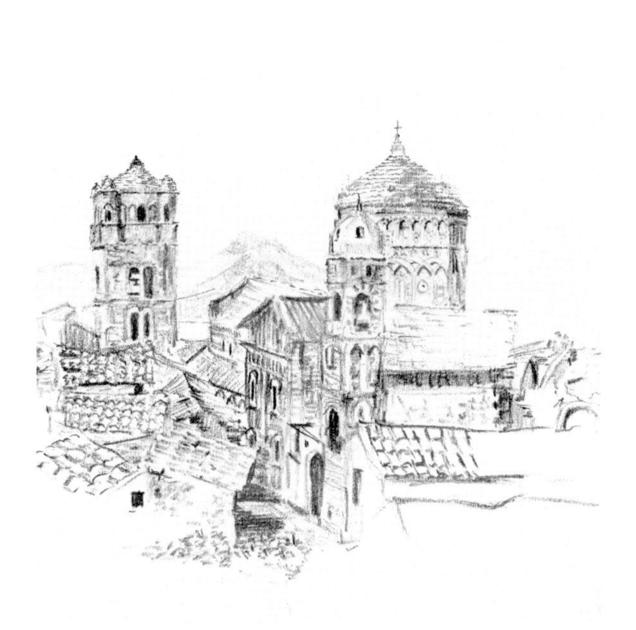

25 James S. Ackerman, *Caserta Vecchia*, 1944

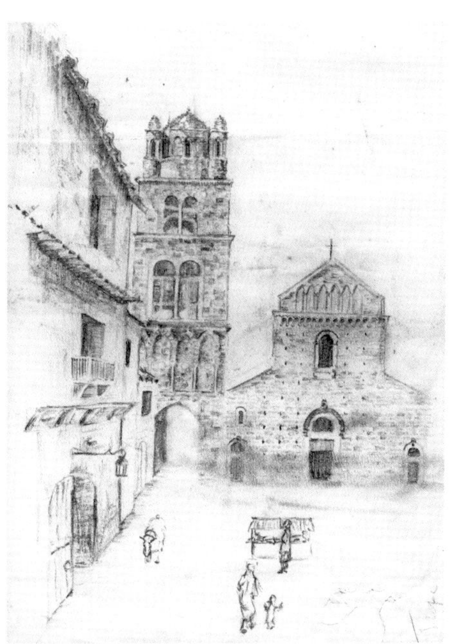

26 James S. Ackerman, *Caserta Vecchia*, 1944

Our initial assignment was in the mountains north of Florence. When we were given a day off to go into the city, we rushed for the public baths (a now obsolete institution) to get clean. But on a later visit we were given a tour of the principal monuments by a professional guide, and I did find time to make a sketch of the Ponte Vecchio, the only Arno bridge that the Germans had not blown up.

Shortly after, four of us were ordered to join a British unit in the mountains to find out about local interception issues. Our team was composed of three technical corporals and a lieutenant, recently upgraded from corporal (he later became a professor of sociology at Columbia – many of the crypto teams became academics, including Nobel Prize economist Robert Solow at MIT (who had been reassigned to a different company). I was the driver, having been given a very short course in truck driving at Caserta, and was still trying to figure out how to shift. My companions were terrified.

The Brits had a tiny group in which three or four cryptographers, graduates of Oxford, were keeping track of enemy communication with none of

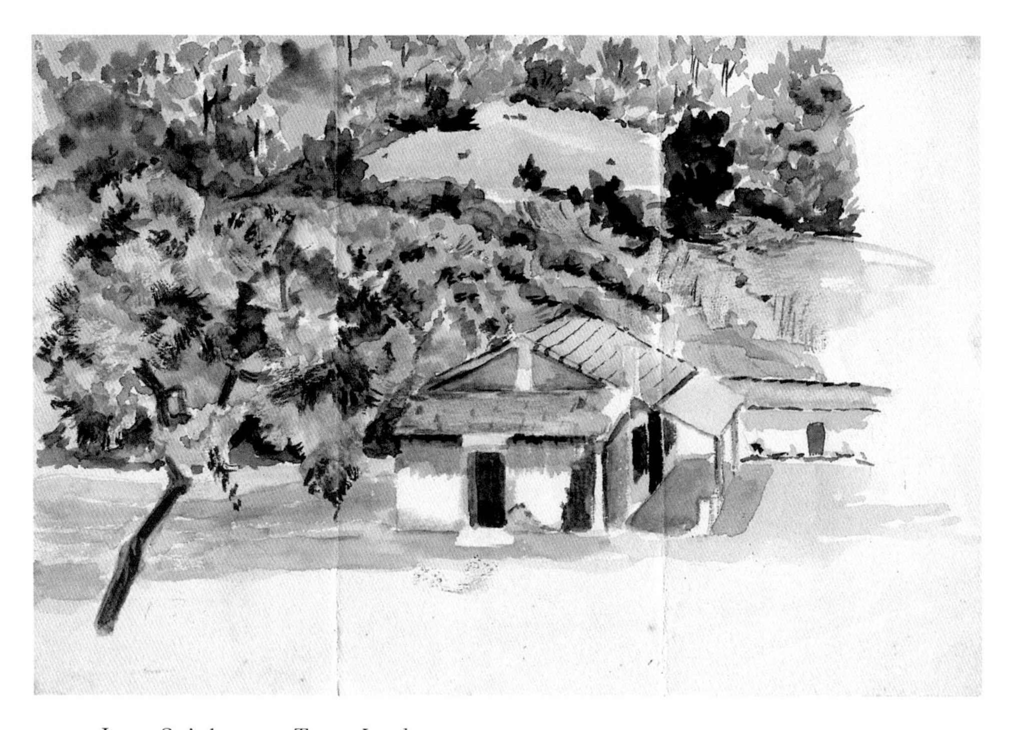

27 James S. Ackerman, *Tuscan Landscape*, 1945

the fancy systems we had developed for archiving the addresses and messages of enemy operators – they just piled papers on the floor and counted on their extraordinary memories to find one they needed in the mess. Food was minimal: meals would be delivered from the rear once a week, and after four or five days there was nothing left but the Brits' favorite snack, toast soaked in fat.

At this time, in late 1944, our Fifth Army and the British force were stalled south of Bologna, along what was called the Gothic Line, extending across the peninsula at the base of the mountains. The outdoor life in the snow was challenging. We spent most of the time on a height far above Bologna, which was visible from the seat of a latrine the carpenter had constructed at the high point. We were a couple of hundred yards in front of an Artillery company, which made it very noisy. I think my present deafness may be attributed to this. The Germans beneath us fired sporadically in our direction; they were short of ammunition.

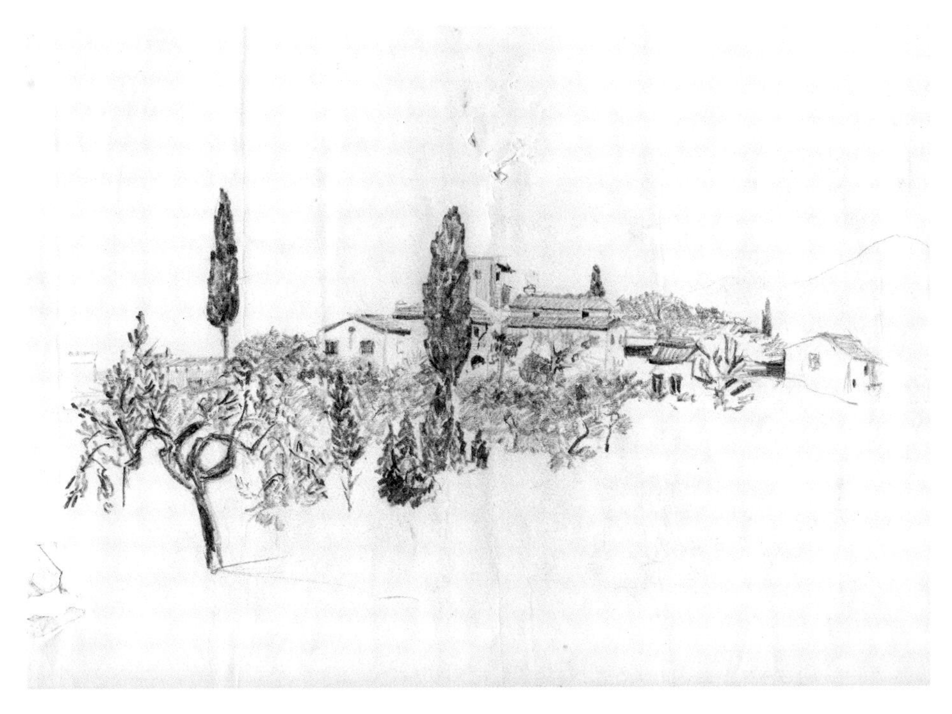

28 James S. Ackerman, *Tuscan Village*, 1945

Because the German front was stabilized across the width of the Italian peninsula, the troops could safely be supplied with small machines with eight spinning wheels so that every letter could be encoded differently. Messages could be deciphered only by mainframe computers in Washington. We didn't get the results for two weeks; they would describe intended deployment of platoons that had long since occurred.

Just before the collapse of the German front, a few of us were sent to Viareggio on the west coast. The enemy encryption system had broken down, and hectic messages were coming in plain language, but at that moment a bomb or shell exploded in a building next door, and I was too terrified to keep track of them. Our group returned to the base and the whole company packed into trucks and started to move down to Bologna. Halting for sleep on the first night, we were strafed by a single enemy plane, but none of us was hit. By the next day we were passing the infantry and became the first Fifth Army arrivals at villages where joyous inhabitants hailed us as saviors,

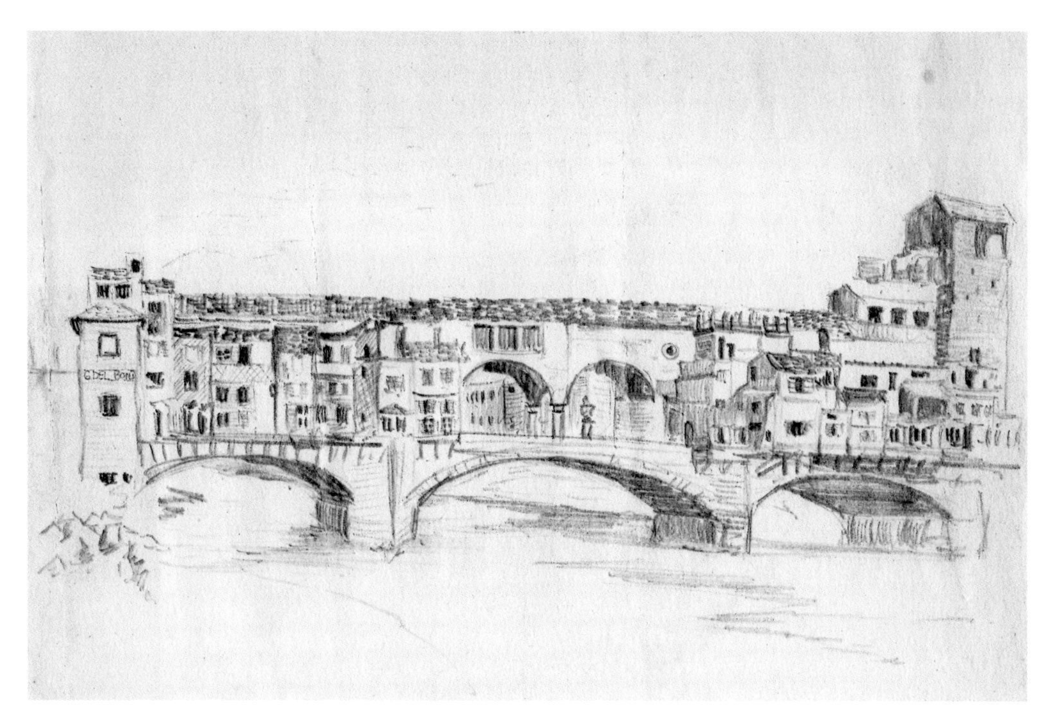

29 James S. Ackerman, *Ponte Vecchio, Florence*, 1945

and we responded by tossing packets of cigarettes and food rations. On the second day we forded the wide Po river, I can't remember how (either the Germans hadn't had time to destroy the bridges or our Engineer Corps had arrived ahead of us). Once across, we camped in a field and set up our two-person pup tents.

The next night there were rumors that a German unit was nearby and we were ordered to form concentric rings and to load our carbines. Since no one had instructed us on how they worked, the chances of being victims of friendly fire were worrisome – but the enemy did not appear. When the major decided to stay until his adjutant could determine the viability of the route north, my pup tent partner and I were permitted to go along in the Jeep to have a look at the nearest town.

The Jeep driver turned off the main road onto a causeway crossing the river toward Renaissance fortifications and passed through a portal leading to a large piazza framed by porticoes. I gradually realized that this was

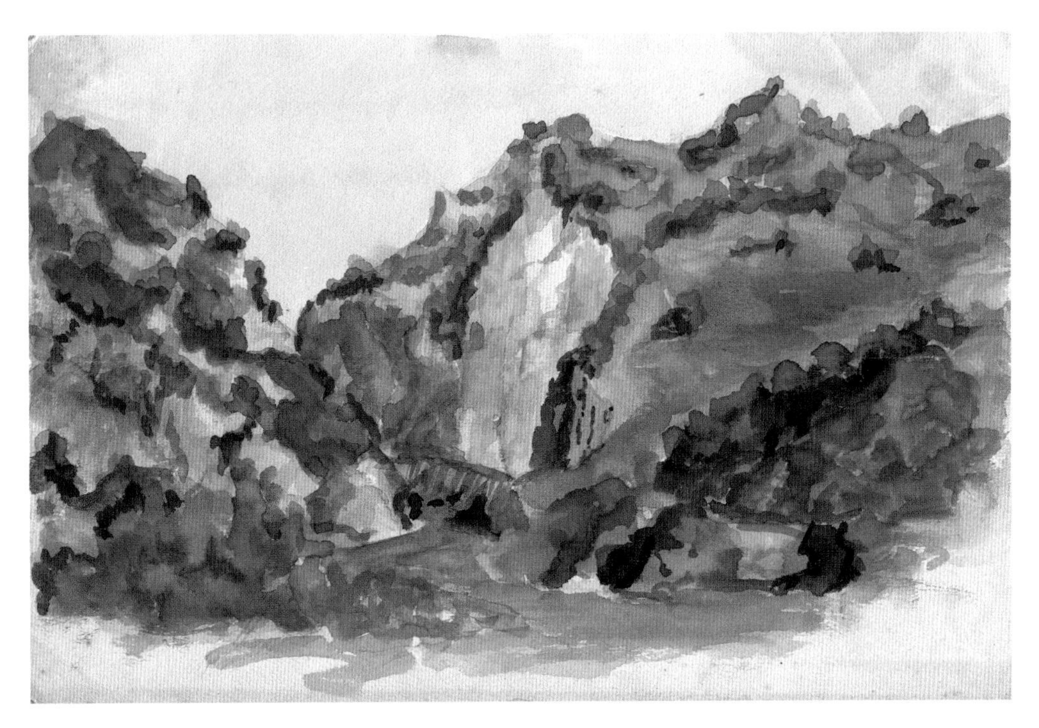

30 James S. Ackerman, *Tuscan Landscape*, 1945

Mantua – churches by Leon Battista Alberti, the father of Renaissance architecture, paintings by Mantegna in the palace, the Palazzo del Te by Giulio Romano on the periphery, and the promise of a few hours of tourism! That was not to be: slowly and cautiously a few people emerged from the shadows of the loggias towards us, seeing that we were we unarmed – and having been told that the forward troops of the allies were black cannibals – to ask who we were. When we told them they went wild with enthusiasm; some rushed away to spread the news.

A horde of citizens gathered and decided to organize a victory column headed by the mayor together with his two daughters, who linked arms with us for a procession through the town, which terminated shortly with the return of the Jeep.

The following day we continued northward to Lake Como, but were told to return to the town of Monza, a short distance from Milan, where the company would be billeted in a pleasant light-filled structure that probably

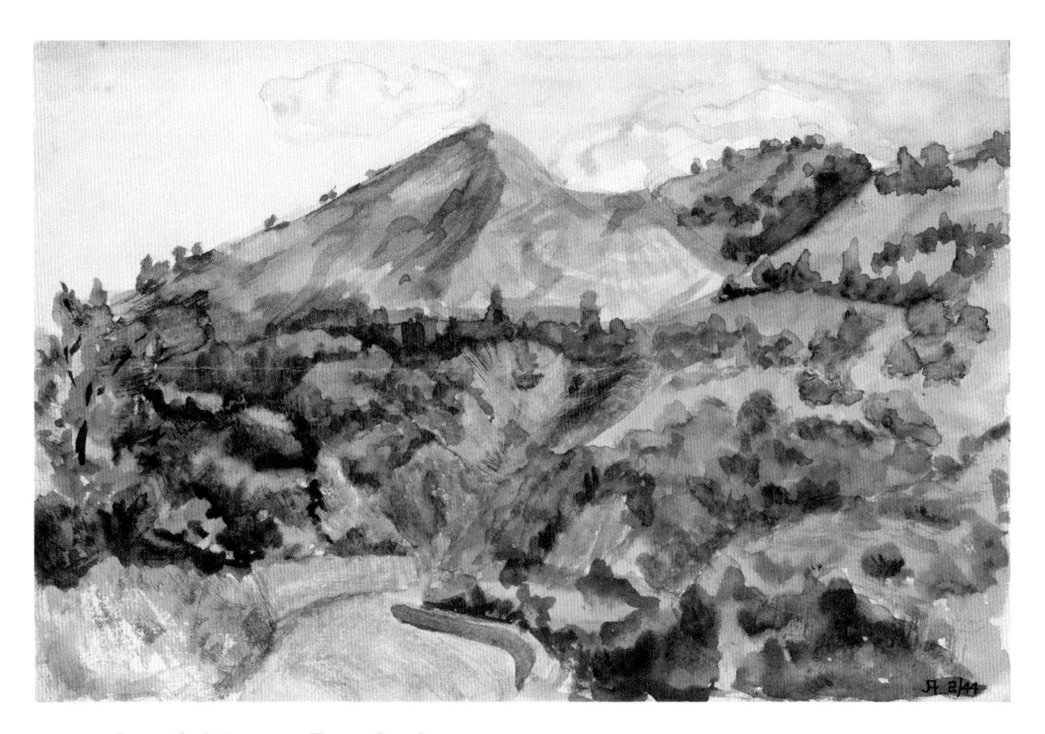

31 James S. Ackerman, *Tuscan Landscape*, 1945

had been a small factory. There we were to wait until we could be sent home – among the first units in Europe – for training in Japanese (this was the ultimate in incompetence – it would have required several years of intense study!).

I got bored playing cards and reading all day and got permission to work with the Monuments and Fine Arts office in Milan. I was housed in an old hotel and assigned to take a truck each day to retrieve papers sent by the Royal Archives for safeguarding in the nearby Certosa di Pavia, a Carthusian monastery. As the loading of the material was delegated to Italian workers, I wandered about the cloisters and their extraordinary church, and my passion for architectural history was kindled; in 1949 my Master's thesis, "The Certosa of Pavia and the Renaissance in Milan," became my first published article. Essentially, this brief experience, which had had nothing to do with the allied victory, solidified my decision to make the art and architecture of Italy the focus of my work as a scholar and teacher.

The company was repatriated shortly as planned. Because I was the only enlisted man promoted from a technical rank to staff sergeant, I was told to take charge of enlisting members of the many units on board to clean the ship. But at this point military discipline had dissolved; no one showed up as ordered and the officers were not interested in enforcement, so I had to do it all myself, cursing my promotion.

We arrived at Fort Dix in New Jersey in late July 1945, and were released for two weeks of home leave. I returned to San Francisco to comfort my parents who were mourning the death of my brother – he was ten years older, a major in the Army assigned to supervise the transfer of US funds and equipment to military units in China. Having been wrongly accused by the Chinese of misappropriating funds, and under stress from working alone with allies whose language he barely knew, he had committed suicide.

During this visit the atomic bombings of Hiroshima and Nagasaki hastened the surrender of Japan and, on returning to Fort Dix, my company was demobilized. The irony of my service was that while I was not given an opportunity to use the cryptoanalytic skills I had been given, my civilian career richly benefited from what I learned of Italy and its landscape and architecture, and I was able to return to my studies at the Institute of Fine Arts of New York University at the start of the fall semester in 1945, with tuition and books paid by the GI Bill, while many of my fellow soldiers who had experienced the brutality of combat were unable to return to civilian life for a year or two after.

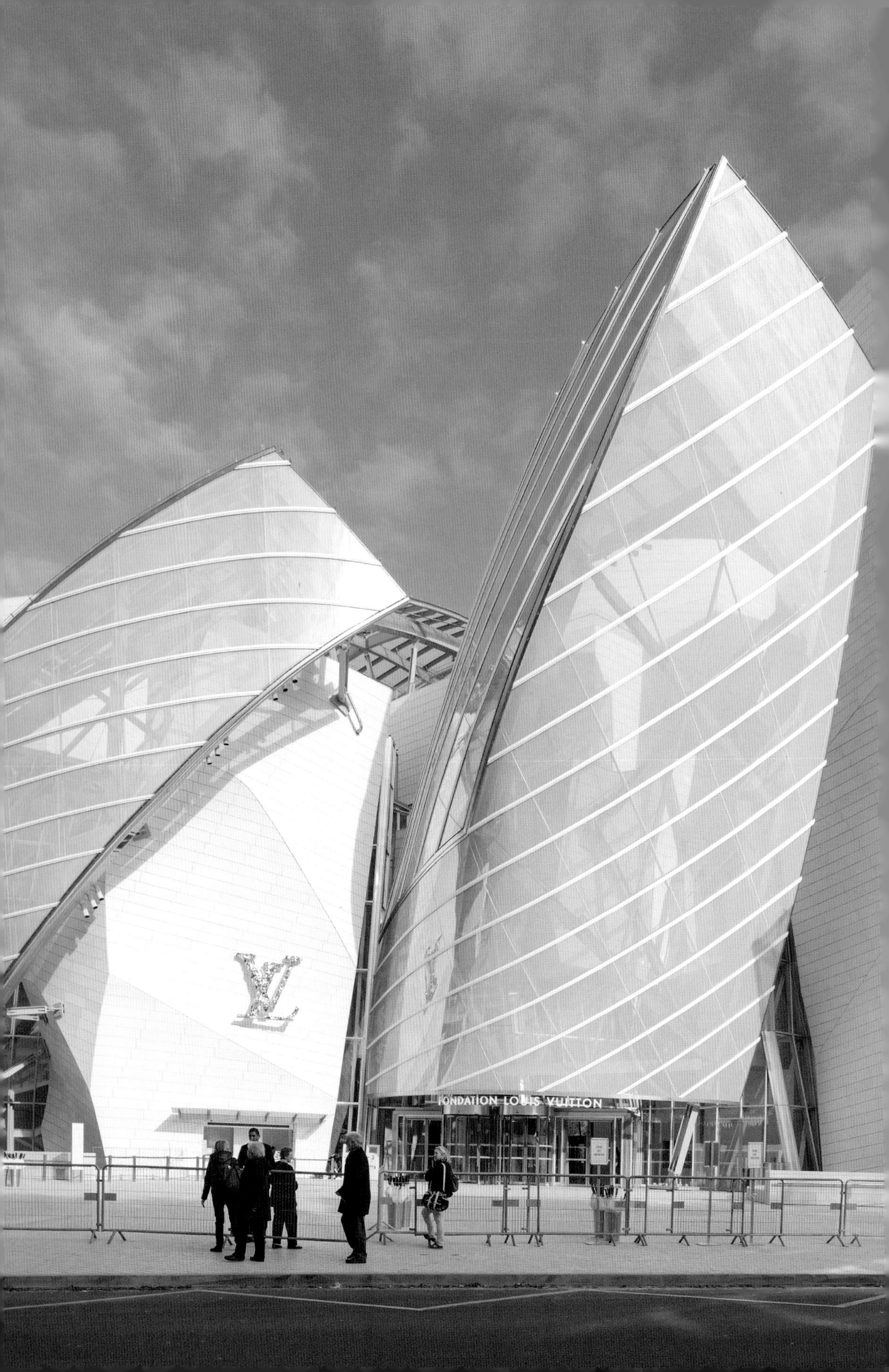
FONDATION LOUIS VUITTON

4

La Fondation Louis Vuitton

THE ARCHITECT

Thirty-eight years ago Frank Gehry told an interviewer:

> My approach to architecture is different – I search out the work of artists and use the art as a means of inspiration. I try to rid myself and the other members of the firm of the burden of culture and look for new ways to approach the work. I want to be open-ended. There are no rules, no right or wrong.[1]

Gehry is one of a small number of architects who rejected the millennial practice of initiating a design by sketching (or, recently, by computer) one or more versions of the plan, elevation, and section of a proposed building, first advocated by Vitruvius, the first-century-BCE Roman architectural theorist. Gehry begins with loose curvilinear sweeps of a pen (made in what the Renaissance theorist Vasari called *furor*), conveying not so much the form of a building as its dynamic, as can be seen in plate 33, an early study for the Vuitton Foundation building (pl. 32). In Gehry's architectural practice, these drawings and loose cardboard models are translated by members of his team from CATIA programs, originally employed in aircraft design, into one adapted for architecture. An early example of this method was realized in the Guggenheim Museum in Bilbao. The program was sent directly to a factory, which produced the curvilinear roofing and delivered it to the site ready for placement (pl. 34).

Detail of pl. 32

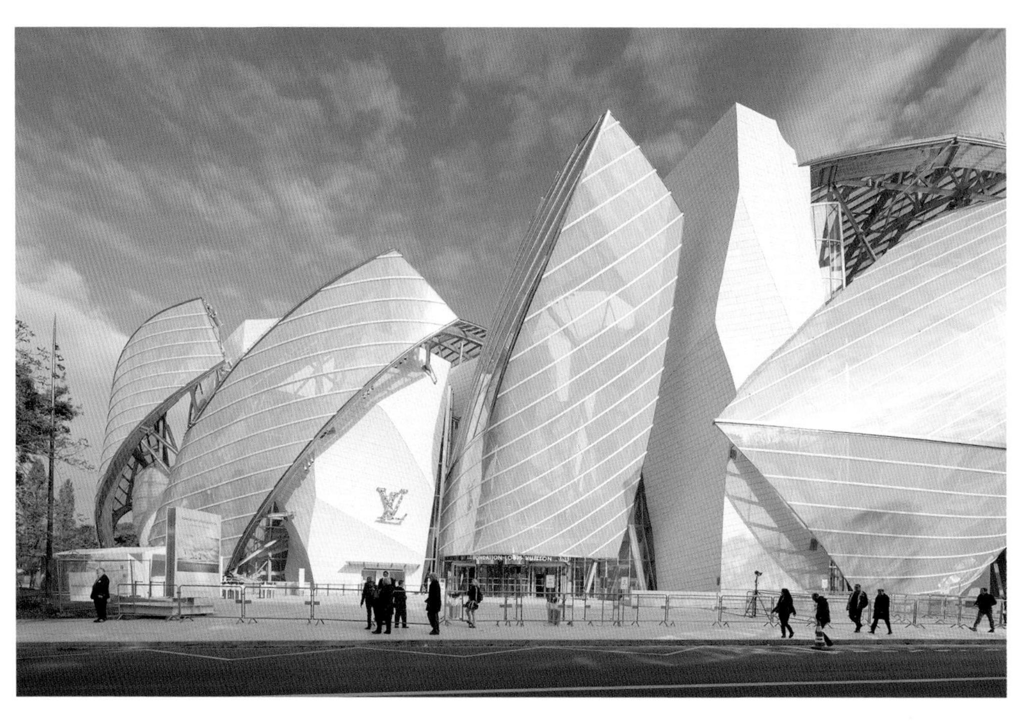

32 Exterior view of the Louis Vuitton Foundation, Paris

33 Frank Gehry, preliminary sketch for the Louis Vuitton Foundation project, 2006

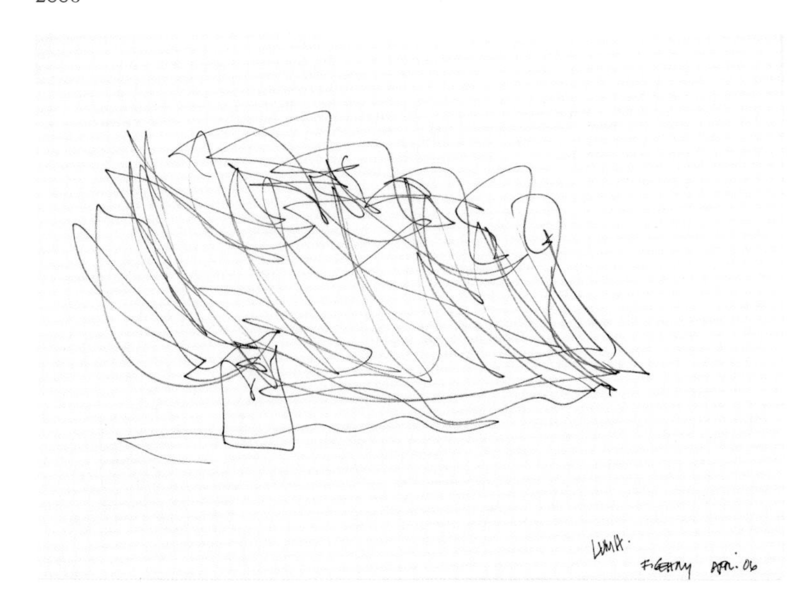

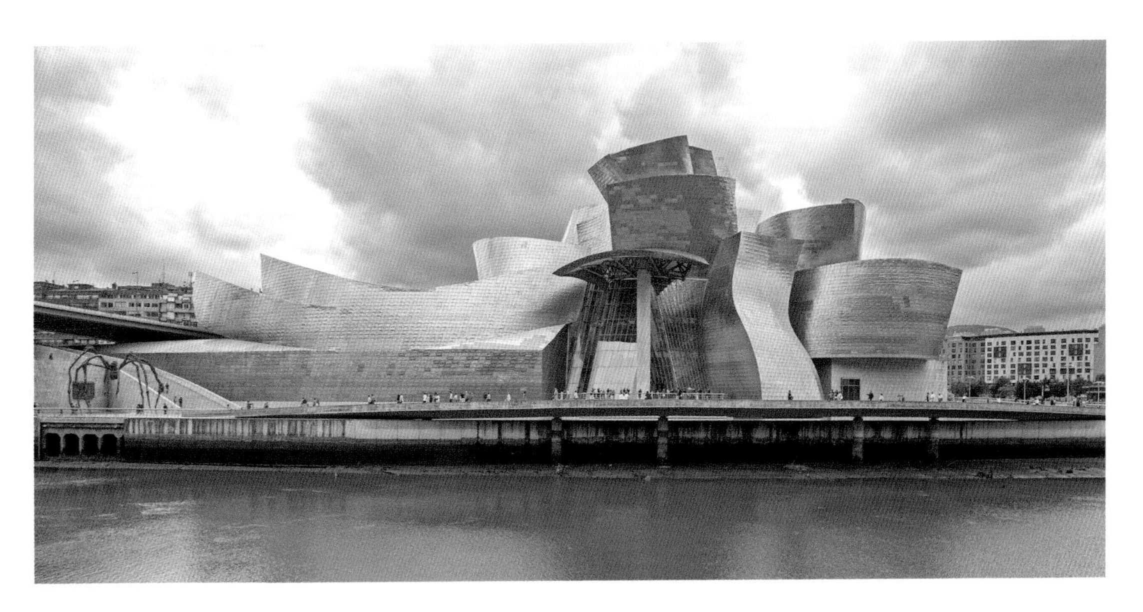

34 Guggenheim Museum, Bilbao

35 Michelangelo, *Waking Slave*, 1530–34

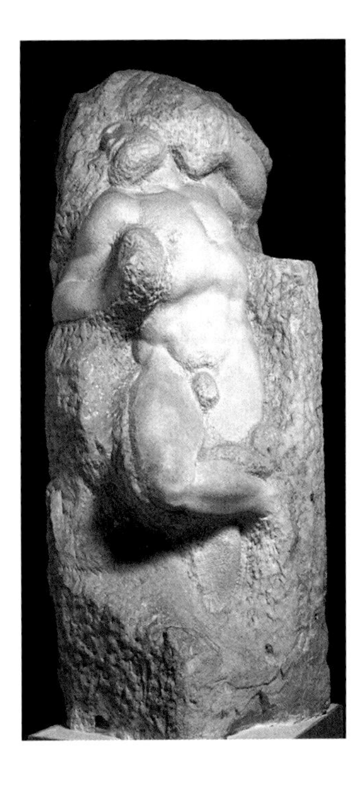

Having throughout my career visualized architectural projects in the Vitruvian mode drawn or printed on paper, I found it challenging to imagine how artisans could work from a three-dimensional presentation of a design of the whole and parts of a building. But it helped me to recall this similar skill displayed in Michelangelo's unfinished sculptures of slaves intended for the tomb of Pope Julius II, now in the Accademia in Florence (pl. 35). The artist made only slight sketches on paper before starting because he could visualize the figures so completely that he was able to work from one or two sides of the block to carve from the outside in, gradually allowing the completely three-dimensional figure to emerge. As he wrote in one of his sonnets: "In the marble the image is there, rich and tender, waiting for our genius to bring it forth."

PRECURSORS IN TWENTIETH-CENTURY ARCHITECTURE

In the early years of modernism, occasional departures from traditional rectangles, ovals, and circles in buildings opened new paths: Frank Lloyd Wright's Guggenheim Museum in New York (1943–59) and the Morris store in San Francisco (1948), and Scharoun's concert hall in Berlin (1960–63) all employed traditional masonry and reinforced concrete. Several encountered design problems: the spiraling ramp of the Guggenheim Museum in New York forces the visitor to see art works from a slope. Erich Mendelsohn's Einstein Tower in Potsdam (1919–21) was built with stucco-covered brick rather than poured concrete as planned, owing to the shortage of building materials in Germany following World War I (pl. 36). In the years before computers were adapted to architectural design, between 1951 and 1953 Le Corbusier encountered difficulties calculating the surface undulations of the roof of Notre Dame du Haut at Ronchamp, a building that Gehry says he tries to visit every year (pl. 37). As Robin Evans has demonstrated, he sought help from the engineer André Maissionier, who used the mathematical system of ruled surfaces to resolve the problem.[2] Like Gehry, Maissonier understood that aircraft design could be applied to architecture. The Danish architect Jørn Utzon resigned from supervision of his Opera House in Sydney (1958–73) when public protest against cost overruns caused the government to commission local architects to design a different interior (pl. 38). Still, all of these buildings are examples of great leaps of imagination that inspired the expansion of the limits of architectural design.

THE VUITTON BUILDING IN THE CONTEXT OF THE HISTORY OF PRIVATE ART COLLECTIONS

In 1435, before the advent of printing, the brilliant Florentine humanist Leon Battista Alberti wrote a treatise, *Della pittura*, intended to inform his readers of the importance of painting to the revival of antiquity, which must have stimulated them to build collections. The book was dedicated to his friend Filippo Brunelleschi, whose success in building the dome of Florence Cathedral surpassed the Romans in its ingenuity. Alberti's treatise on architecture, *De re aedificatoria* (1452), provided a similar instruction to patrons of architecture.

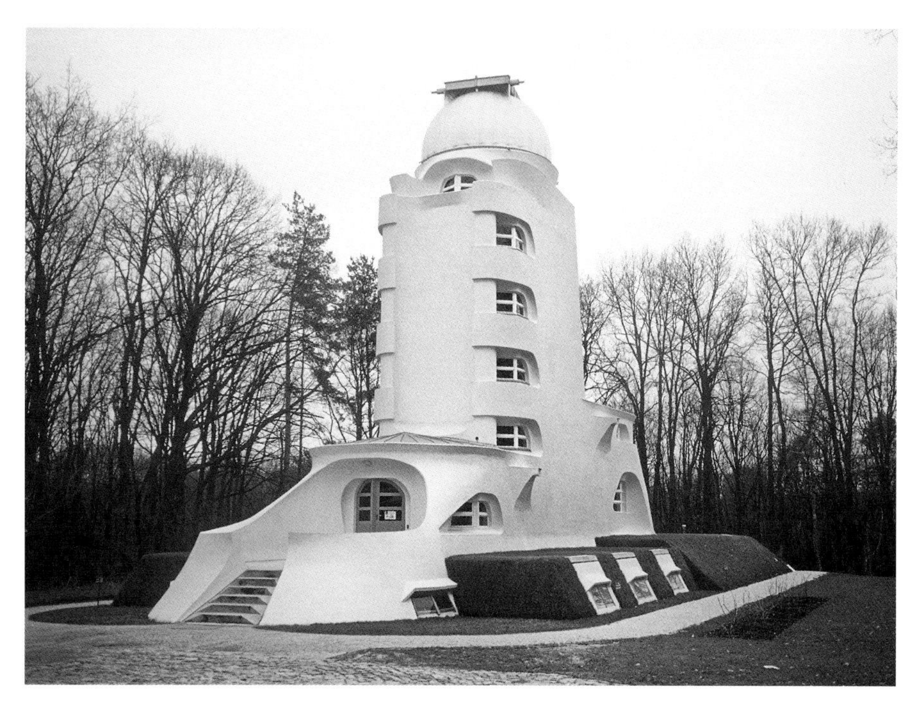

36 Einstein Tower, Potsdam

37 Notre Dame du Haut, Ronchamp

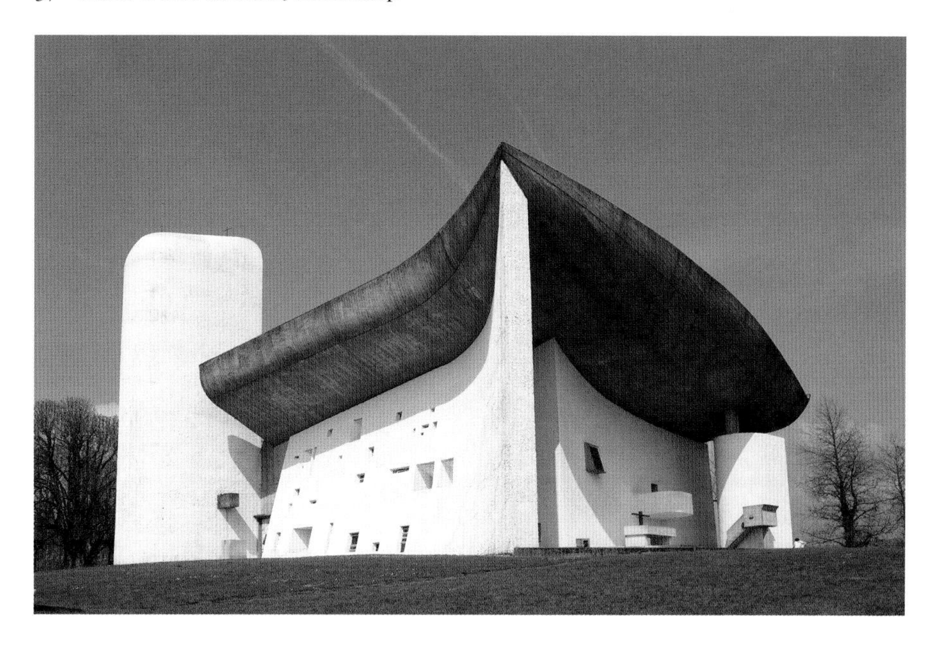

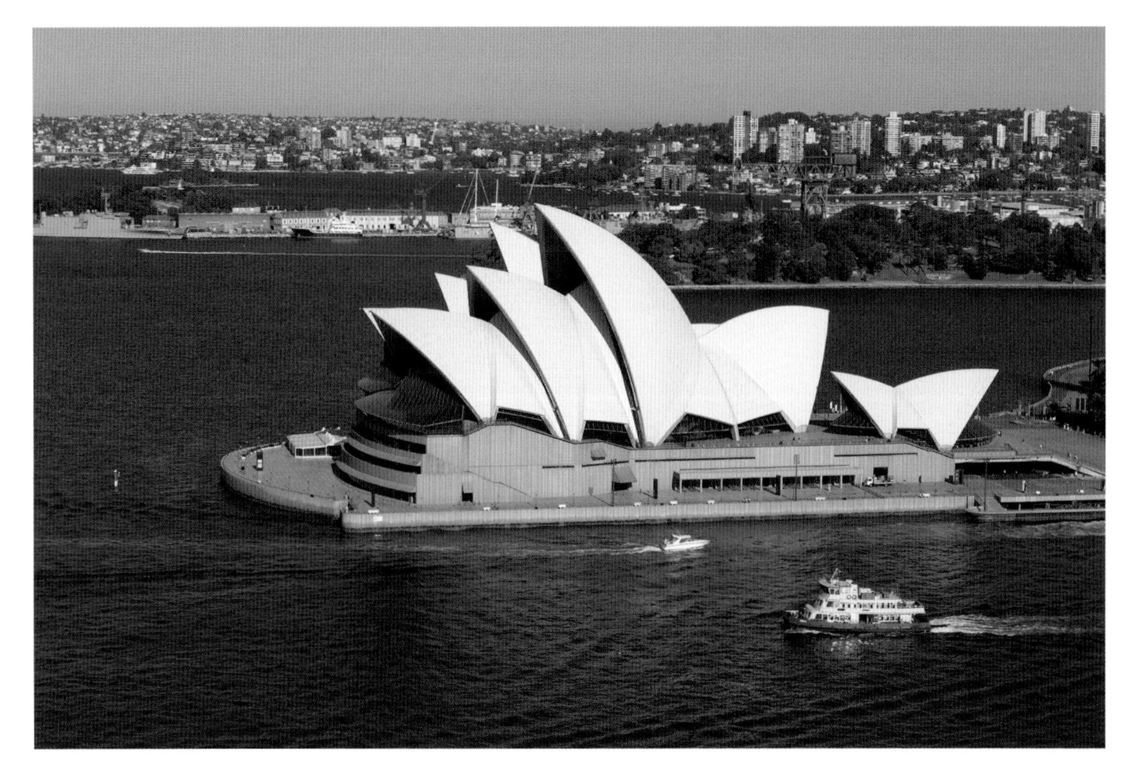

38 Sydney Opera House

In early Renaissance Italy, private collections were commonly acquired by the nobility of the many small states, by popes and cardinals, and by the affluent citizens of the republican states of Florence and Venice. At the close of the sixteenth century, the largest of them all was acquired by the Holy Roman Emperor and king of Spain, Charles v. These collections were ultimately opened to the public in the bequests of descendants.

Apart from collections devoted to sculpture, painting, and drawing, many families, especially in northern Europe, built *wunderkammern* to display curiosities of scientific interest, fossils, totems and tribal arts, tools, weapons, clothing, and sea shells. But the Italian model survived in Paris to the late nineteenth century in the Musée Jacquemart-André, housed in a grand palace – a merger of the collections of the wealthy Edouard André and Nélie Jacquemart, a successful portrait painter. In 1913 the palace and the collection were willed to the city as a public museum. Other collections in private houses, such as the Querini Stampalia in Venice, the Barnes in Philadelphia, and the Phillips in Washington, DC, have also been open to the public by the owners' bequests.

In 1997 the age of the house museum was virtually superseded (except for those of exceptionally wealthy collectors, not accessible to the public) by the construction of the Beyeler Museum in Basel, designed by the architect Renzo Piano for the collection of Ernst Beyeler, a successful art dealer in Bern. This innovation spread rapidly throughout western Europe but to a far greater extent in the USA, for example, Louis Kahn's Kimbell Museum in Fort Worth (pl. 39) and Tadao Ando's Pulitzer Museum in St. Louis. These showcases for private collectors could be lavishly funded and became architects' access to many other commissions, both private and public, and to international recognition. At the same time, other types of museums – natural history, local historical, scientific – have remained in old structures in a variety of styles or in bland commercial and industrial spaces.

39 Kimbell Art Museum, Fort Worth, Texas

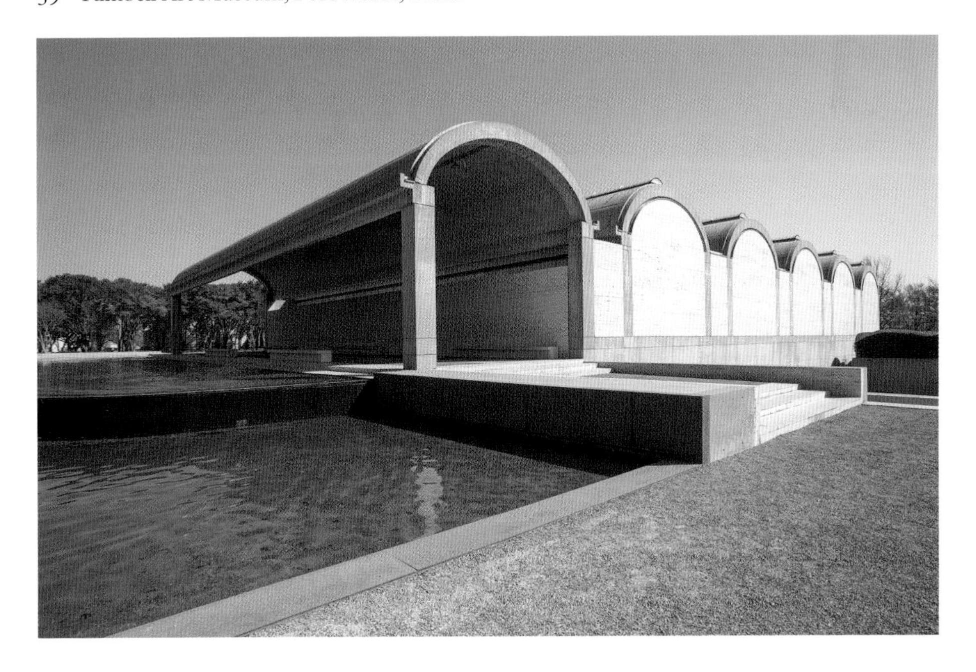

Art museums replace for many in contemporary society a kind of spiritual experience – an opportunity to encounter profound insights, universal stories, and to be introduced to new ideas and art forms. Attendance at art museums in the west has surpassed that of all other kinds of leisure activity. In the year 2013 more than eight million people visited the Louvre in Paris, and more than six million visited the Metropolitan Museum in New York.

THE COMMISSION

In 2006 Bernard Arnault, chairman of LMVH, the Vuitton fashion enterprise, created the Fondation Louis Vuitton pour Création in Paris as a center for cultural events, independent of the company's business operations. He commissioned Frank Gehry, whose museum in Bilbao had impressed him, to design a building alongside the Jardin d'Acclimatation at the edge of the Bois de Boulogne as a unique gift to his city and country. It was designed to function not as a museum, where works of art are permanently stored, but rather as a place for the exhibition of selections from his large collection of modern and contemporary art that is located elsewhere.

Although construction began in 2008, the civic organization Coordination pour la Sauvegarde du Bois went to court in 2011 claiming that crowds of visitors would increase traffic and pollution damaging to the Bois; it persuaded a judge to cancel the building permit, but in April of the same year the City Planning Commission reversed the judge's decision, allowing the project to proceed.

STRUCTURE

The construction of the Vuitton Foundation required two teams: one team in the factory outside of Paris that fabricated the structural materials and components – the wood and metal supports, the white masonry slabs for the exterior, and the complex framework that supports them – and one team on site who installed these supports and slabs. All major contractors on the project were required to utilize the software Digital Projects as the base platform for creating and exchanging three-dimensional project data for engineering purposes as well as for fabrication and installation.

The canopies follow the traditional gravity load concept and are not necessarily related to floor plates. The glass is framed by secondary members that, in turn, are framed by tertiary members, which are then supported by "tripod" structures. These tie into the building's primary steel and concrete elements. The Gehry team reviewed all exposed joints, and in the case of the canopy, joint details, with the engineers.

In an early model of the building, the masonry components appear as separate blocks distinct from the glass covering. In their curved and concave surfaces the white slabs recall stereotomy, the virtually lost technique of stonemasonry used in France in late medieval and Renaissance buildings.

The exterior of the blocks, faced with what appears to be white masonry (it is in fact composed of 25mm-thick Ductal plates, a fiber-reinforced concrete developed by Lafarge), are set into thin steel frames, on the rear of which are instructions for their placement. Almost every panel differs from its neighbors. The masonry structures become dominant at the topmost levels of the building, where they rise above the glass sails into the open air, providing views of the woods to the north and the city to the west, and open to the sky. In one of the terraces, a small raised concrete bed is planted with a dwarf palm tree, an homage to the Palmarium, the glass-covered building that previously occupied the site.

In Gehry's initial sketches for the Vuitton Foundation, the building was almost entirely covered in glass, suggesting sails (both he and M. Arnault, the client, are avid sailors). As the building's functions were eventually clarified, he designed the complementary white masonry structures to accommodate offices for the Foundation, an entrance hall, library, and theater, in addition to the exhibition spaces.

The glass sails are unique in their forms and functions. They are composed of two layers, an underlying layer of ceramic frit (fifty per cent density) that provides a measure of sun and glare protection, and an outer layer, called Ipasol, that reflects the landscape, atmospheric conditions, neighboring structures, and visitors circulating around and entering the building, constantly changing.

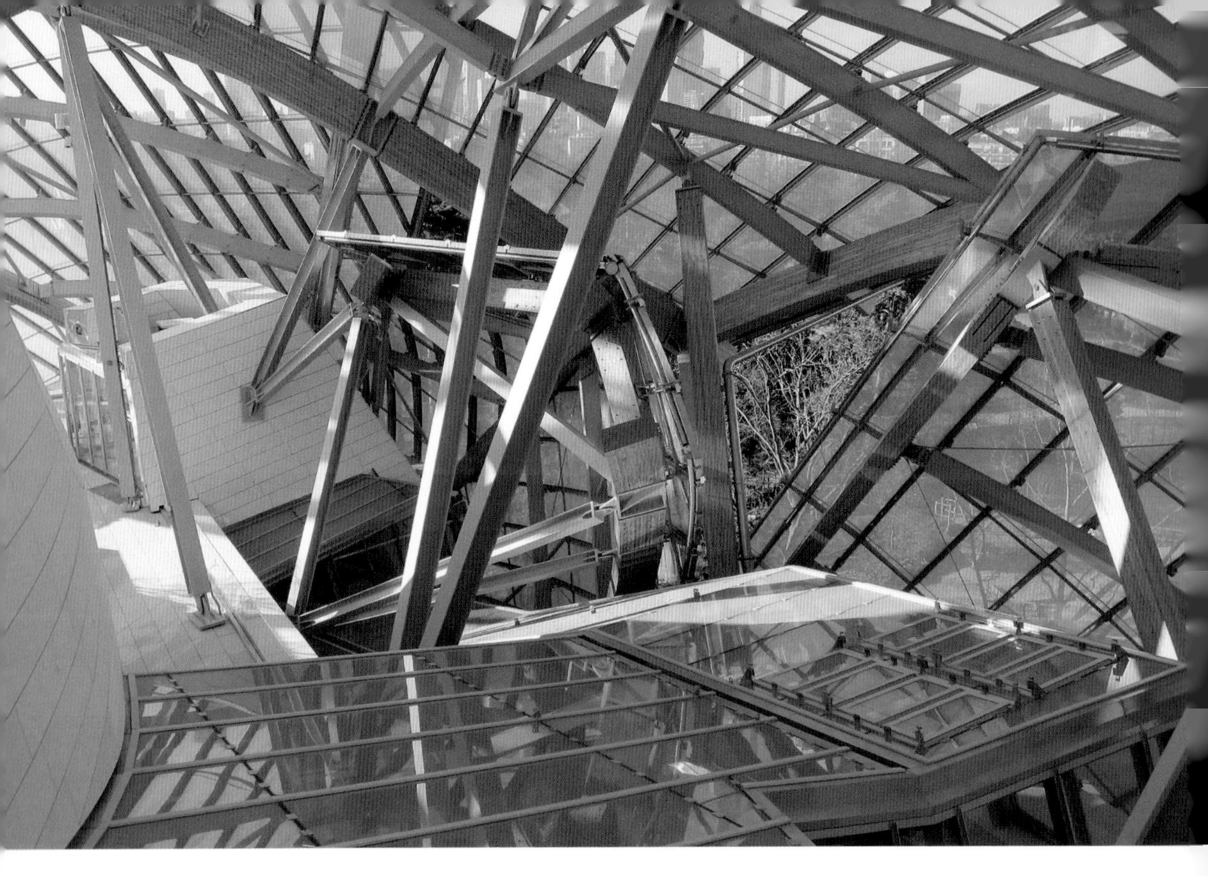

40 Support system for clear glass area of the covering, Louis Vuitton Foundation, Paris

41 Structural detail, Louis Vuitton Foundation, Paris

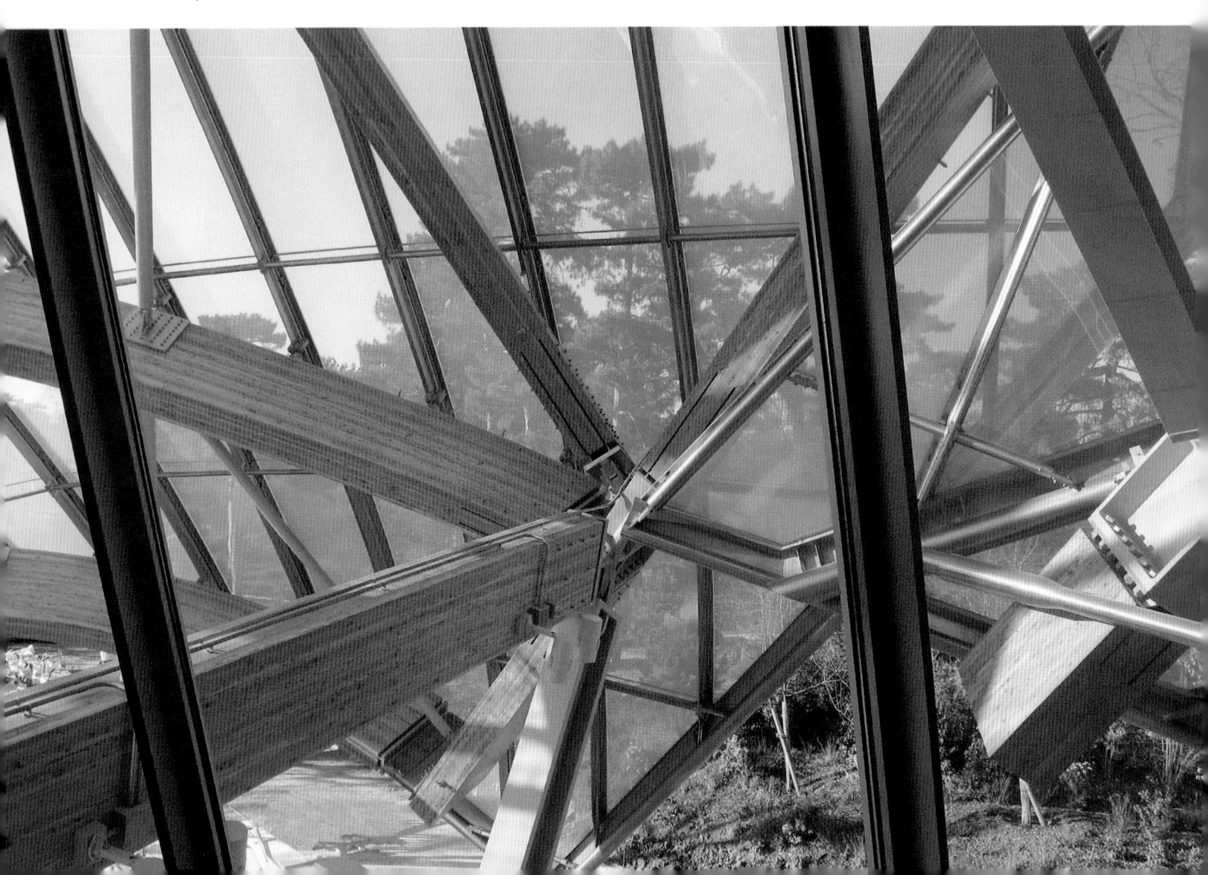

ART IN ENGINEERING

I want to address Gehry's achievement in joining his passion for art while observing the demands of engineering. His statement quoted at the opening of this study underlies his decisions to turn structural elements into sculpture, drawing, and painting, giving them a variety of color, form, and materials that illustrate his personal expression. It even becomes filmic as the shadows on the sweeping curves of the supporting beams change with the angle of the sun's rays (pls. 40 and 41).

Specific references to modern and contemporary art seem to include the "Cubi," the burnished steel sculptures of David Smith (pl. 42) – especially the outward burst of supporting members from a complex steel joint designed by the architect, and two segments of beams that have no structural function but are directed downwards to draw the eye to the gardens alongside – and also to the fantastical sculptures of Alice Aycock (pl. 43) and the monumental steel compositions of Richard Serra (pl. 44). Views through clear glass windows from the interior of the building (pl. 47) recall the framed paintings of Franz Kline and Emilio Vedova (pls. 45 and 46).

42 (left) David Smith, *Cubi XVIII*, 1964

43 (right) Alice Aycock, *Studies for a Town*, 1977

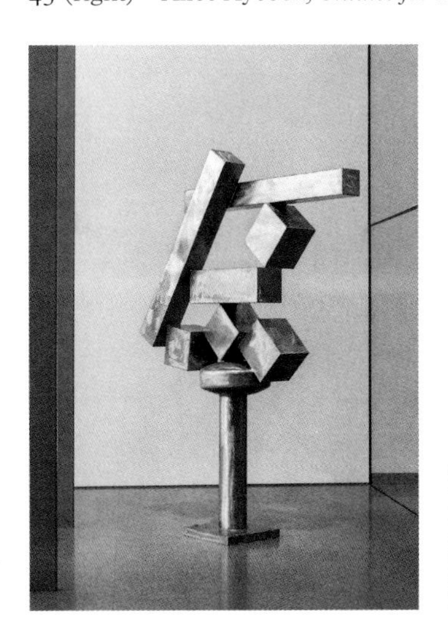

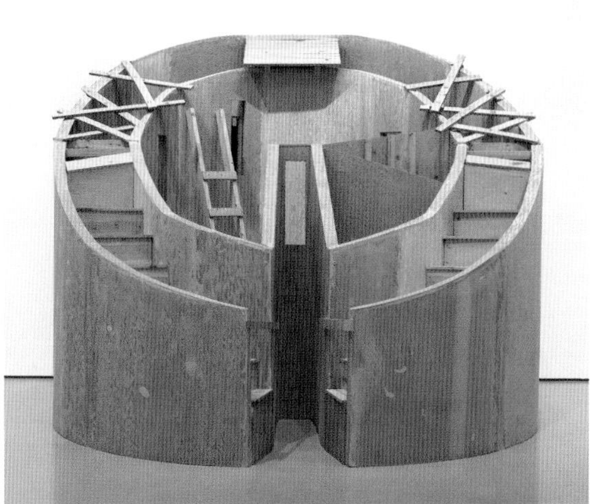

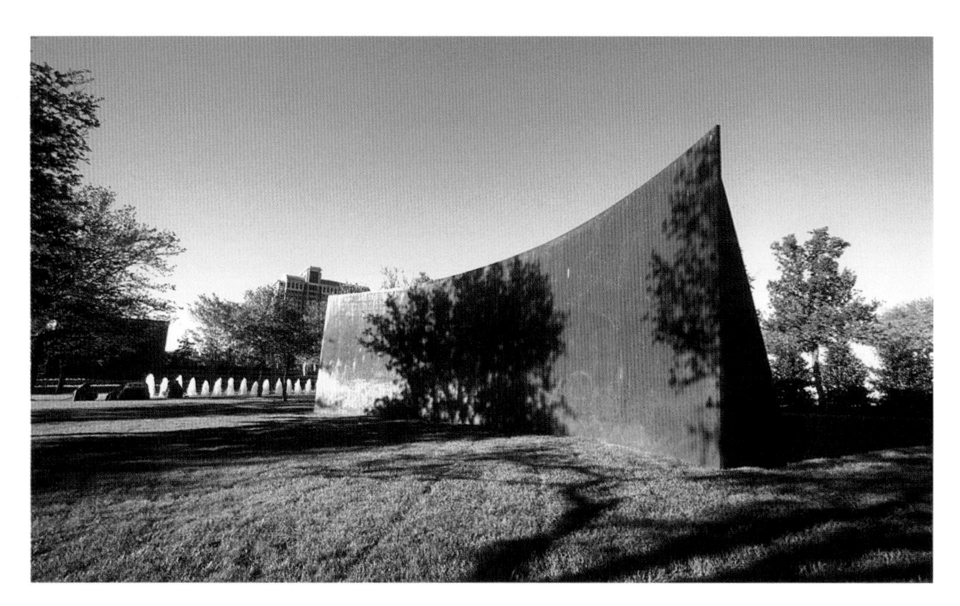

44 (above) Richard Serra, *My Curves are Not Mad*, 1987

45 (below left) Franz Kline, *New York, NY*, 1953

46 (below right) Emilio Vedova, *Ciclo Spagna 1936/76 n.5: Rottura*, 1936/76

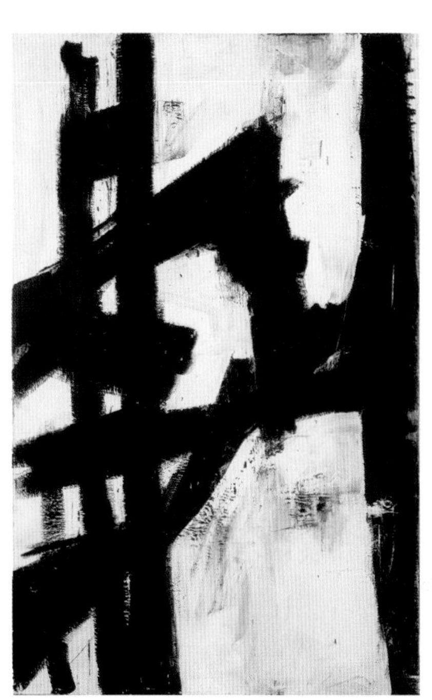

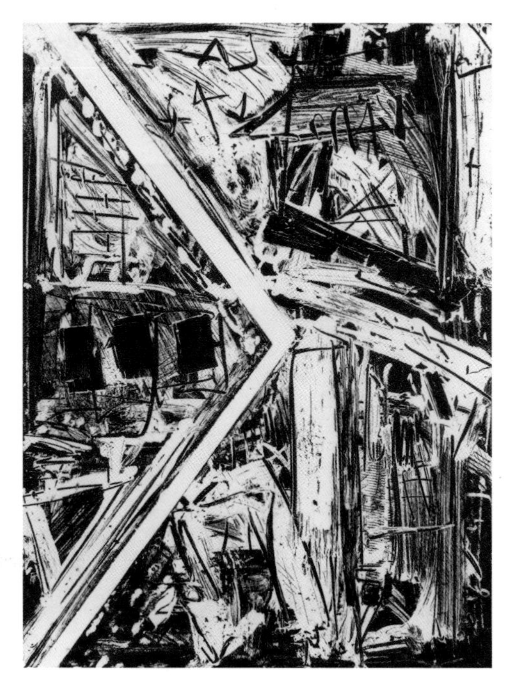

ENVOI

I find Frank Gehry's design for the Vuitton Foundation to be a work of unique invention and imagination, an architecture that embraces air, from the exterior in the billowing of its glass coverings, and from the interior of free-standing portions supporting girders, earth, in its interaction with the natural forest of the Bois de Boulogne and in the placement of structural elements of larch wood that share the supporting functions with those of steel, and water, rippling down the broad stepped masonry cascade west of the building into a shallow moat below ground level that surrounds and reflects the building.

Gehry's glass and metal structure evokes the Palmarium of 1893, and other nineteenth-century iron and glass buildings, such as the Grand Palais and Les Halles, which were the pride of Paris.

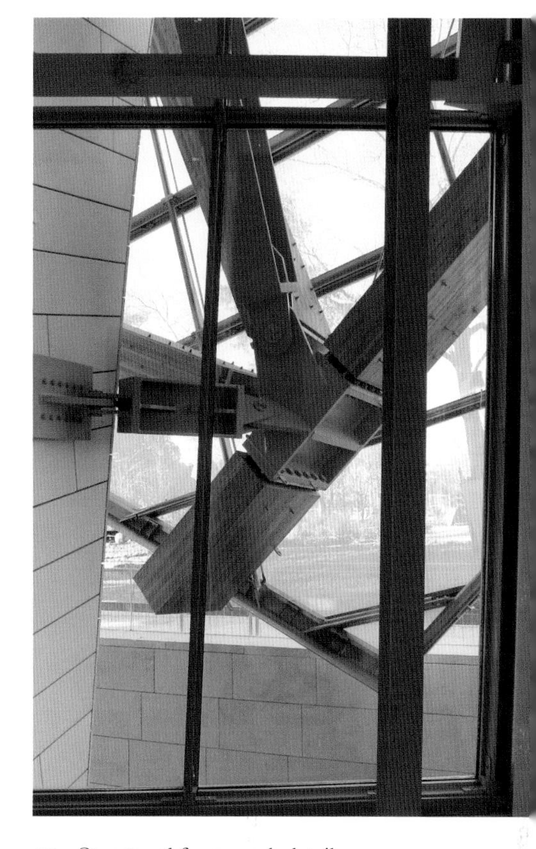

47 Structural framework detail, Louis Vuitton Foundation, Paris

NOTES

1 Janet Nairn, "Frank Gehry: The Search for a 'No Rules' Architecture," *Architectural Record* (June 1976), pp. 95–102.

2 Robin Evans, *The Projective Cast: Architecture and its Three Geometries*, Cambridge, MA, 1995.

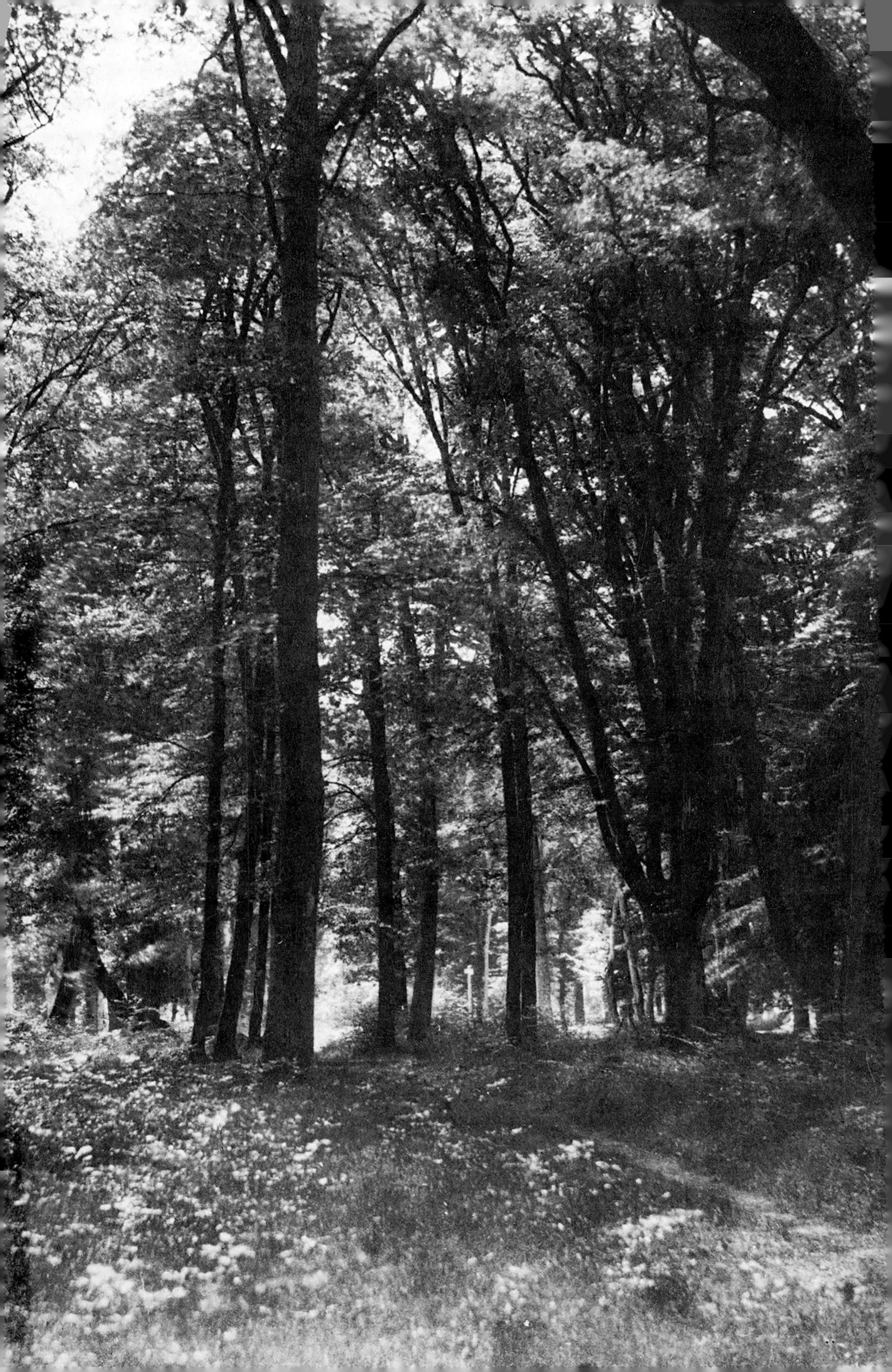

5

The Photographic Picturesque

THE ANNOUNCEMENT IN 1839 OF TWO photographic techniques – the daguerreotype and the calotype – was one of the very rare moments in history when an entirely new form of representation made it possible to record the visual world. It was not immediately clear how the new technique might be used. There were those who foresaw its utility in documentation, as in the reproduction of works of art and architecture and the recording of scientific and technological subjects, and those who anticipated that it might make possible a new genre of image-making. Understanding the aesthetics of the Picturesque as it was regarded in the early eighteenth century leads to insights into how people made photographs in the period from 1839 to 1860.

The early attempts to find the most efficient materials and techniques for photography were based on laboratory experiments that culminated in the capacity to fix an image on a metal plate or sheet of paper. The techniques built upon the long history of the camera obscura, a box with a lens that projected on its rear or top surface (by way of a frosted glass or a periscope) an inverted image of what the lens was facing. Daguerre announced in 1839 his success in the recording of images by coating copper plates with iodized silver.[1] Shortly after, the British amateur scientist Henry Fox Talbot described his invention of the calotype, or talbotype,[2] using a paper negative from which multiple photographic prints could be made. Talbot wrote in a late memoir:

Detail of pl. 65

> In the summer of 1835 I made in this way [i.e., with the use of a small *camera obscura* and short-focal-length lenses] a great number of representations of my house in the country, which is well suited to the purpose, from its ancient and remarkable architecture. And this building I believe to be the first that was ever yet known to have drawn its own picture.[3]

Like many early photographers, Talbot, a mathematician, physicist, and chemist who communicated regularly with other scientists, chose to emphasize the technical aspect of his craft because he foresaw its value in providing evidence and as a means of documentation. But he also must have been aware of the mistake of defining photographic images simply as reproductions of reality, ignoring various elements of choice (of subject, position, framing, lighting, and focus), that reflected and addressed the ideology and taste of their time, and of the degree to which the techniques of photography themselves imposed certain expressive results (for example, the speed of exposure, the capacities of the lenses, the graininess resulting from the use of paper negatives, the tonal effects of colored objects, which are altered as they are transferred to the black-and-white gradations of photographic emulsion). Talbot had, indeed, written in a published volume of photographs, *The Pencil of Nature*, of 1844: "A casual gleam of sunshine, or a shadow thrown across his path, a time-withered oak, or a moss-covered stone may awaken a train of thoughts and feelings, and picturesque imaginings."[4] He and his family enjoyed, like many of his contemporaries of the middle class and gentry, trips into the countryside to make sketches of the natural (non-agricultural) landscape.

Talbot's interest in photography may have been stimulated by his failure to master the camera lucida, a device with a prism on an arm attached to a drawing board, which permitted the operator to see the subject and the drawing paper simultaneously.[5] Sir John Herschel, his contemporary and adviser in the development of the paper negative technique, was especially adept in the use of this instrument (pl. 48).[6] While the selected subject contains elements that might appeal to the connoisseur of the Picturesque, it inevitably lacks an organizing composition; the instrument gives the user little freedom to choose what it projects, and even lacks the framing capacity of the camera obscura.

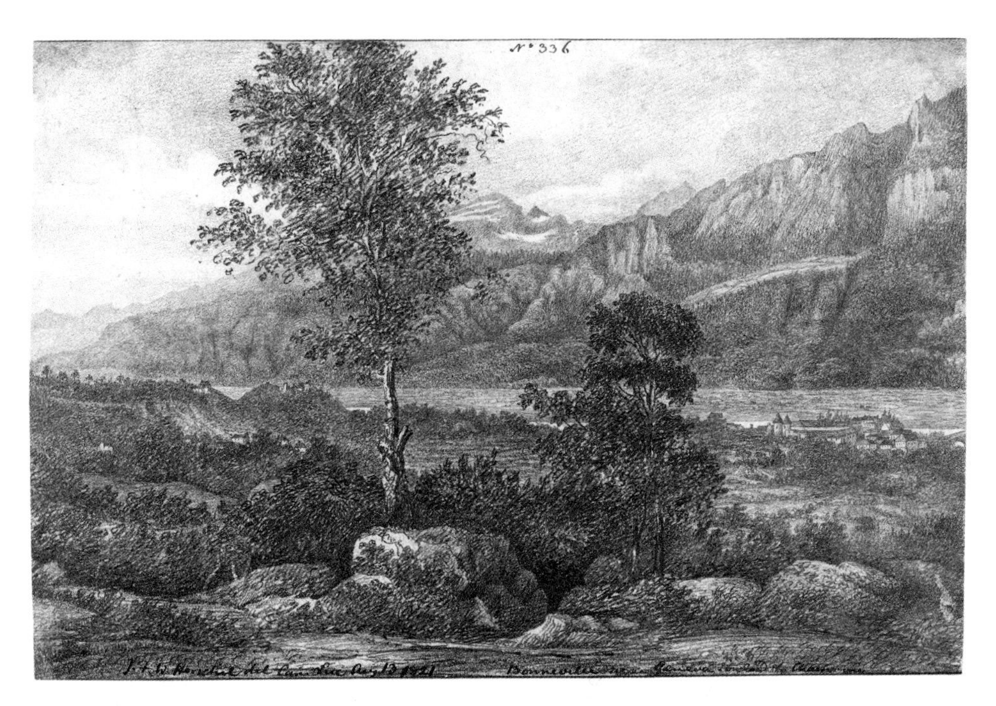

48 Sir John Herschel, *Bonneville near Geneva on the Road to Chamonix*, 1821

Plate 49 is characteristic of Talbot's photographic views of Lacock Abbey, his "ancient and remarkable" residence, in that it does not attempt to be either a documentary record or a work of art; it is, rather, one of his many tests (of lighting, depth of field, focus, etc.) employing the most easily available objects. The depiction of the country houses of the aristocracy and gentry had long been a genre of painting and printmaking that engaged painters of the time.[7]

Jacques-Louis-Mandé Daguerre's invention of the daguerreotype was announced in France only weeks before Talbot's. The initial response to the strikingly clear and detailed silver plates also compared the craft favorably to drawing. The earliest critic of photography, Jules Janin, wrote about daguerreotypes in the first year of the perfection of the techniques, articulating the amazed reaction of the public to this new means of reproduction:

> Never did the art of drawing of the great masters produce such drawing. While the mass is admirable, details are infinite. Imagine then that it's the

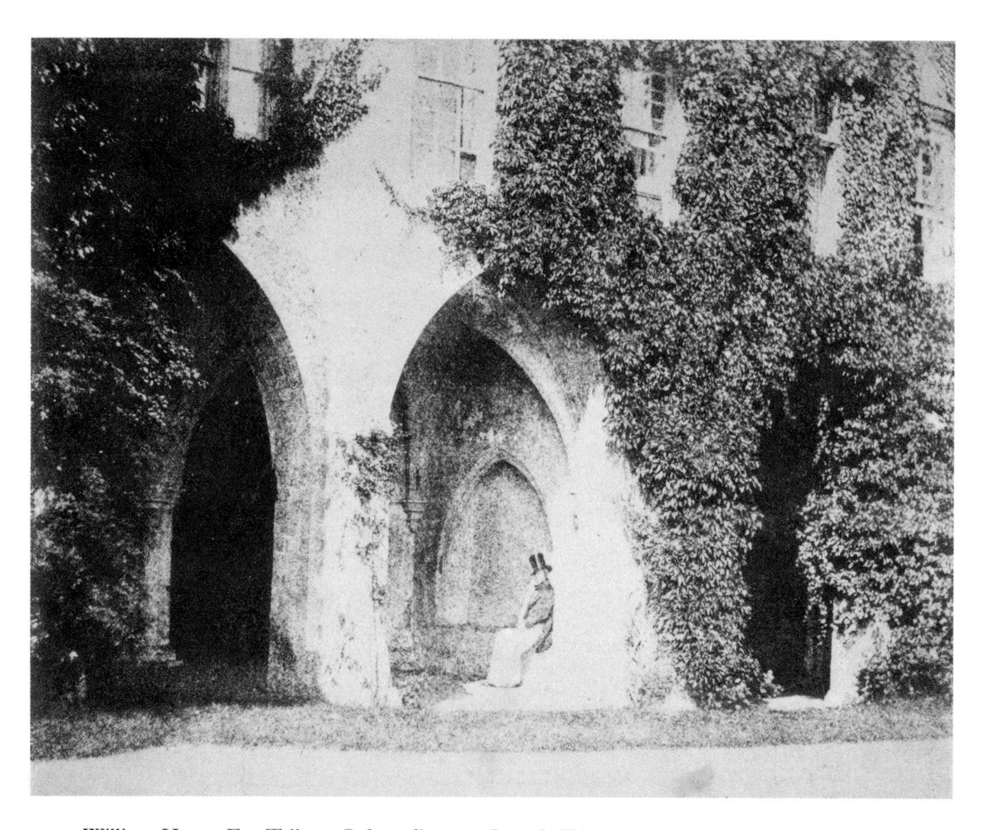

49 William Henry Fox Talbot, *Calvert Jones at Lacock Abbey*, c.1845

sun itself introduced now as the all-powerful agent of an entirely new art that produces these unbelievable works. Now it's no longer the uncertain gaze of a man who finds in the distance shadows and light, no more his trembling hand that reproduces on a shifting paper the changing scene of this world. No longer is there a need to spend 3 days at the same spot only to barely achieve a lifeless shade . . . this wondrous operation does its work in a moment, as swift as thought, as fast as a ray of the sun.[8]

Even today one can still share Janin's response to such impressive plates as that of the Propylaea on the Acropolis in Athens by the painter Baron Gros (pl. 50). Gros, like many early French architectural and landscape photographers, traveled to the eastern Mediterranean, most often to Egypt

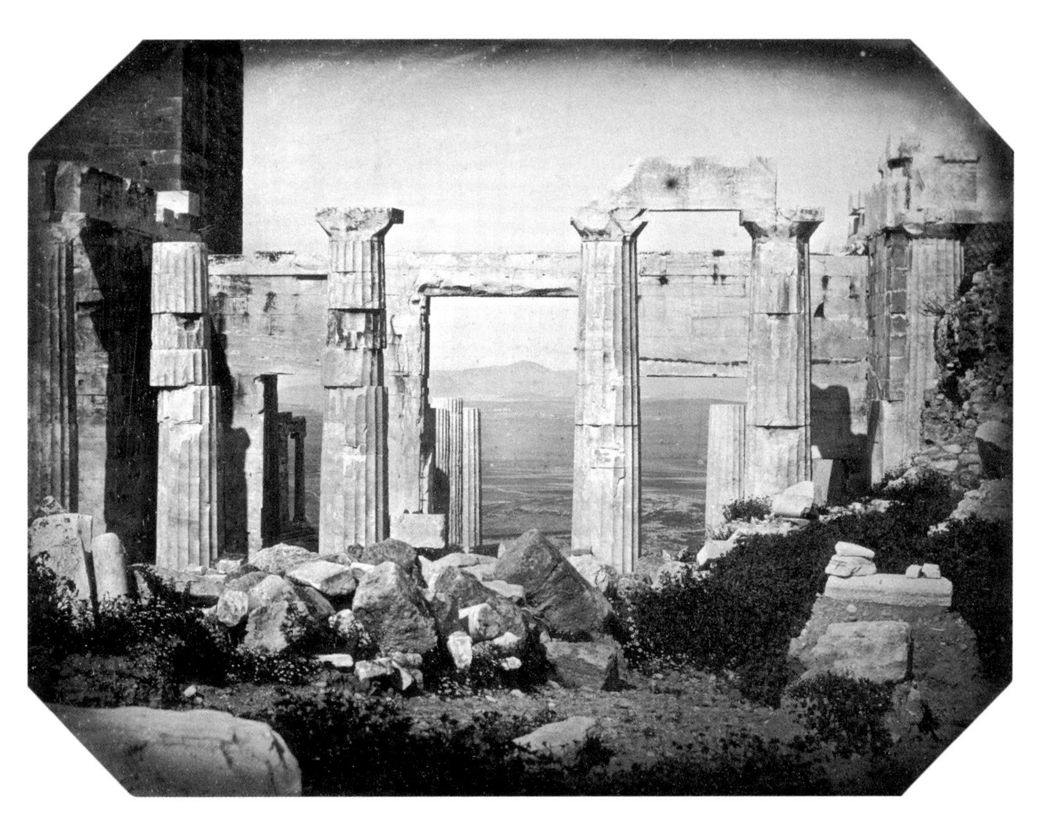

50 Baron Jean-Baptiste Louis Gros, *View of the East Façade of the Propylaea on the Acropolis*, 1850

and the Holy Land, to photograph monuments of the ancient world. Before long, those who used calotype negatives could make a career of photographing and selling the prints to tourists and to people interested in foreign places. Because daguerreotypes were unique prints on metal they were not, despite their precision and brilliance, suited to wide distribution – their commercial adaptation was primarily portraiture (pl. 51). For middle-class patrons the modestly priced daguerreotype portrait was an alternative to a costly painted one. As a result, few images of architecture and landscape in this technique have survived to the present day.

As the quoted texts indicate, the earliest photographs were associated with drawing rather than painting, perhaps because artists had used the camera obscura to make drawings, and because one function of drawing had long

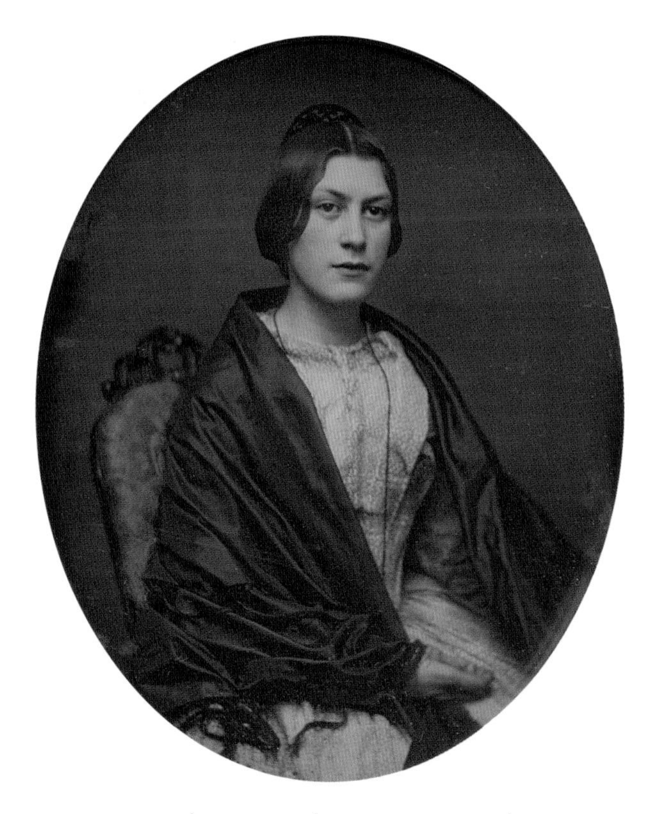

51 Anonymous daguerreotype portrait

been to record views and monuments seen in travel. But a difference is reflected in language: I "make" a drawing; that is, I project out onto a surface what I have in mind, or what I think I see before me. But I "take" a photograph, bringing it in from the outside. Indeed, the camera is modeled on the eye; its lens is like the pupil, similarly receiving light emissions, reversing and inverting them. However, it does not have a retina in its rear in which the central cones provide a sharper focus, nor is the lens a mobile part that can scan the object viewed; further, unless it is a stereoscopic camera, it is monocular. But the analogy is part of the mystery and complexity of photography.

During the first fifteen years of photography the need for long exposures favored immobile subjects or persons who could hold still for the requisite exposure time. The repertory in addition to portraiture included landscapes, buildings, still lifes, art works, and certain scientific subjects. The architectural and landscape images I am discussing represent a particularly rich area of investigation because they reflected or awakened in their viewers a pride in the uniqueness and beauty of their countries.

The sudden emergence of a totally new technique of representation did not at this moment generate a new mode of imaging. Both the photographer and the public had formed a clear concept of what a landscape or a representation of architecture should look like from the vast number of prints and paintings of the half-century preceding 1839. While studies of early photography have sometimes recognized the impact of the flourishing group of naturalistic landscape painters and watercolorists from Gainsborough (1727–1788) to Turner (1775–1851) and Constable (1776–1837), they have rarely examined the impact of the extraordinary fever of production of illustrated (in a variety of printmaking techniques) travel and guidebooks that began to be published, especially in Britain, from the end of the eighteenth century until the 1840s.[9] Images from these sources not only provided models for the photographers to emulate, but they also confirmed a particular taste that had been formulated in eighteenth-century writings on aesthetics, that of the Picturesque.

A major factor in the prominence of architecture and landscape photography in the first decades of the craft was the urge of both the practitioners and the public to celebrate the monuments and scenery they saw as most characteristic of the national identity.[10] These had, already in response to eighteenth-century taste, been identified and celebrated in poetry and prose and in the astonishing efflorescence of illustrated travel literature catering to the widespread attraction to uncultivated natural sites. In Britain the photographer initially chose his subjects, whereas in France the government commissioned the most recognized practitioners to record not only the monumental patrimony (in a program called the Mission Héliographique, launched in 1851), but also the structures and settings of the railroad network (pl. 52).[11]

British travel literature was involved primarily with scenery.[12] The historic architecture that attracted interest was mostly medieval and, within that period, primarily Norman and Gothic. One would expect some interest in Anglo-Saxon architecture, given that it was more indigenous and was not a reminder of French conquest. Anglo-Saxon culture was not much admired in early nineteenth-century Britain; it was felt to represent a cruder, less sophisticated society.[13]

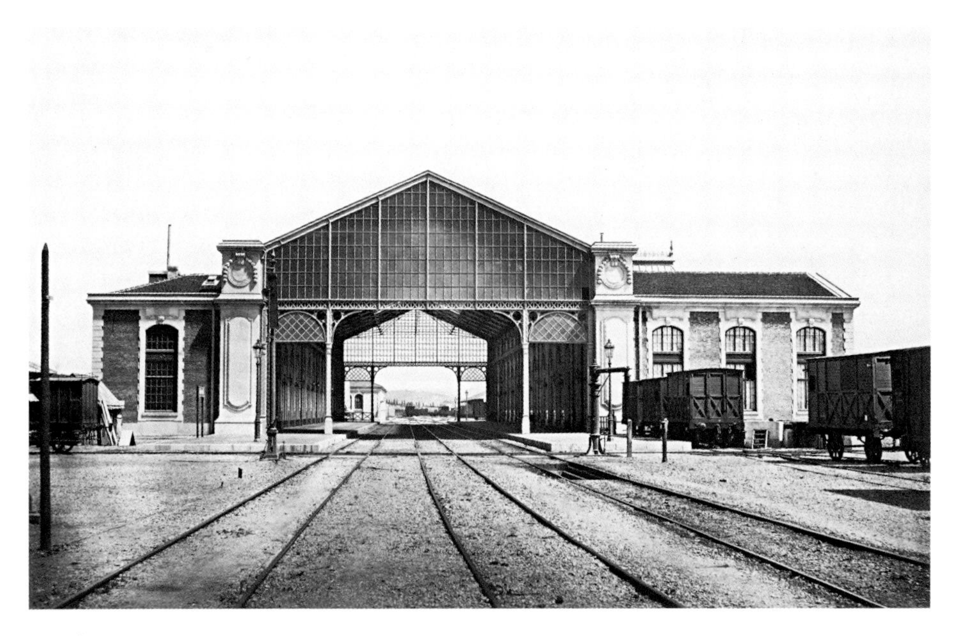

52 Édouard Baldus, *View of the Newly Constructed Train Station with Tracks Running Through, Toulon, France*, 1861 or later

Though a few illustrated books, such as Henry Gally Knight's *An Architectural Tour in Normandy* (1836), and lavish volumes on the universities of Oxford and Cambridge were published in the first quarter of the century, visits to ecclesiastical and civic monuments interested travelers of the time less than the pursuit of undeveloped scenery. Architectural publications were overshadowed by a huge number of illustrated tour books devoted to the river valleys of England and Wales, the Lake District and Scotland, which prepared the ground for a substantial commercial market in photographs in the decades after 1839 for pictures of the landscapes travelers had seen or wished to visit on holiday trips.

After the civil conflicts of the seventeenth century, travel within Britain as well as in Europe and the Middle East became increasingly popular, especially among the gentry and the growing middle class. The beginnings of the Industrial Revolution and the rise of property enclosure, which diminished farming, gave a particular attraction to the search for unspoiled and unimproved land.

Moreover, a dominant style in British poetry and, to a certain extent, fiction, in the late eighteenth and early nineteenth centuries addressed the open landscape; it was not pastoral – that term suggests the classical tradition of rustic settings populated by shepherds – but engaged with the hills, lakes and rivers, downs and cliffs that were seen as emblematic of the national identity.[14] The most influential of the Picturesque writers were Wordsworth, Coleridge and Walter Scott. Wordsworth was a committed trekker and the author of one of the many guidebooks to the Lakes (*A Description of the Scenery of the Lakes in the North of England*, London, 1822). His poetry was so widely read and admired that his home itself became a pilgrimage site, attracting thousands of visitors annually. In a late poem, *The Prelude*, he reflected on his engagement with the Picturesque and regretted his acceptance of the superficiality of its focus on pictorial composition.

At the root of the adoption of Picturesque taste in Britain was a revolution in the theory of the arts that engaged the literary and philosophical establishment throughout the eighteenth century. It took shape in Joseph Addison's essays on "The Pleasures of the Imagination" published in *The Spectator* in 1712. The earliest and most influential study of taste in the eighteenth century was Edmund Burke's book, begun in 1747 and published in 1757, *A Philosophical Enquiry into the Origin of Our Ideas of the Sublime and the Beautiful.* Burke's proposition was that pleasure in the contemplation of natural and manmade works need not be restricted to the enjoyment of beauty (as in the classical goals of smoothness, order, calm, etc.), but could encompass responses to the Sublime, which engendered awe and even terror, as experienced in encounters with immensity, the uncontrollable, wild, and dangerous. But more important and lasting than the admission of a new realm of experience to treatment in the arts was the proposition that the individual response of the observer, listener, or reader was relevant, even essential to interpretation and criticism. In Addison's words,

> We cannot indeed have a single Image in the Fancy that did not make its first Entrance through the Sight; but we have the Power of retaining, altering and compounding those Images, which we have once received, into all the varieties of Picture and Vision that are most agreeable to the Imagination.[15]

Similar views were expressed in pre-Revolutionary France, for example in Condillac's *Traité des sensations* of 1754. This insertion of the individual psyche into the determination of artistic value constituted an essential preamble to the formation of the modern discipline of aesthetics. The classical position, which had dominated the theory and criticism of the arts since the Renaissance, governed taste through fixed rules; the value of a work of art was inherent in the object, and the observer either did or did not have the education and capacity to grasp it. This new philosophical approach empowered the observer to interact with the object, making his/her feelings about it relevant. It therefore represented liberation from oppressive authority and an invitation to freedom of thought and action. Addison proposed that our pleasure in seeing an object came not so much from the object itself as from the train of thought and imagination stimulated by it. Without such a change, it is unlikely that the passion for touring the countryside in search of natural wonders would have developed to the degree that it did.

Burke's alternatives appeared to his contemporaries and successors, who were attempting to formulate a critical approach to the natural and manmade landscape, to demand a third category – the Picturesque – mediating between the two – one more evocative than the bland and smooth character of the "Beautiful" and less overwhelming than the "Sublime."[16]

At the root of the concept of the Picturesque in William Gilpin and other theorists was a tradition, originating in the mid-seventeenth century, of elegiac landscape painting incorporating architectural elements in the work of artists such as Claude Lorrain, working in Italy, and emulators such as Richard Wilson in Britain. The pictures could either be elegiac, recalling a classical past, or sublime (e.g., threatening or brooding), as in the work of Salvator Rosa in Italy and Jacob van Ruisdael in the Dutch Republic. But the habitual identification of the Picturesque with these seventeenth-century origins has concealed its distinctiveness. The style introduced an unprecedented positive evaluation of the characteristics of roughness, irregularity, and decay (e.g., by replacing stately classical buildings with ruins), not at all in harmony with the ideal landscape's classical calm or with the Sublime landscape's dramatic extremes. Uvedale Price, the most incisive theorist of the Picturesque, offered as an example of its distinction from the Beautiful (in "A letter to H. Repton," 1795):

> . . . a scene that exhibits the varied, and strongly marked effects of broken ground; of sudden projections, and deep hollows; of old twisted trees, with furrowed bark; of water tumbling in a deep-worn channel over rocks and rude stones, and half lost among shaggy roots, decaying stumps, and withered fern . . .[17]

The guidebooks available to tourists from the second half of the eighteenth century instructed them not only in what to see, but also in how to see it. Gilpin encouraged his readers to look on natural wonders as if they were paintings of the landscape. His publications strongly influenced the formulation of the taste for the Picturesque.[18] Travelers were directed to sites that had to be not only attractive in themselves but also had to obey the rules of seventeenth- and eighteenth-century pictorial composition. Readers in pursuit of Picturesque sites have been compared to fox hunters, as Coleridge joked:

> Tour, Journey, Voyage, Lounge, Ride, Walk,
> Skim, Sketch, Excursion, Travel-talk –
> For move you must! 'Tis now the rage,
> The law and fashion of the Age.[19]

Their excessive zeal was satirized by William Combe in the popular books entitled *The First Tour of Doctor Syntax in Search of the Picturesque* and *Doctor Syntax's Three Tours in Search of the Picturesque*.[20] In one of the illustrations by Thomas Rowlandson, the Doctor is shown astride a donkey, overloaded with sketching equipment, including his "Claude Glass" (referring to Claude Lorrain), an instrument devised to turn any scene into a painting by framing it. Gilpin suggests a formula for the Picturesque composition of a river scene:

> Every view on a river, thus circumstanced, is composed of four grand parts; the area which is the river itself; the two side-screens which are the opposite banks, and mark the perspective; and the front screen, which points out the winding of the river.[21]

The passage is complemented by his aquatints illustrating his guidebooks, such as plate 53 in which there are "screens" in the foreground, middle ground and rear, and a body of water, the winding contours of which also emphasize recession into the depth. Another common formula of the Pictur-

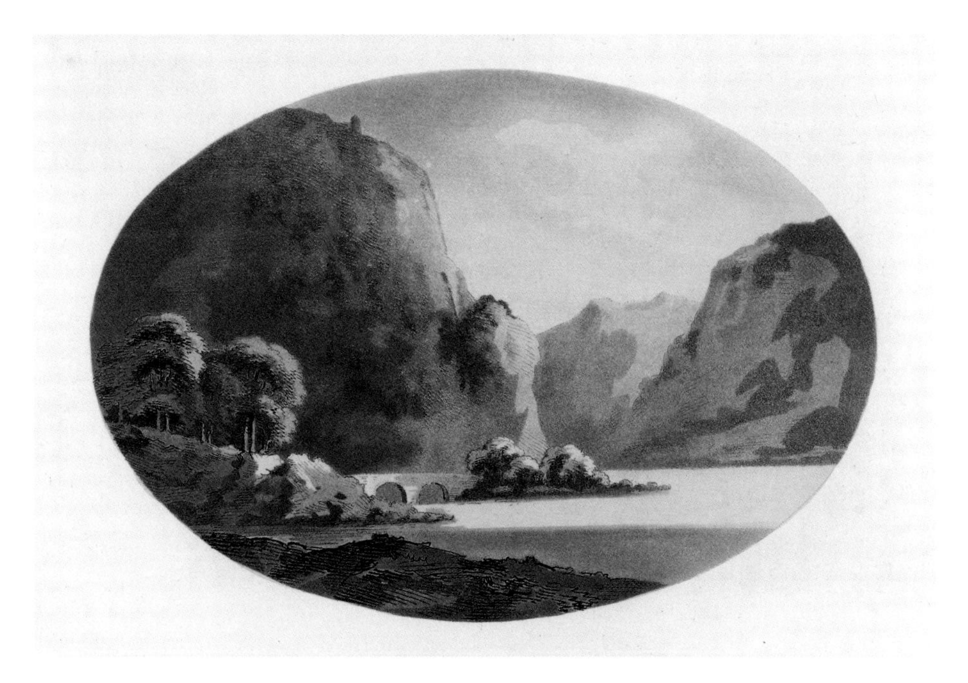

53 William Gilpin, *The Mountain of Doniquaick and the Bridge over the Aray*, 1776

esque view featured a major architectural element – often a ruin – on one side, as in William Westall's "Oystermouth Castle and Harbour" (pl. 54), which retains Gilpin's foreground screens, a descending road providing the perspective, and a plane of water. Photographers emulated these compositional devices, as did William Bedford, a late practitioner of the Picturesque, in his print of the castle and pass at Llanberis (pl. 55).

Not every illustrator, photographer, or tourist was qualified for the pursuit of the Picturesque; in order to recognize it in a view, one had to be familiar with a particular tradition in the history of painting, preferably by having collected pictures. Thus Picturesque taste was linked to class, an association that betrayed itself in a studied avoidance by the most celebrated painters of any depiction of manufacture or rural labor and poverty. Turner, in his landscapes of the first decade of the nineteenth century, was the only major artist who was willing to address these themes.[22]

While the basic rules of Gilpin's composition are derived from seventeenth-century landscape painting, they also reflect, perhaps unconsciously,

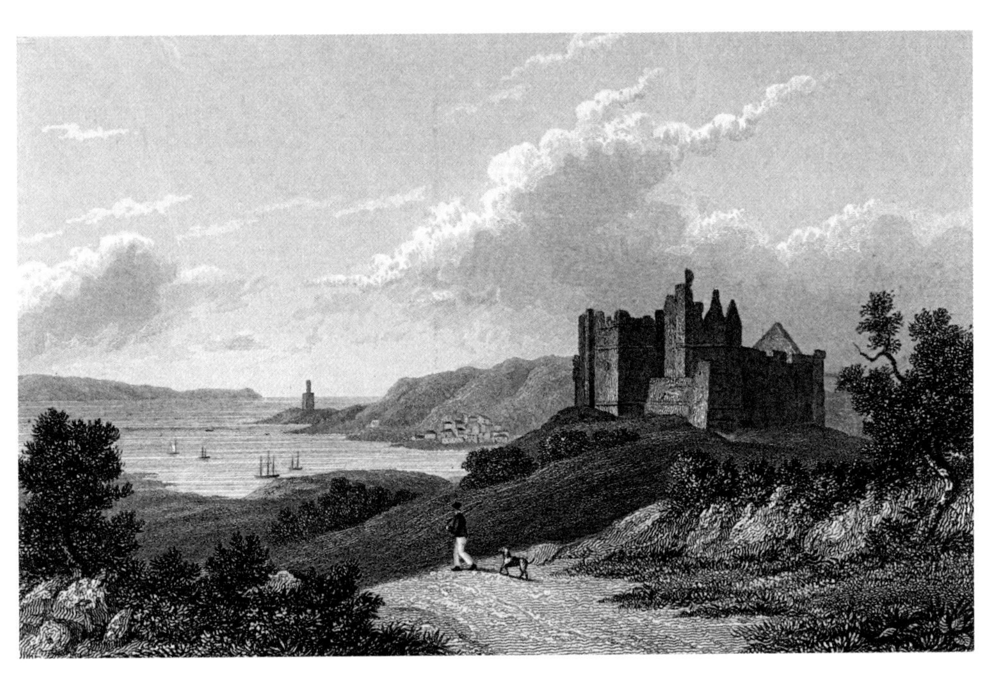

54 William Westall, *Oystermouth Castle & Harbour*, 1830

55 Francis Bedford, *View of Dolbadarn Castle and Llanberis Pass, North Wales*, 1860s or 1870s

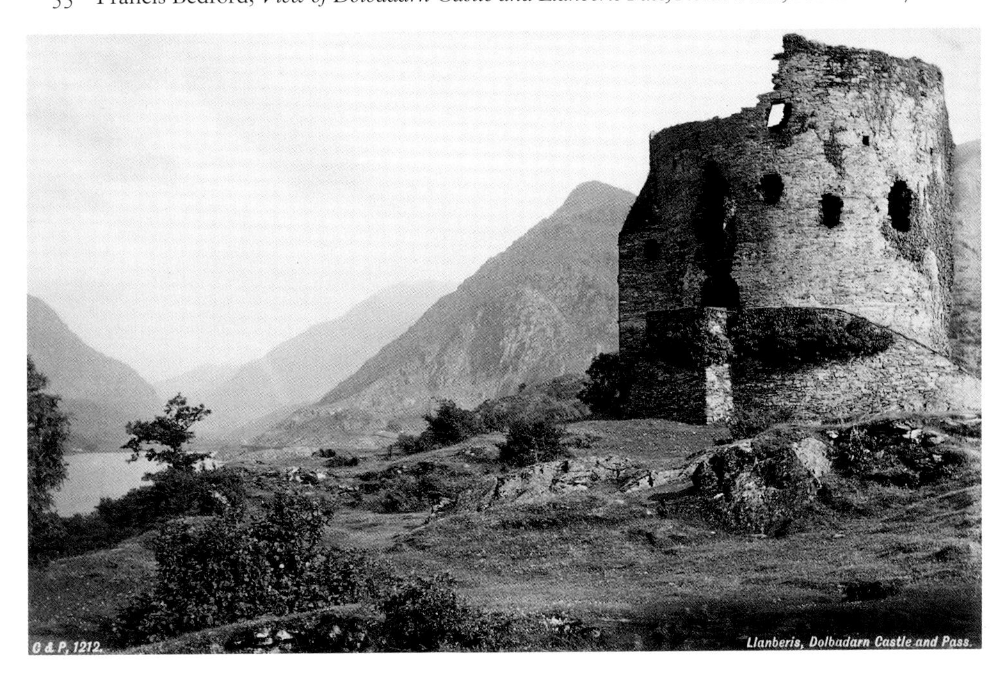

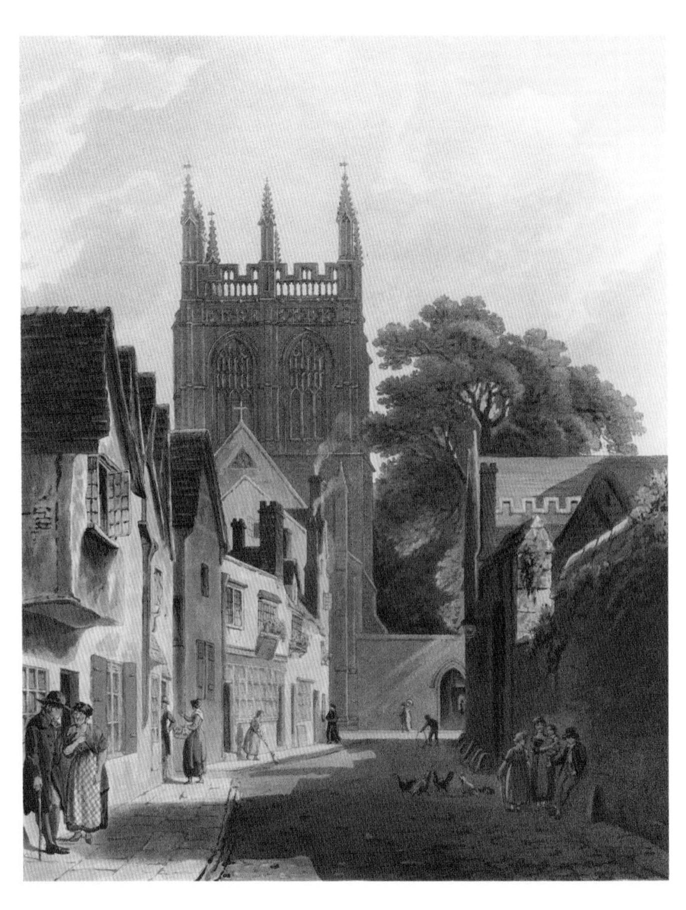

56 J. Bluck after Augustus Charles Pugin, *Magpie Lane, Oxford*, 1813

57 William Henry Fox Talbot, *York Minster from Lop Lane*, 1845

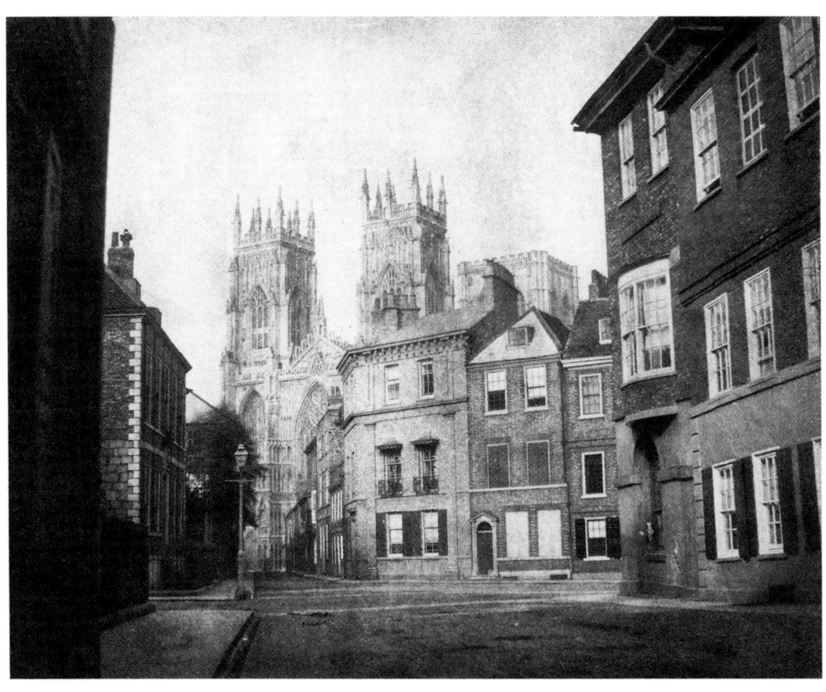

the practice of theater design, in which the proscenium constitutes the outer frame, and is frequently, especially in the case of outdoor sets, re-emphasized by flats or scrims. The rectangular format of most early photographs supports this approach to composition. Some even have curved upper edges, which remind us, possibly unintentionally, of the theater's proscenium arch. Both landscape painting and theater design tended to distance the observer from the scene, establishing it as occupying a different and distant world. David Punter, in an essay on the Picturesque and the Sublime, has interpreted the aim of Picturesque framing as an attempt to establish defined limits to the experience of nature as a psychological and social defense against the uncontrollability and frightfulness of the Sublime.[23]

Picturesque conventions applied as much to city views as to landscapes; on the Continent, where tourists sought out monuments and villages more than open country, they were published in much greater profusion, especially in the books of *voyages pittoresques*.[24] The vogue for naturalistic landscape painting in France did not, as in England, precede the invention of photography. In the standard illustrations in published works (pl. 56), the draftsman positioned himself in the center of a street, which recedes in perspective to a terminus in a tall building. The vernacular structures on one side are rendered in shadow and those on the opposite side in the light. People are represented, strolling, standing in conversation, or offering things for sale from carts or baskets. Talbot's view of York (pl. 57) follows the same format, except that it is the left side that is in shadow, and the need for long exposures enforced the elimination of figures. The towers terminating the two perspectives are of virtually the same design, in a High Gothic style that is as distinctively British as the landscapes I have discussed. The same style was favored in the innumerable depictions of ruins, well before the first evidence of the Gothic Revival.

Gilpin was more an artist and a guide than a philosopher, and soon a more persuasive theoretical foundation of the Picturesque was formulated not by the mentors of travelers but by writers – in particular, Uvedale Price and Richard Payne Knight – landscape designers who specialized in country houses. They shared a distaste for the blandness of the contemporary vogue of gardens represented by the popular work of Capability Brown, in which trees with smooth curvilinear contours were casually dispersed over acres of

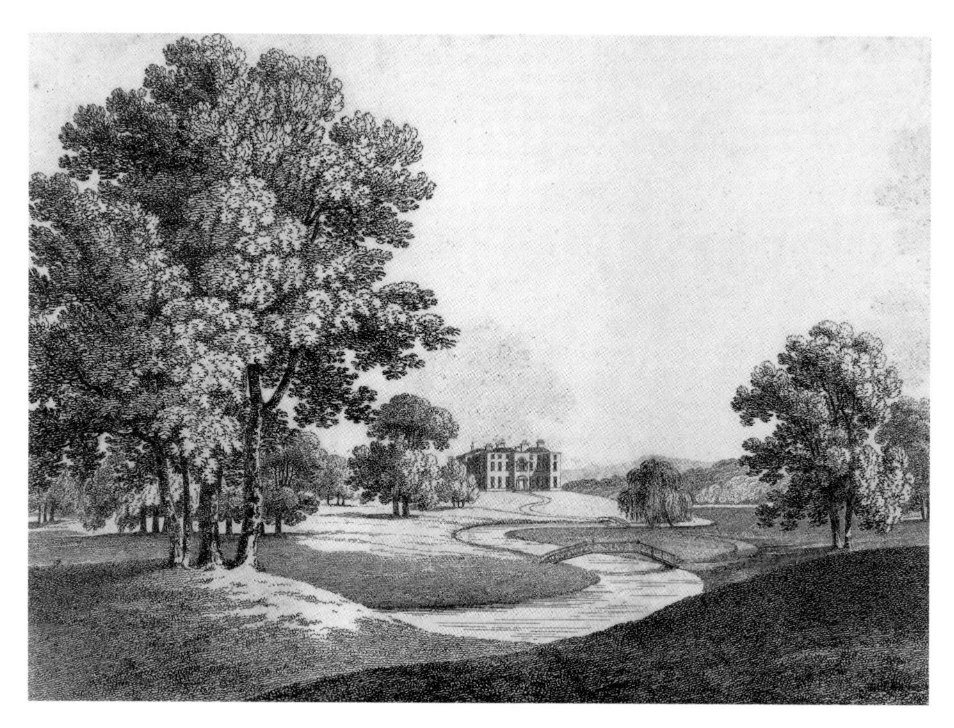

58 Thomas Hearne, *The Beautiful*, 1794

rolling green lawn. Through their influence, the Picturesque became the principal model for garden and landscape design and eventually for public parks and cemeteries.

Knight commissioned Thomas Hearne, an emulator of Turner, to provide drawings for the two etchings illustrating his theoretical poem "The Landscape" (pls. 58 and 59), which express the contrast of the two fashions. The "Beautiful" presents an isolated house set in a Brownian lawn sparsely scattered with clumps of trees. In the same setting, a Tudor mansion, with no trace of the classical tradition, exemplifies the Picturesque. Not only is it irregular in design, but it is also almost obscured by randomly placed trees and shrubs; the subject of the picture is not a work of architecture but an environment in which patterns of light and shadow are more evident than any individual element. The manmade is almost indistinguishable from the natural. A similar but more extreme expression of this approach is the illustration in a contemporary guidebook of the cottage of William Wordsworth,

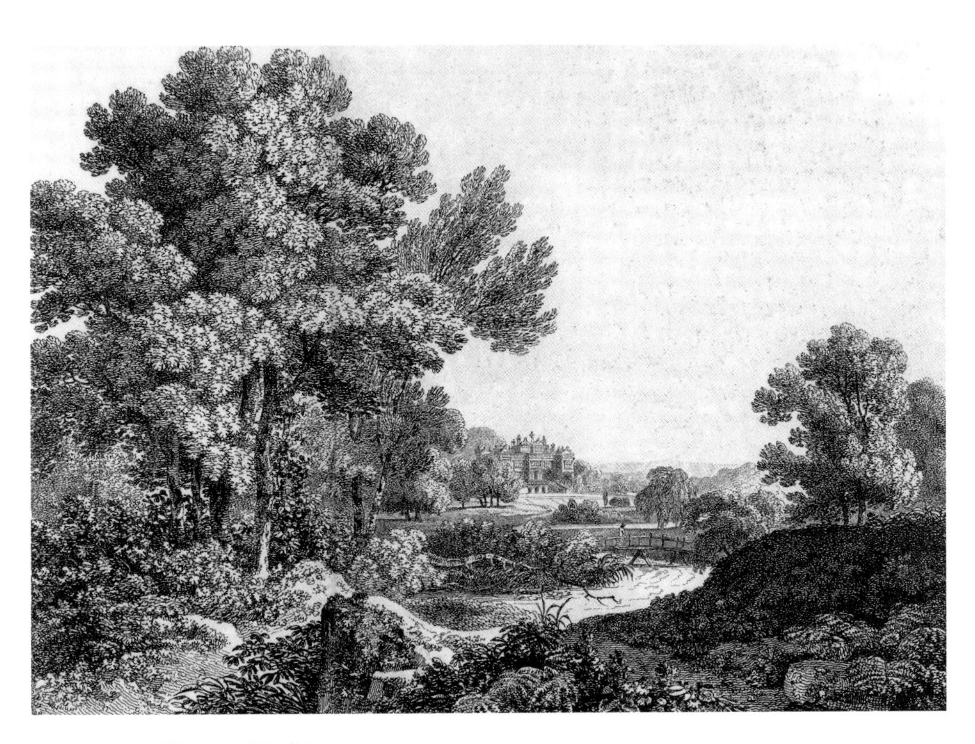

59 Thomas Hearne, *The Picturesque*, 1794

himself the most eminent literary exponent of the Picturesque. The building is hardly discernible behind the enveloping greenery. The illustration was anticipated in a passage from Knight's poem:

> Not yet unenvy'd, to whose humbler lot
> Falls the retired and antiquated cot' –
> Its roof with weeds and mosses covere'd o'er
> And Honeysuckles climbing round the door;
> While mantling vines along its walls are spread,
> And clustering ivy decks the chimney's head.[25]

In a stimulating discussion of the two images, Ann Bermingham demonstrated that, in Knight's mind, the contrast between them had a political message: the open prospects of the Brownian estate stood for "the leveling tendencies of democratic governments and revolutions" (as represented by the recent revolution in France), while the Picturesque disorder represented,

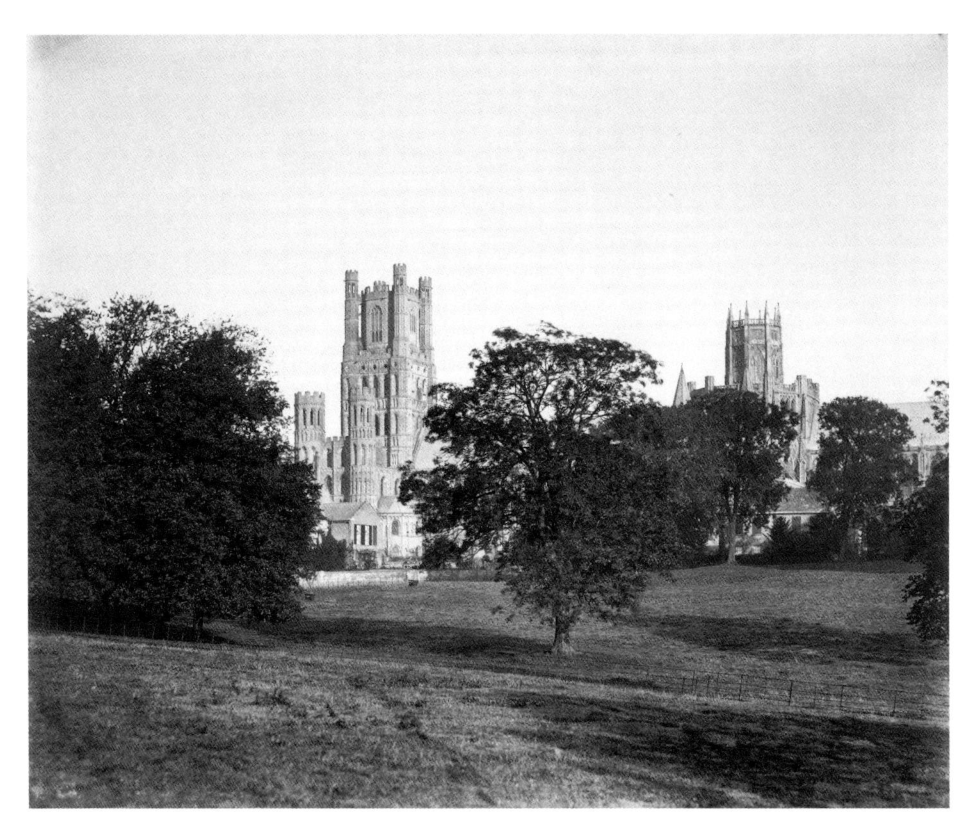

60 Roger Fenton, *Ely Cathedral, from the Park*, 1857

as Knight's fellow theorist wrote, the "love of seclusion and safety [which] is no less natural to man, than that of liberty" – a view that patently supported the privileges of the landowning class.[26]

This submersion of architecture into its setting characterizes many early "architectural" photographs (see pls. 60, 62, 64). In Picturesque aesthetics, the uniqueness of a work of architecture had to be subordinated into a pictorial composition in which a bush could be as important as a colonnaded porch.

Yet, despite the more coherent theoretical positions of Knight and Price, Gilpin's less rigorous formulation of the Picturesque had a greater impact on painters and sketchers – and through them, on photographers – than that of the landscape designers who, by the nature of their interests, were not engaged in exploring and recording the undeveloped countryside.

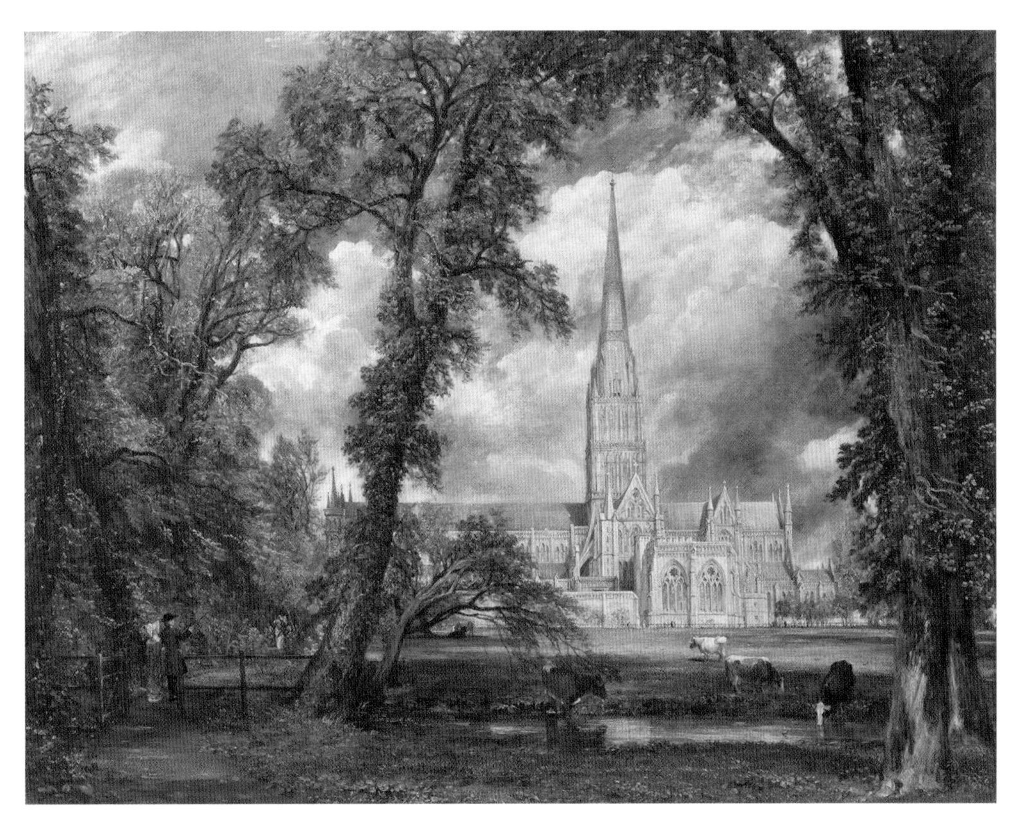

61 John Constable, *Salisbury Cathedral from the Bishop's Ground*, 1823

Early British photographers, from Talbot on, echoed the paintings of J. M. W. Turner and John Constable, especially in their approach to ecclesiastical monuments. When Roger Fenton, in photographing Ely cathedral (pl. 60), chose to favor foliage over architecture in such a way that one can find out very little about the building, he must have had in mind John Constable's *Salisbury Cathedral* (pl. 61) rather than the interests of the planners of inventories or architectural historians.

The characterization of decay and roughness as basic values of the Picturesque was best illustrated in the representation of ruins, in which the architectural image merged with the landscape. Gilpin wrote of Tintern Abbey:

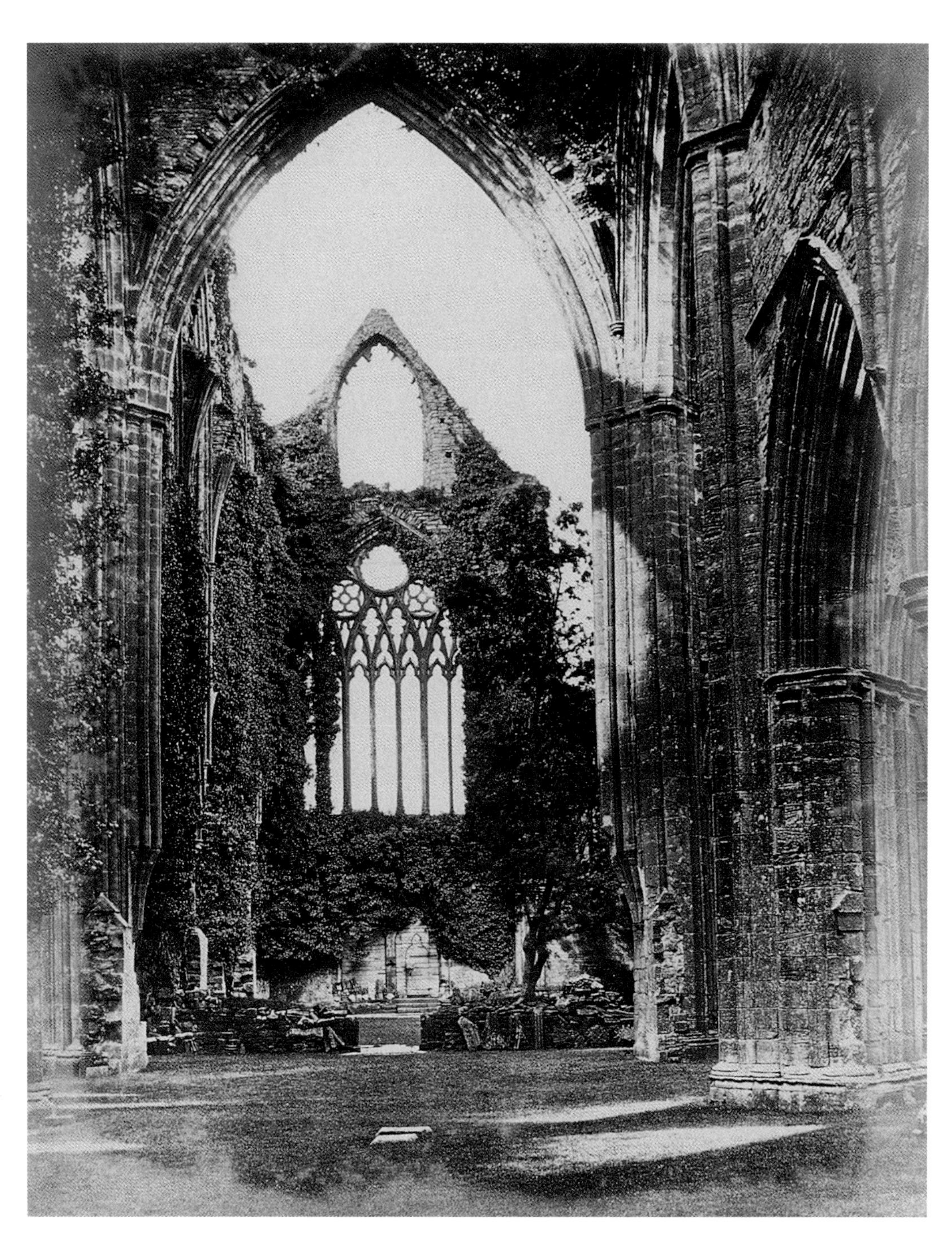

62 James Mudd, *Tintern Abbey, Interior of Nave, looking East*, c.1850

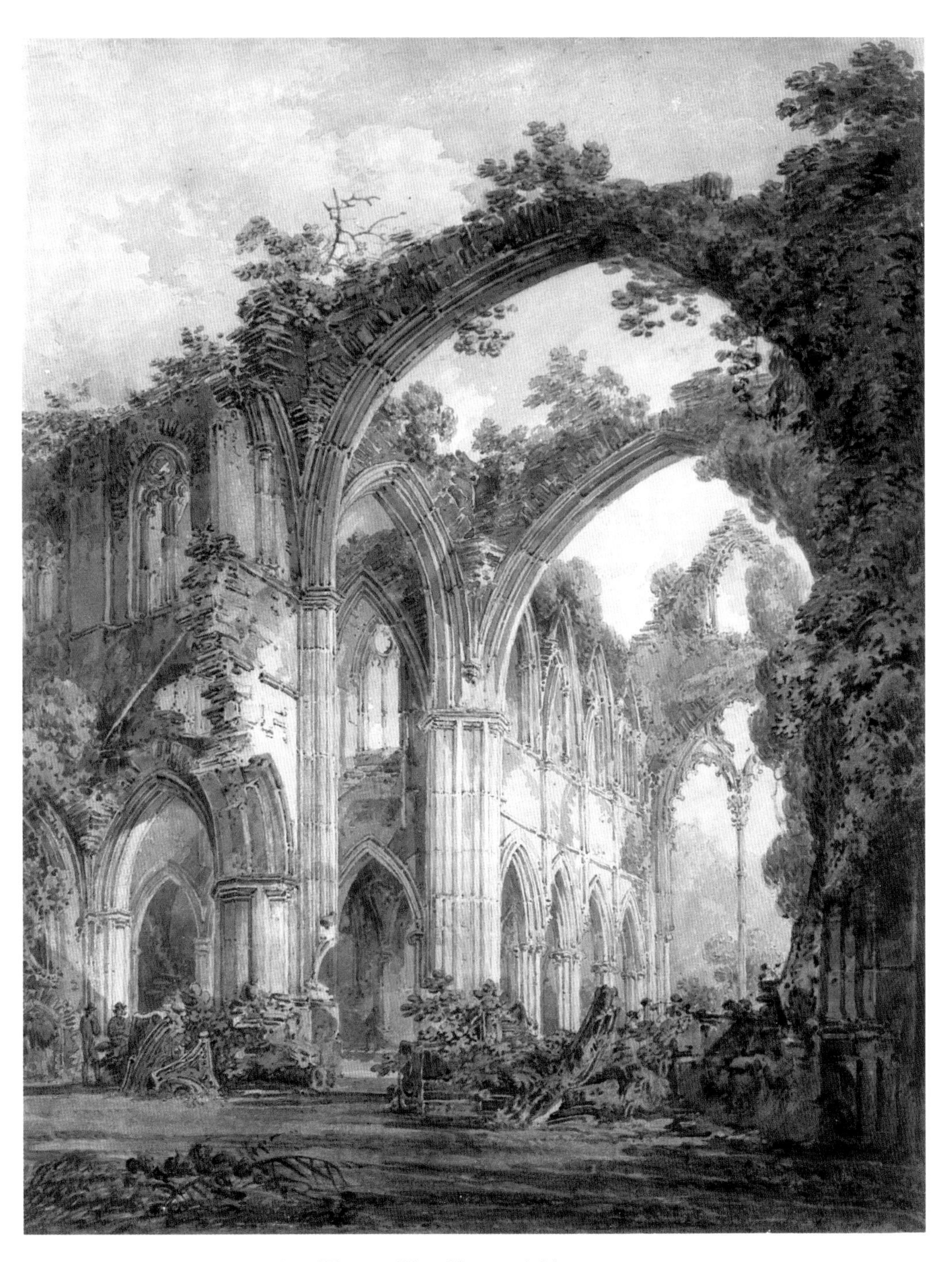

63 J. M. W. Turner, *Interior of Tintern Abbey, Monmouthshire*, *c.*1794

Bless'd is the man in whose sequester'd glade,
Some ancient abbey's walls diffuse their shade;
With mouldering windows pierced, and turrets crown'd
And pinnacles with clinging ivy bound.
Bless'd too is he, who, 'midst his tufted trees,
Some ruin'd castle's lofty towers sees . . . [27]

Photographers, following the lead of poets, painters, and printmakers, were drawn to decayed abbeys and castles, which had been preserved ubiquitously in the British landscape – more because they fulfilled the criteria of Picturesque beauty than because of an impulse to document the monuments of the medieval past. In fact, they were drawn to ruins as places for melancholic contemplation, meditation on the impermanence of worldly goods and power, and by delight in their evidence of the triumph of natural growth and disintegration, as voiced by Gilpin in his description of Tintern Abbey.

The depiction of ruins constitutes an astonishingly high proportion of the images in guidebooks and of early landscape photographs. Tintern Abbey, the subject of Gilpin's remarks quoted above, stimulated innumerable prints and watercolors, including plates 62 and 63.[28] Most of these are interiors, looking out from the nave or transept. Exterior views apparently did not generate the same depth of rumination. Turner's striking watercolor emphasizes the growth of foliage at ground level, upon the piers, in the arches and vaults, and expresses a conflict between man's work and nature. In the picture by James Mudd, who was best known for urban photographs of Manchester, the interior of the ruin has been landscaped, an enterprise of the property owner, the Duke of Beaufort, who planted a lawn in the nave and transept and placed fragments discretely about, in an effort to appeal to and to control tourists.[29] Roger Fenton's portrayal of Rievaulx Abbey (pl. 64) is more evocative; he did not see the architectural remains as being invaded by natural growth, but as a foyer opening onto a landscape (of salvation?) bathed in light.

The photographers favored ruins. For example, castles were impenetrable blocks, best seen as inapproachable features in the landscape. When Henry VIII made himself Supreme Head of the Church in England, the abbeys were forcibly vacated, and their decay was accelerated by the Crown's appropriation of their more expensive materials, particularly the lead roofing that

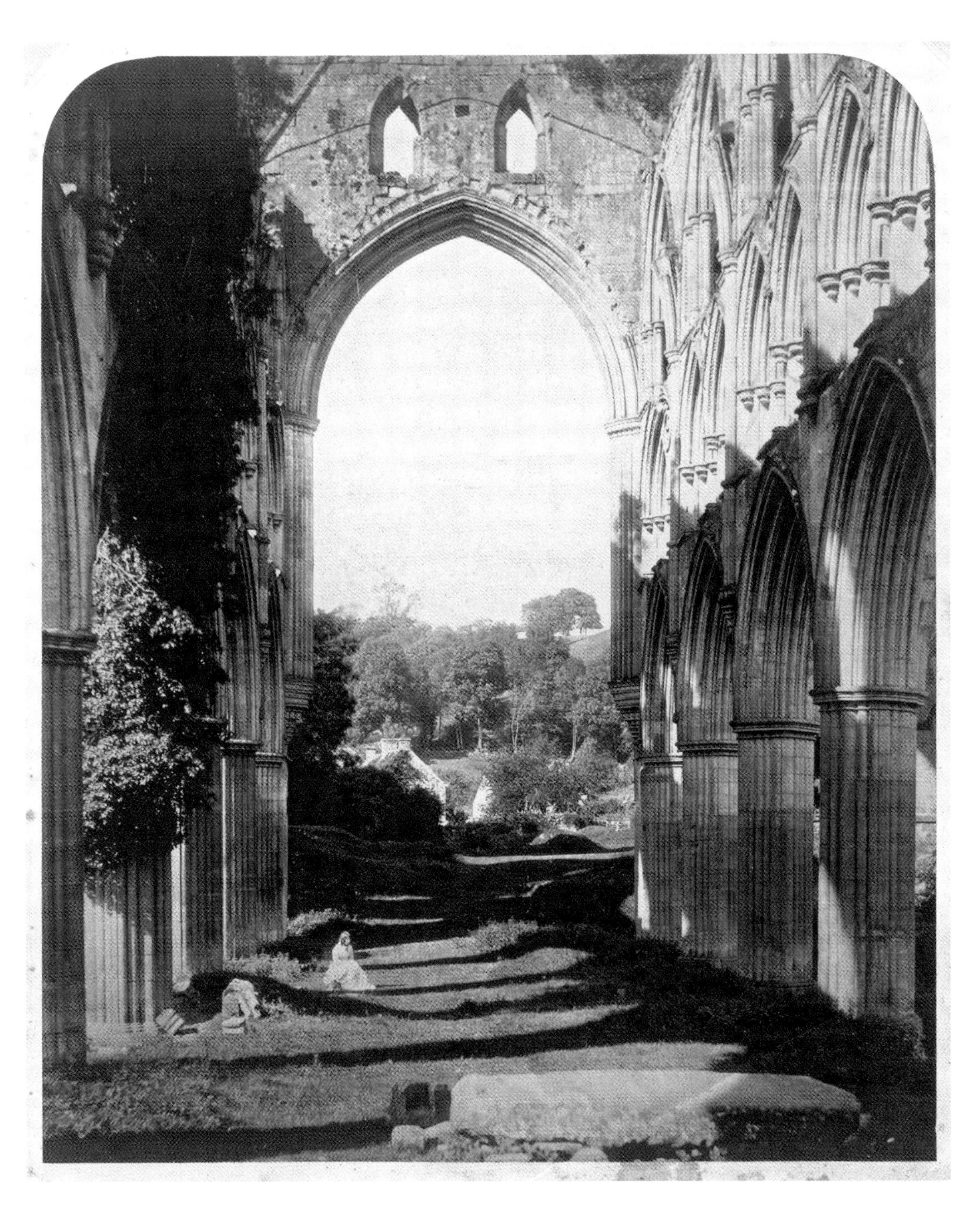

64 Roger Fenton, *Rievaulx Abbey*, 1854

protected interiors from the weather. English mistrust and even hatred of Roman evangelism, expressed in tales of the dissolute life of monks, remained intense in the eighteenth century, refueled by Jacobite revolts aimed at the restoration of a Catholic monarch (1745–79).[30] William Shenstone, the sponsor of the most impressive Picturesque landscape garden of the period at his estate, Leasowes – which featured an artificial Gothic priory as a reminder of the evils of superstition – articulated this attitude in a poem of 1746:

> Here if my vista point the mould'ring pile,
> Where Hood and Cowl devotion's aspect wore,
> I trace the tott'ring reliques with a smile,
> To think the mental bondage is no more.[31]

But, toward the end of the eighteenth century, once the danger of a Stuart restoration had passed, the abbeys could become sites for Picturesque reflection free of historic echoes. The nostalgia for medieval life that was to become a feature of the Romantic movement (as articulated by Augustus Welby Pugin and John Ruskin, both writing during the early years of photography) was in one sense a reaction against the Picturesque.[32] Because Picturesque taste was so exclusively visual and so indifferent to political, social, and moral issues, those who espoused it overlooked the original function of the monasteries and their role in England's cultural history. Changes of taste in the middle of the nineteenth century combined with the development of technique moved photography away from the Picturesque toward the more expressive and individualized, on one hand, and toward the more refined documentation, on the other. Picturesque painting, illustration, and photography began to decline, primarily because advances in the craft of photography made other, more varied and expressive options possible, and partly because the taste for it began to seem old-fashioned. The landscapes of Gustave Le Gray, initiated shortly after his participation in the Mission Héliographique, introduced an entirely different aesthetic; he favored subjects in the forest of Fontainebleau and other woods in the vicinity of Paris, like contemporary painters of the Barbizon school.[33] The example in plate 65 is unrelated to Picturesque principles of enframing and overlapping topographic side screens, distant perspectives, and architectural incidents central to the landscape tradition. It intentionally defeats traditional convergence to a dis-

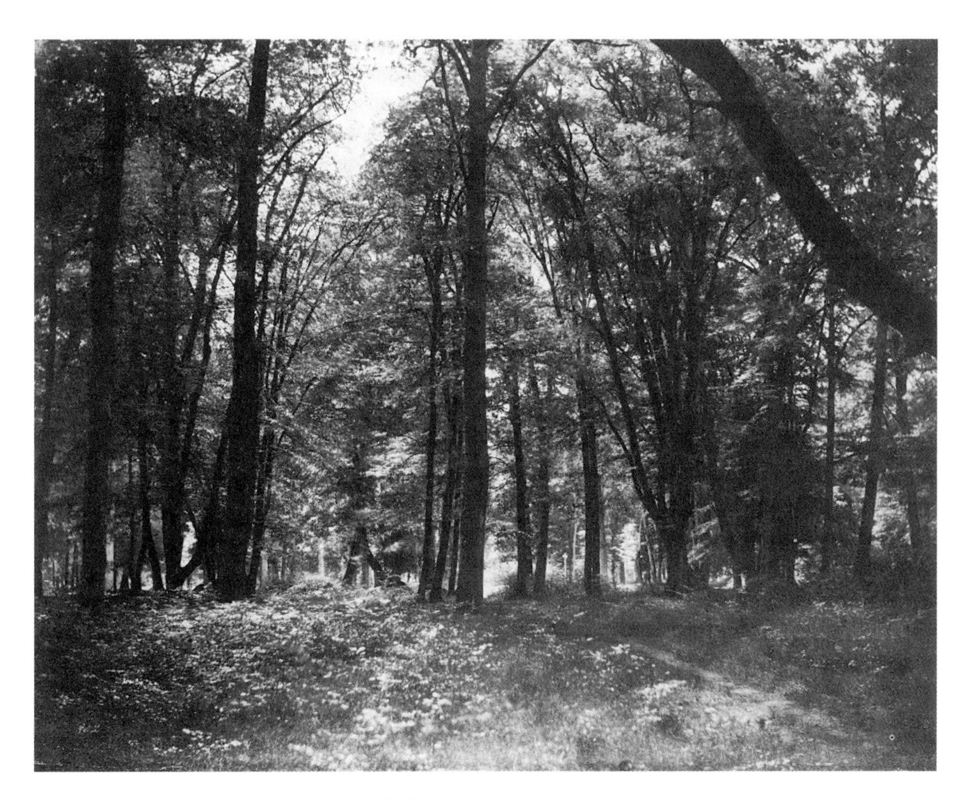

65 Gustave Le Gray, *Forest of Fontainebleau*, 1852

tance point; planes extend horizontally, and the image presents itself as a segment of a continuum, casually but sensitively cut off by the borders on the top and to the left and right. The rapid response of the wet collodion negative encouraged the photographer to study ephemeral effects of light and shadow. Le Gray's plate is remarkably close in sensibility – except for the absence of cattle – to Théodore Rousseau's canvas *Le vieux dormoir de Bas-Bréau* (a painting started in 1835 but completed in the 1860s) (pl. 66). Rousseau also defeats perspective and constructs horizontal layers; though the composition is more studied, he courts the appearance of a casually chosen section of the woods.

Early photographers had rarely tackled the Sublime; the long exposures, which made for flat skies and blurred the movement of water and people, were not conducive to the production of awesome images. But by the mid-

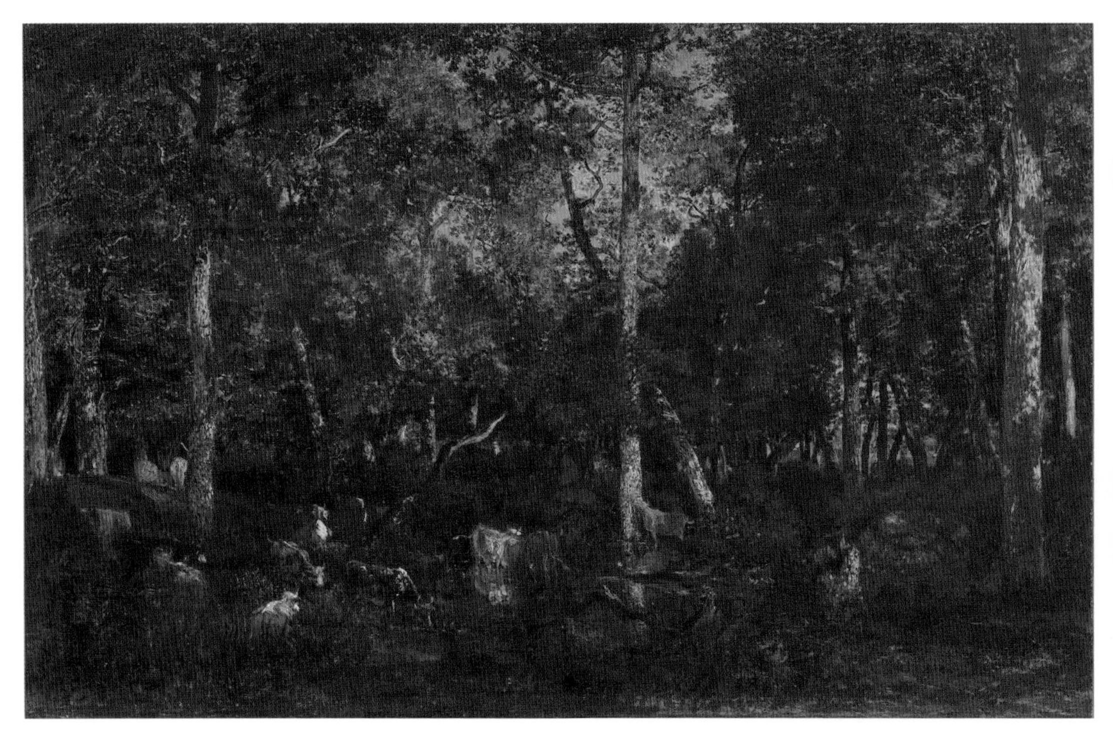

66 Théodore Rousseau, *Le Vieux Dormoir du Bas-Bréau, Forest of Fontainebleau*, 1836–7

nineteenth century, as the aesthetic of the Sublime waned with that of the Picturesque, some of the best photographers did produce prints that reflected that tradition in painting and printmaking. Among these were Le Gray's seascapes (pl. 67),[34] which conveyed an atmospheric intensity and an immediacy unachievable during the era of the calotype and the daguerreotype. Le Gray employed the wet collodion process, which had been in use since 1851: the chemicals, poured onto glass plates, greatly reduced exposure time and gave the negative a transparency that effected a greater clarity in the highlights and shadows. Albumen prints, which had a precision, tonality, and smoothness different from those of the preceding period, were most commonly made from these negatives.[35] In many of Le Gray's seascapes, the sky was printed from separate negatives; indeed, in several instances, different sea views were given the same sky, dramatically and effectively exemplifying photography's qualification as a fine art. The glowering sky, the range of the

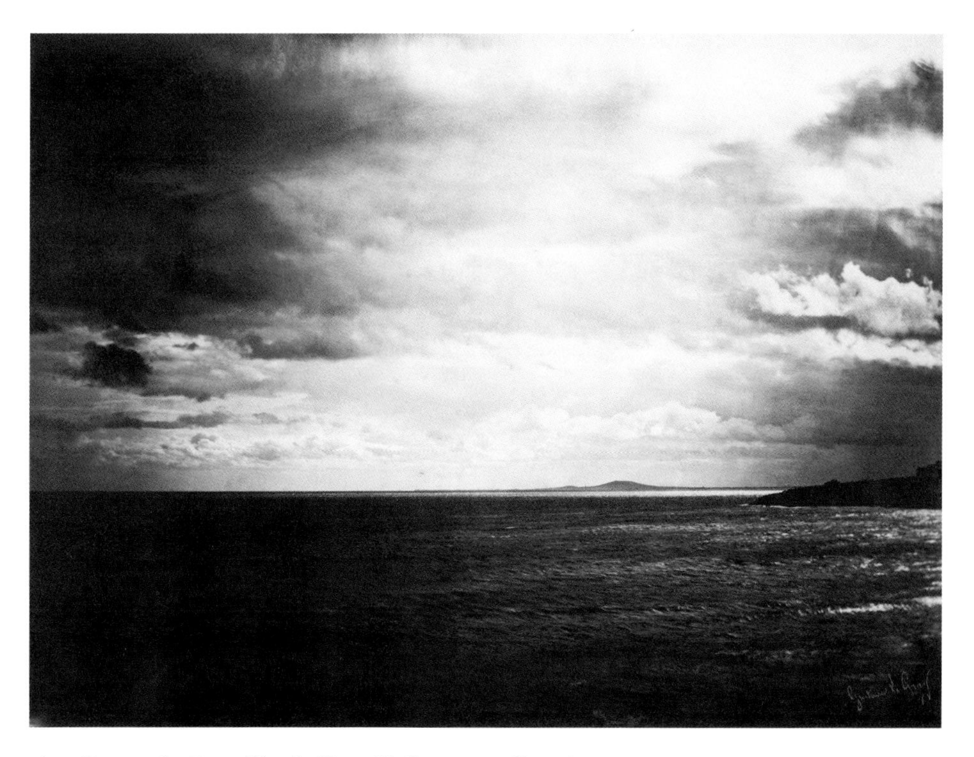

67 Gustave le Gray, *Cloudy Sky – Mediterranean Sea*, 1857

lighting effects and the shimmering surface of the ocean in plate 67 illustrate the difference from earlier processes and the immensely expanded expressive potential of photography.

The foregoing examination of the role of the Picturesque aesthetic in early photography differs from the familiar art-historical exercise of revealing the influence of one artist or style upon a subsequent one. When photography was invented, it was not even evident that works of art should be the photographer's model: the process opened up the potential of a virtually unlimited range of imagery. That many practitioners chose fine art as a model was due to its elevated status. The obvious alternative choice was naturalism, which, in photography, took the form of documentation, serving the interests of science, technology, and programs for building inventories of national monuments and works of art. Most career photographers whose names and reputations have survived pursued both paths. The documentary option was as loaded with ideological nationalism as the aesthetic: Fenton, for example, was employed to document a colonialist campaign of the British army, while Le Gray recorded military maneuvers, and both were engaged as portraitists for the ruling monarchs and their families. They could not have earned a living making landscapes. Private, and ultimately commercial photographers responded to travelers' interests as well as to people who did not travel but who were curious about foreign places, and to educators. Their photographs of ancient sites capitalized on conquests and ambitions in recording the buildings, landscapes, and the "natives" of Egypt, the Holy Land, and the Middle East.

The Picturesque aesthetic imposed the formal precepts of an established taste, and was retrospective, to a quintessentially eighteenth-century disposition. The documentary approach was utilitarian and modern, a manifestation of a faith in the scientific and technological promise of the Industrial Revolution; it had no formal agenda, though the most perceptive photographers could make the recording of a historic building or of the phases of the moon into what today is regarded as a work of art.[36] By the mid-nineteenth century, aided by major improvements in technique (such as rapid exposure times), the Picturesque focus on landscape photography was abandoned in favor of urban and industrial subject matter. Edouard Baldus, the distinguished photographer of the Middle East, was commissioned to photograph the French railroad system.[37] Architectural photography continued to inventory monuments, favoring sites frequented by tourists in western Europe and the eastern Mediterranean and Middle East.

Consciously or not, the photographers of the Picturesque legitimized photography's claim to be accepted as an art form by placing it in the established tradition of landscape painting and prints. The work of Gustave Le Gray, the late work of Baldus with landscape and dwellings, and that of MacAndrew and Adams, marked the moment when photography no longer needed the support of other arts and of literature and was free at once of primitive techniques, of pictorial tradition, and of the choice of iconic national scenery. Its subjects had no specific locus – they represented the photographer's responses. In plates 65 and 67, to the overcast ocean and sunlit forest, their close affinities to contemporary painting did not represent dependence but a common interest in visual effect rather than the specifics of place.

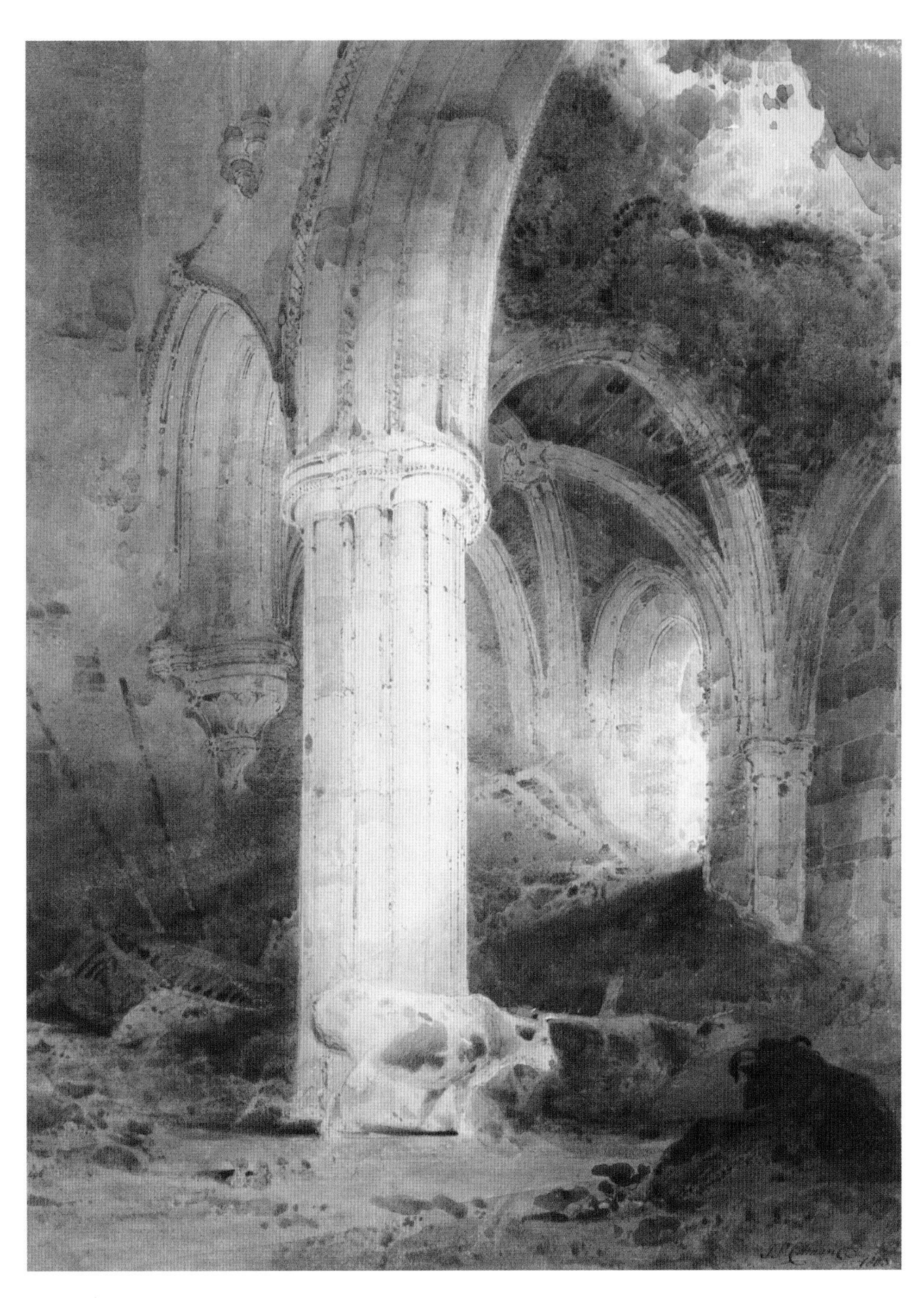

68 John Sell Cotman, *Ruins of Rievaulx Abbey, Yorkshire*, 1803

AFTERWORD

THE PRESERVATION OF DECAY: RUINS IN THE PICTURESQUE LANDSCAPE

Painters, particularly watercolorists, have made innumerable images of ecclesiastical ruins, especially churches and chapels. A watercolor by John Sell Cotman (pl. 68) emphasizes the piles of rubble from the collapsing superstructure of the church. James Mudd's *Tintern Abbey* (see pl. 62) shows the skeleton of a decaying roof, which was reconstructed to provide shelter or to forestall the collapse of the structure; it is unlikely that the original timbers would have survived uncovered for half a millennium. Conditions of this sort led some owners of noteworthy ruins to undertake campaigns to facilitate access to the many tourists seeking the Picturesque experience by leveling the ground and planting grass to reduce mud. The appearance of grazing cows in both of these images is a unique exception to the exclusion of agricultural landscape and labor mandated by arbiters of Picturesque taste.

Ecclesiastical ruins served as a reminder of the liberation from the dominance of the papacy over Britain, a response fueled by fear of a return of the Catholic Stuart monarchy. But early eighteenth-century scholars of British antiquities took a more detached view of the remains. Though they showed little interest in their original condition, they supported their preservation as ruins.

NOTES

Recently a version of this article, originally published in *Artibus et Historiae,* was published in *Composite Landscapes: Photomontage and Landscape Architecture*, Boston, MA: Isabella Stewart Gardner Museum, 2013.

I am grateful to the Centre Canadien d'Architecture in Montreal for the award of a Mellon Senior Grant to pursue preliminary research for this study, and to Gordon Baldwin for his thoughtful comments on the manuscript.

1 Extremely thorough, even exhaustive cleaning and polishing of the silver was the first essential step in the making of a daguerreotype. Next came the suspension of the shiny plate over iodine in a closed container. Rising revapors from the iodine united with the silver to produce a light-sensitive surface coating of silver iodine. The sensitized plate, inside a lightproof holder, was then transferred to a camera and, in the earliest days, exposed to light for as long as twenty-five minutes. The plate was developed by placing it in a container suspended over a heated dish of mercury, the vapor from which reacted with the exposed silver iodine to produce an image in an amalgam of silver mercury. The image was made permanent, i.e., fixed by immersion in a solution of salt or hyposulfite of soda and toned with gold chloride to improve its color, definition, and permanence. The image thus produced had startling clarity. See Gordon Baldwin, *Looking at Photographs: A Guide to Technical Terms*, Los Angeles and London, 1991, p. 35.

2 Mike Weaver, ed., *Henry Fox Talbot: Selected Texts and Bibliography*, Oxford, 1992, p. 50.

3 Martin Kemp, "Talbot and the Picturesque View," *History of Photography*, 21 (1997), pp. 270–82. On the social and nationalist overtones of Talbot's views of Lacock, see Carol Armstrong, *Scenes in a Library: Reading the Photograph in the Book*, Cambridge, MA, 1998, chapter 2.

4 Henry Fox Talbot, *The Pencil of Nature*, London, 1844, pl. 6.

5 On Talbot's problems with drawing, see Larry Schaaf, *The Photographic Art of William Henry Fox Talbot*, Princeton, 2000, p. 13.

6 Larry Schaaf, *Tracings of Light: Sir John Herschel and the Camera Lucida*, San Francisco, 1989.

7 Ian Ousby, *The Englishman's England: Taste, Travel, and the Rise of Tourism*, Cambridge, 1990.

8 Andre Rouillé, *La photographie en France, textes et controverses: une anthologie, 1816–1871*, Paris, 1989, p. 40.

9 In searching a bibliographical base for the title keywords, "voyages pittoresques," I found 489 titles, primarily from the early nineteenth century.

10 For discussion of the appreciation of native landscape in Britain, see Esther Moir, *The Discovery of Britain: The English Tourists, 1540–1840*, London, 1964; W. G. Hoskins, *The Making of the English Landscape*, 2nd edn., London and Toronto, 1988; Elizabeth K. Helsinger, *Rural Scenes and National Representation: Britain, 1815–1850*, Lawrenceville, NJ, 1997; A. Howkins, "Land, Locality, People, Landscape: The Nineteenth-Century Countryside," in *Prospects for the*

Nation: Recent Essays in British Landscape, 1750–1880, ed. Michael Rosenthal et al., New Haven and London, 1997, pp. 97–114.

11 Philippe Néagu, *La mission héliographique: photographies de 1851*, Paris, 1980.

12 On scenic touring, see Moir, *The Discovery of Britain*, Ousby, *The Englishman's England*, and Hoskins, *The Making of the English Landscape*; Malcolm Andrews, *The Search for the Picturesque: Landscape Aesthetics and Tourism in Britain, 1760–1800*, Stanford, CA, 1989; Andrews, "A Pictorial Template: The Tourists and their Guidebooks," in *The Picturesque in Late Georgian England*, ed. Dana Arnold, London, 1994. For the different approach to travel in France, see C. W. Thompson, "French Romantic Travel and the Quest for Energy," *Modern Language Review*, 87 (1992), pp. 307–19. For extensive study of tourism directed to scientific interests, see Barbara Stafford, "Toward Romantic Landscape Perception: Illustrated Travels," *Art Quarterly*, 62 (1977), pp. 89–124; Stafford, *Voyage into Substance: Art, Science, Nature, and the Illustrated Travel Account, 1760–1840*, Cambridge, MA, 1984.

13 See Matthew Arnold, *On the Study of Celtic Literature*, London, 1867 (a shamelessly racist tract denigrating the Irish), and L. P. Curtis, *Anglo-Saxons and Celts: A Study of Anti-Irish Prejudice in Victorian England*, Bridgeport, CT, 1968.

14 For analysis of the role of literature in the Picturesque movement, see Martin Price, "The Picturesque Moment," in *From Sensibility to Romanticism: Essays Presented to Frederick A. Pottle*, ed. Frederick W. Hilles and Harold Bloom, New York, 1965, pp. 259–89; J. N. Watson, *Picturesque Landscape and English Romantic Poetry*, London, 1970; J. D. W. Murdoch, "Scott, Pictures, and Painters," *Modern Language Review*, 67 (1972), pp. 31–43; John Barrell, *The Idea of Landscape and the Sense of Place, 1730–1840*, Cambridge, 1972; Marcia Allentuck, "Scott and the Picturesque: Afforestation and History," in *Scott Bicentenary Essays*, ed. Alan Bell, Edinburgh, 1973, pp. 188–98; Matthew Brennan, *Wordsworth, Turner, and Romantic Landscape: A Study of the Traditions of the Picturesque and the Sublime*, Columbia, SC, 1987.

15 Joseph Addison, "The Pleasures of the Imagination," in *The Spectator* (1712).

16 Essential contributions to the definition of the Picturesque are Richard Payne Knight, *An Analytical Inquiry into the Principles of Taste*, London, 1794; Uvedale Price, *An Essay on the Picturesque, as Compared with the Sublime and the Beautiful*, London, 1794; Christopher Hussey, *The Picturesque: Studies in a Point of View*, London, 1927; Walter Hippie, *The Beautiful, the Sublime, and the Picturesque in Eighteenth-Century British Aesthetic Theory*, Carbondale, IL, 1957; Price, "The Picturesque Moment"; J. Carré, "Le pittoresque, art national britannique?," *Revue française de civilisation britannique*, 3 (1985), pp. 39–53; S. K. Robinson, *Inquiry into the Picturesque*, Chicago, 1991; K. I. Michasiw, "Nine Revisionist Theses on the Picturesque," *Representations*, 38 (1992), pp. 76–100; D. Punter, "The Picturesque and the Sublime: Two Worldscapes," in *The Politics of the Picturesque: Literature, Landscape, and Aesthetics since 1770*, ed. S. Copley and Peter Garside, Cambridge, 1994, pp. 220–37. See also the invaluable anthology of Picturesque writings in Malcolm Andrews, ed., *The Picturesque: Literary Sources and Documents*, 3 vols., Mountfield, 1994, and the works of William Gilpin cited in note 18 below.

17 "A letter to H. Repton, esq., on the application of the practice as well as the principles of landscape painting to landscape gardening, intended as a supplement to the 'Essay on the Picturesque,'" Hereford, Printed by D. Walker for J. Robson, London, 1798.

18 The principal publications of William Gilpin: *Forest Scenery*, London, 1791; *Observations on the River Wye, and Several Parts of South Wales, etc., Relative Chiefly to Picturesque Beauty; Made in the Summer of the Year 1770*, London, 1782; *Observations Relative chiefly to Picturesque Beauty, Made in the Year 1772, on Several Parts of England, Particularly the Mountains, and Lakes of Cumberland and Westmoreland*, London, 1782; *Remarks on Forest Scenery and other Woodland Views, Relative Chiefly to Picturesque Beauty*, London, 1791; *Three Essays: On Picturesque Beauty; On Picturesque Travel; and On Sketching Landscape*, London, 1803. See the detailed study by C. P. Barbier: *William Gilpin: His Drawings, Teaching, and Theory of the Picturesque*, Oxford, 1963.

19 "The Delinquent Travelers," lines 18–21, 120–27 (from *Poetical Works*, ed. Ernest H. Coleridge, London and New York, 1969, pp. 445ff.), quoted by John Whale, "Romantics, Explorers, and Picturesque Travelers," in *The Politics of the Picturesque*, p. 175.

20 W. Combe, *The First Tour of Doctor Syntax in Search of the Picturesque*, London, 1820; Combe, *Doctor Syntax's Three Tours in Search of the Picturesque*, London, 1871.

21 Gilpin, "River Wye," as quoted by Malcolm Andrews in *The Picturesque: Literary Sources and Documents*, vol. I, p. 245; Stephen Copley, "Gilpin on the Wye: Tourism, Tintern Abbey, and the Picturesque," in *Prospects for the Nation*, pp. 115–32.

22 John Gage, *A Decade of English Naturalism, 1810–1820*, Norwich, 1969; Michael Rosenthal, "The Rough and the Smooth: Rural Subjects in Later Eighteenth-Century Art," in *Prospects for the Nation*, pp. 37–60; Howkins, "Land, Locality, People, Landscape."

23 David Punter, "The Picturesque and the Sublime: Two Worldscapes," in *The Politics of the Picturesque*, pp. 220–37. For a further valuable study on landscape sensibilities, see Martin Kemp, "The Art of Seeing Nature: Points of View in the Perception of Landscape in Britain, 1770–1850," in *De la beauté à l'ordre du monde: paysage et crise de la lisibilité*, ed. L. Mondada, Lausanne, 1992.

24 Malcolm Andrews, "The Metropolitan Picturesque," in *The Politics of the Picturesque*, pp. 282–98. For an example of the *voyages pittoresques*, see Frognall Dibdin, *Voyage bibliographique, archéologique et pittoresque en France*, Paris, 1825.

25 *The Landscape, A Didactic Poem. In three books. Addressed to Uvedale Price, esq. by R. P. Knight*, part II, London, 1794, pp. 288ff.

26 Ann Bermingham, "System, Order, and Abstraction: The Politics of English Landscape Drawing around 1795," in *Landscape and Power*, ed. W.J.T. Mitchell, Chicago, 1994, pp. 80–86. She cites a supporting opinion of Price from *An Essay on the Picturesque, as Compared With the Beautiful . . .*, London, 1810, vol. I, p. 342.

27 Gilpin, "River Wye," as transcribed in Andrews, ed., *The Picturesque: Literary Sources and Documents*, vol. I, pp. 254f.

28 These are among the many images of the abbey published in the catalog by Robert Woof and Stephen Hebron, *Towards Tintern Abbey*, Grasmere, 1998. For an introduction to the British attraction to ruins, see William Howitt, *Ruined Abbeys and Castles of Great Britain*, Kindon, 1862; Paul Zucker, *Fascination of Decay: Ruins: Relic–Symbol–Ornament*, Ridgewood, NJ, 1968; Rose Macaulay, *Pleasure of Ruins*, London, 1953; Margaret Aston, "English Ruins and English

History: The Dissolution and the Sense of the Past," *Journal of the Warburg and Courtauld Institutes*, 36 (1973), pp. 231–55; Stuart Piggott, *Ruins in a Landscape: Essays in Antiquarianism*, Edinburgh, 1976; Louis Hawes, "Constable's Hadleigh Castle and British Romantic Ruin Painting," *Art Bulletin*, 65 (1983), pp. 455–70; Anne F. Janowitz, *England's Ruins: Poetic Purpose and the National Landscape*, Oxford, 1990; Ian Ousby, "A Proper State of Decay: Ruins and Ruin-Hunters," in *The Englishman's England*, pp. 100ff.; Raimonda Modiano, "The Legacy of the Picturesque: Landscape, Property, and the Ruin," in *The Politics of the Picturesque*, pp. 196–219; Christopher Woodward, *In Ruins*, London, 2001.

29 See the account of Henry Gastineau, *South Wales Illustrated in a Series of Views . . . Engraved on Steel From Original Drawings by Henry Gastineau*, London, 1830, vol. II, unnumbered pages on Tintern Abbey.

30 See Aston, "English Ruins and English History"; Michael Charlesworth, "The Ruined Abbey: Picturesque and Gothic Ruins," in *The Politics of the Picturesque*, pp. 62–80.

31 William Shenstone, *The Poetical Works*, ed. C. Gilfillan, New York, 1854 (reprinted 1968), Elegy XXI: "Taking a View of the Country From His Retirement, He is Led to Meditate on the Character of the Ancient Britons. Written at the Time of a Rumored Tax upon Luxury," 49, Stanza 5.

32 On the shift from the Picturesque to the Gothic Revival, see Martin Price, "The Picturesque Moment"; J. Mordaunt Crook, *The Dilemma of Style: Architectural Ideas from the Picturesque to the Post-Modern*, Chicago, 1987, especially chapter 2.

33 Eugenia Janis, *The Photography of Gustave Le Gray*, Chicago, 1987; Sylvie Aubenas et al., *Gustave Le Gray, 1820–1884*, Los Angeles, 2002 (also published in French), with essays by various authors on different aspects of Le Gray's work.

34 On the seascapes, see Janis, *The Photography of Gustave Le Gray*, pp. 45–83.

35 See Baldwin, *Looking at Photographs*, pp. 27f. Earlier, Le Gray had been the inventor of a technical process to increase the transparency of paper negatives by impregnating them with wax.

36 See the excellent monograph by Malcolm Daniel and Barry Bergdoll, *The Photographs of Edouard Baldus*, New York and Montreal, 1994.

37 I have discussed the early evolution of architectural photography in "The Origins of Architectural Photography," in *Origins, Imitation, Conventions*, Cambridge, MA, 2002, pp. 95–124.

6

Art and Evolution

ART CHANGES FROM ERA TO ERA: some styles vanish quickly; others survive and evolve; still others spring up in place of the old and in different parts of the world. At the end of the nineteenth century, historians, noticing a parallel to biological evolution, picked up some Darwinian metaphors to support a theory of history, but the fact that they misinterpreted Darwin – as did so many of his successors, even in biology – as giving support to an ineluctable sequence of events directed by some internal or external destiny. So when I became interested in the implications of historical theory for criticism, it was as an opponent of "evolutionism," and I realized only later that it was not the use but the misuse of evolutionary concepts that had caused the misunderstanding. Historians had cut off contact with biologists just during the period when the latter were abandoning finalism and vitalism, and were producing a view of life capable of stimulating fresh approaches to cultural history.[1]

The fact that nineteenth-century historians fell into a trap when they adopted the evolutionary metaphor does not mean that their attempt was misplaced or doomed from the start; the fundamental hypotheses about evolution are historical and it would be presumptuous to assume that there was nothing to learn about history from the students of life on earth. Though there are radical differences in the data of natural history and of cultural history, their operational hypotheses are formulated in similar ways.[2] The data collected by scientists and historians are mere raw materials to be arranged into rational structures according to hypotheses and principles that are not empirically discovered but created. Since these creations crystallize and represent the point of view of the moment in which they are made, one can expect to discover in them a bridge between the humanities and sciences at any given time. At this generalizing level, technical barriers to understanding – the professional jargon and the mystifying formulas – fall into the background.

SIMILARITIES AND CONTRASTS OF METHOD

While speaking of change or evolution in the visual arts one is not thinking about single works, which are mostly inorganic physical objects altered only by damage or decomposition, but of patterns observed in collections of such objects arranged in a linear – usually a chronological – order. In this case, like biologists, one does not observe primarily individual things but trends that can be deduced by comparing them. Comparison is the fundamental method of both fields. The technique is viable only when a number of such things are sufficiently alike to make comparison meaningful, yet sufficiently different that change is apparent. In evolutionary theory, the class of like things is called a taxon (species, genus, family, etc.); in art history, it is called a style.

Both taxa and styles are organized according to a hierarchic, pyramidal classification. As a species, lion (*Panthera leo*) is a class of a genus (cats with retractable claws), which is in turn in a class of a family (Felidae) and so on up to a phylum (Vertebrata), so the style of an artist (Botticelli) is classed as belonging to a local period style (early Renaissance, Florentine), which is part of the Renaissance, Italian, and so on up to the whole span of western art. I am going to compare styles (at the level of the individual and the period) to species rather than to taxa from this point on.

The borderlines between one species and another and one style and another are not always apparent. They may be recognized initially by likenesses and differences in physical characteristics, but the biologist has a more precise basis for classification. Species are interbreeding groups defined by genetic relationship, whereas styles, like other manifestations of culture, cross promiscuously with other styles – even extinct ones. Tortoises always descend from tortoises, but a modern English sculpture may "descend" from a modern French, ancient Roman, or Gothic one, or from all three. So biology differs from history in that its categories are internally organized, and would be so even if there were no biologists (we can make tortoises race, but not mate, with hares), while historical categories like style have to be invented by historians. This is one reason why biological classifications are more descriptive in character (*Vertebrata*, *Amphibia*) than historical ones, which show their creators' bias toward a particular interpretation of history and usually are either denigrating (Middle Ages, Gothic, Baroque) or approving (Renaissance, Risorgimento, Enlightenment). Yet the biologist also is influenced by his interpretation of history; thus not all of his *Amphibia* are amphibious, and not all amphibious animals are *Amphibia*.

As evolutionists employ fossil evidence to construct an image of change in the past, so art historians examine the products of extinct styles. The historical evidence is much richer, but this advantage obscures the fact that our links can be missing, too. Whole phyla of art are lost, such as Classic Greek wall painting, a major art of antiquity, or much of medieval and Renaissance gold- and silversmithery, too precious to survive the poverty and cupidity of later times. The fate of the former affected the entire evolution of later western art, since adherents of the recurrent revivals of antiquity, including painters, saw the Greeks primarily as sculptors; the greatest revival of all – the Renaissance – was well on its way before any Roman painting was known. The losses were due mostly to chance and indifference, not willful destruction; our ancestors generally kept even what they disliked, and any visitor to provincial American museums will find that bad art has survived as well as good.

But it is the character, not the quantity, of the evidence from the past that makes the fundamental contrast in the nature of the evidence; while the Gothic style as such is as extinct as the Brontosaurus, every surviving, well-preserved example of that style can be as lively today as it was when it was made.[3] Indeed, it often happens that products of an extinct style are more influential in the origin of new forms than those of a living style. In the early twentieth century traditional tribal images and figures were adopted, notably in Picasso's *Demoiselles d'Avignon*.

THE ORIGIN OF STYLES

The origins of art are as little known as the origins of life, because works of art precede other records. It might have originated simultaneously in several parts of the world and at intervals of many thousands of years, and wherever it occurred, it thrived. Rarely has an art been extinguished except by force or by the substitution of another type more congenial to the environment. The art of prehistoric and so-called "primitive" people was also their science and magic, or means of investigating and controlling their environment. But it cannot be common utility that explains its perseverance, because art that has served no social function other than the aesthetic has survived and propagated, as in recent centuries, with unabated vigor.[4]

Art does not persist by the approval of each successive generation in human history, but by a principle of inertia. Except by the exercise of extreme repressive power, it could not be stopped, any more than language. The comparison does not imply that the survival of art is assured by its symbolic, communicative function; that is one factor, but another is the drive to create which is indifferent to a prospective audience. The impulses that produce art are found in most, if not all humans, and may be related somehow to our survival in evolutionary competition.

Life does not repeatedly appear by spontaneous generation (as was believed not long ago on the evidence of the appearance of bacteria in sealed solutions and maggots in decaying organic matter); nor does art. Every style of the past and present descends in some way from previous works. In the whole span of recorded time, no art can be proven to have been initiated without some stimulus from preceding forms. The Renaissance threw off some characteristics of late medieval art, but with the aid of still earlier art; and hardly any of the most experimental painters of our time relinquished the Renaissance problems of easel painting. Art since the nineteenth century has been promiscuously historical in resurrecting Japanese prints, African sculpture, Persian miniatures, and so on. Whenever we believe that a radical change of direction in the art of the past was wholly unprecedented, it is likely that some evidence is missing. Evolution does not follow a straight course; each source produced many offshoots, of which a few survive, while the huge majority became extinct.

NATURAL SELECTION

According to the principle of natural selection, the evolution of a species is the product of differential reproduction occurring genetically, and of the interaction between the organisms produced and their physical and organic environments. Individuals better adapted to successful life in a given environment tend to be favored by their ability to produce more offspring. Natural selection does not favor change over stability; in a relatively stable and congenial environment, mutations are likely to be unfavorable, and certain animals such as the opossum and the bat have managed to survive without much change for more than fifty million years; the phenomenon is known as stabilizing selection.

The evolution of the modern horse offers a good example, since it is especially well documented.[5] The line can be traced to a mammal of the Eocene era, perhaps sixty million years ago, called *Eohippus*, a tiny, four-toed browsing creature with a very small brain. His descendant, *Mesohippus*, was nearly twice as large, had three padded toes and was much smarter. This was the end of a simple linear development. From here on, a number of distinct genera emerged of which only one led to the modern horse; in time the remainder disappeared. Most continued as browsers, but in the Miocene era one line (*Parahippus-Merychippus*) made a significant step from browsing to grazing that favored a wholly new kind of tooth composition and structure (thus altering the skull), and digestive system. Meanwhile, the rotation of the fore and hind legs had become severely restricted, and the three-toed foot, thus specialized for running, began to operate like a spring, with the aid of ligaments, in order to propel the increased weight at the speed attained by lighter ancestors. One descendant of this group, the *Pliohippus*, lost his auxiliary toes to develop the single hoof of his modern descendant; the most advanced members of this line are already *Equus*.

OPPOSING INTERPRETATIONS OF THE EVOLUTIONARY PROCESS

There are two ways to interpret this evidence; the one, which minimizes the factor of chance and the role of the environment, takes many forms, from the extreme of finalism (according to which the modern horse – or man – was "meant to be"; his development was steered along the path it took by an external guiding force, necessarily of a supernatural character) to the more moderate principle of orthogenesis (development-in-a-straight-line; usually strictly determined by an internal component, though not progressing toward a foreseen goal). The other – natural selection – postulates variations occurring by chance, which gave some horses advantages over others that aided them in escaping predators, in competing for mates, and in producing and protecting offspring. There was no plan involved, and no step in the direction ultimately taken implied by any or all of the subsequent steps. At any moment, a number of variants were brought into a world that ultimately favored some more than others; the shifting conditions of that world might be as important in horse development as anything peculiarly horsy. Finalism, the first of these interpretations, involves a plan beyond our comprehension and ultimately a Maker of this plan, while natural selection, with its emphasis on the free operation of the genetic mechanism, leaves nothing outside the scope of potential investigation. Both systems have their appeal, but scientists and scholars have no real choice but to accept the latter, since ultimately the former can be handled only by theologians or metaphysicians.

THE FUNCTION OF NATURAL SELECTION

The story of the horse, then, is to be explained by the selection of characteristics favoring grazing over browsing, a change that occurred at a time when grass was increasing – and the ability to avoid predators by speed of flight rather than by, say, the armor developed by such horse relatives as the rhinoceros. From fossil evidence it is not possible to agree conclusively on the selective advantage of every feature; for example, the general increase in size, which did not occur in a constant development (there were long periods without notable size change and some branches even became smaller). Though the overall evolution can be represented as linear and destined to produce the modern horse, the major trends have been, in fact, anything but predictable and represent shifts in evolutionary direction (e.g., from short browsing teeth to long grazing teeth; from pad feet to hooves). The rate of change was not regular; shifts occurred at an accelerated rate, since transitional forms are disadvantageous (middle-sized teeth would be poorly adapted to either grazing or browsing). Finally, the lines that shifted radically from early branches normally did not supplant more primitive ones but shared the earth with them over millions of years, and of course many radical but impractical shifts failed so quickly as to leave no record.

THE APPLICATION OF NATURAL SELECTION TO ART

The practice of art historians involves choosing between solutions of the kind once so fiercely debated in biology. Every past style has been interpreted as a linear sequence of achievements progressively nearing the goal of a perfected or "classic" form of that style. Just as the spokesman of orthogenesis would have the line from *Mesohippus* to *Parahippus* aimed in the direction of *Equus*, Notre Dame in Paris and Sens cathedral may be represented as early and only partially fulfilled attempts to build Amiens, or the Italian "primitives" (revealing word!) as would-be Raphaels. By contrast, the theory of natural selection convincingly explains the apparently systematic evolution of styles toward optimal solutions without relying on a guiding agency.

In the evolution of a style, variants appear in different works of art, of which some are "well adapted" and some are not. Adaptation in this sense is the capacity to stimulate emulation among artists and favorable response in the society at large. What makes style evolve is the incorporation of new elements into the complex. Each generation of artists – and of patrons – keeps what it wants from the generation before and rejects what it has no use for. But, as in life, the well-adapted variant tends to produce more offspring. Usually the most compelling innovations – and traditions – are kept, but there are also periods when the facile and inconsequential fares better; evolution is not a synonym for progress. There cannot be a predestined or predictable development because the process depends not only on the achievement represented in any work of art but also on the ability and desire of later artists and laymen to accept it. The phenomenon of apparent growth toward classic forms (as at Amiens) is explained by an initial conception. Not all works of art now regarded as masterpieces have been so well received; they were disliked or misunderstood (for example, the late *Pietà*s of Michelangelo).

RADIATION

As styles radiate into divergent paths, adapting to different environments, it often happens that the so-called mainstream is less long-lived than a provincial offshoot, since the provinces tend to be conservative and slow to change. The Gothic style of architecture, which spread throughout Europe from the Ile-de-France in the twelfth and thirteenth centuries, was nearly extinct in France by the end of the 1400s, but flourished in a South German branch of delicately vaulted hall churches for another century and a half.

Art historians speak of one style "succeeding" another. But a true case of succession would be even harder to find in art than in life, where there have been rare and intriguing cases of "phyletic evolution," in which the whole of a single population – always geographically isolated – changes from one species to another without splitting. It is questionable whether there is convincing documentation for a comparable cultural isolation and uniformity; in any case, the typical pattern of historical process is represented by the Renaissance, which, though it outlasted the Gothic, did not really succeed it, as demonstrated by the survival of Gothic art so long after Masaccio and Donatello.

THE MULTIPLICATION OF SPECIES AND STYLES

Early evolutionists explained the origin of new species by sudden gross mutations in individuals (saltations) which then immediately became the source of distinct lines. How these individuals propagated without the simultaneous aid of more-or-less normal mates and a compatible environment could not be explained, and recent theories of speciation have made the population rather than the unit the prime object of study. Similarly, the initiation of major new styles cannot be attributed to the isolated creation of a single great artist. They can be recognized and defined only in terms of related characters in large groups of works, and the great artist is the one whose work epitomizes a tendency and stimulates certain trends in its evolution.

Speciation usually proceeds gradually and imperceptibly, though radical and relatively sudden shifts in direction may occur, as with some of the horse's ancestors. The same is true of art, though the shifts often are called, misleadingly, "revolutions,"[6] a concept that prompts historians to refer loosely to a "first Renaissance building" (the Foundling Hospital, Florence) or a "first Cubist picture" (Picasso's *Demoiselles*), as if those works were miraculously successful mutants that sprang into the artist's mind without preparation.

Dialectic theories of art, particularly in Germany, have encouraged revolutionary rather than evolutionary interpretations of history. So the change from late Archaic to early Classic Greek sculpture has been represented as a revolution overthrowing a refined, linear, and abstract style in favor of a more vigorous, blocky, and representational one.

THE INTERPLAY OF INNOVATION AND ENVIRONMENT IN EVOLUTION

The emergence of period styles, like that of species, is studied in terms of aggregates; but art history, unlike biology, cannot ignore the role of the individual. Differential variations occurring genetically can be attributed to chance, but variations in works of art are consciously willed (or produced unconsciously and consciously capitalized on). So the prime mechanism in the evolution of art is the individual imagination.

This is not to say that the artist alone controls evolution. Change is not essentially generated by what artists want, but by the effect of the works they produce – artists' manifestos and theoretical writings reveal what a difference there can be. Those who aim to direct evolution can only orient their work within or away from tradition and hope that contemporaries and successors may follow the lead. Once a work leaves the studio, the process of natural selection begins to operate: the cultural environment, by accepting or rejecting it, provides the structure of the evolution. In a limited sense, this selective process is also creative; though it does not produce the raw materials – the variants – it determines the extent to which they prosper or decline and the way in which they are integrated into the culture.

★ ★ ★ ★

ADAPTATION: THE ENVIRONMENT OF ART

Since life depends on a dynamic equilibrium between an organism and its environment, the principle of adaptation (adjustment to the environment) is the core of the theory of natural selection. An organism that has changed through differential variation prospers only if its new characteristics are adapted to its environment and, conversely, a change in the environment favors only organisms that can adapt to the new conditions. This environment includes the physical area(s) in which the organism lives, and the population of the area(s), including members of its own species.

The obstacle to applying the principle of adaptation to works of art in their cultural environment has been the realization that at times the most meaningful art has been rejected and ridiculed by society, and thus seems to be poorly adapted. But this has been due to a curious failure to admit that artists make an important contribution. Artists, indeed, provide the essential mechanism of evolution: if they reject an innovation, it cannot be sustained, no matter how many others approve it; if they accept one, it cannot perish, though it has no other sponsors. When artists are not believed to be essential to culture, it is because they are forced into a romantic role – rejected and isolated by society and economic failures. Yet for a century and a half the evolution of style has been dominated by "rejected" artists, while their colleagues who adapted to prevailing tastes failed to keep their styles alive. Cézanne illustrates the point: during his life few people understood his work, but through those few it changed the future of art. Art requires an engaged viewer, but not a socially dominant one; a few sympathetic artists can constitute the most influential class of all. The effectiveness of artist's judgments is proven by the fact that some have written the finest criticism since Vasari.

The evolution of style, then, is not necessarily guided by taste, though in every age some or all artists are led or pushed by patrons and social pressures – especially in eras when all art is commissioned and performs specific functions. Art adapted to the prevailing taste[7] may prove to be overspecialized for long-term survival, since taste is one of the most mutable aspects of culture. In nearly every historical instance of conflict between what artists produce independently and what fashion demands, the judgment of time has shown the former to be a better fit.

"SURVIVAL OF THE FITTEST"

Darwin's term "survival of the fittest" (or "struggle for survival"), which appealed so much to *laissez-faire* capitalists, schoolmasters, and diplomats of the nineteenth century, is misleading. To be "fit" or adapted in an evolutionary sense is not, as is commonly thought, to be exceptionally powerful and far-ranging; if that were so, jungles would contain only lions, which would then die of starvation. The defenseless mouse and slug are as "fit" as the king of beasts, and fitter than his relative the saber-toothed tiger, which failed to survive. Within species the same applies: human evolution shows that intellectual ingenuity can compensate amply for lack of physical power (as illustrated by the comic-book image of the superior being from outer space as a man with a tiny, feeble body, an enormous head, and antennae symbolizing extraordinary cerebral equipment); and that aborigines with a stone-age technology can survive as well as highly civilized atom-smashers. So fitness is not a determinate condition; a population may be more or less fit, and in improving its fitness allow it to survive for long periods only to be replaced by another still more viable.

Similarly, individuals within any population vary in fitness. Extreme cases are monsters incapable of adaptation to any environment (in art, incompetent or meaningless work); more relevant are variants that might function successfully in a somewhat different environment (animals with coloration poorly suited to their habitat; art that is not welcomed in its time or place). Since these variants may be as vigorous and as fertile as their fitter relatives, their unfitness cannot be taken as evidence of their intrinsic inferiority.[8] The implications for history and criticism are clear: in the evolutionary metaphor, a work of art may be evaluated according to its fitness – in the sense of adjustment to the taste of its time and place – but this position is relative, since there are many degrees of fitness, and even unfitness has no necessary value implications. To say that the rejection of a work of art by its cultural environment is good or bad is to judge the environment as well as the work.

★ ★ ★ ★

STABILITY AND CHANGE

Adaptation is not synonymous with change; the conservative Egyptian culture nurtured a style that evolved less in the course of millennia than recent styles did in a generation; it quickly extinguished the only radical shift in its history – the style of the eighteenth dynasty – in favor of a return to something like the previous status quo. But the term "stability" as applied to a culture or style is relative; absolute stability is stagnation. When artists reproduce works without individual variation, their art is soon extinguished for lack of vitality; this is comparable to inbreeding in organisms, which tends to inhibit adaptation. In art or in life, a line is strengthened by individual variation and moderate admission of foreign strains, although excessive outbreeding may weaken adaptation to specific local conditions. Variation, then, cannot be thought of as the antithesis of stability; it is rather a prerequisite for it. Styles can be sustained over long time spans only by admitting constant inventiveness to challenge the imagination of their practitioners.

In unstable and complex cultures such as those of recent centuries, the arts change often. It appears that the rate of change in western art has been accelerating regularly; but we lack perspective on our own time, and someday the evolution of Florentine art of the fifteenth century may seem to be faster than that of modern architecture, for example, which leveled off to a relatively stable condition after a period of rapid change from 1910 to 1935.

DO STYLES "DECLINE"?

The extinction of styles in the past is often described as the end product of a gradual "decline" from a classic moment of maximum vigor. The source of this trope is an archaic application from biology to criticism represented in Vasari's statement (1568) that style, "like human bodies, has a birth, a growth, an ageing and a death." Vasari's metaphor may have satisfied Renaissance humanists and their descendants, but it obscures more than it illuminates. The individual works that we group into styles are not organically interdependent as cells are in the body, nor is the so-called life cycle alike in different styles – it varies in character as much as in duration. The cyclical analogy warps criticism by implying that the early phases of every style are infantile or primitive while the later phases are enfeebled by age.

The evolutionary metaphor does not constrict criticism because the life and extinction of species obeys no fixed pattern. When extinction is due to a change in environment, the species itself may not decline in vigor but only in numbers; in other words, it may remain perfectly adapted to an environment that is in the process of shrinking away. This analogy can explain styles that disappear without in any way degenerating – the Gothic, for example, which was vital and creative at the time it was being displaced by the Renaissance: brilliant innovations of the late medieval International style and English Perpendicular architecture were contemporaneous to those of Masaccio and Brunelleschi; Monet's *Water Lilies* series, now so highly praised and priced, were painted long after Impressionism had been "supplanted" by other styles (one of them absurdly called "Post-Impressionism" – imagine calling horses "Post-Parahippi"!). The new culture to which styles adapt gradually replaces the old, but the old lingers on in a segment of the same population or away from the great centers, and fosters the traditional forms. So "old" styles do not suddenly vanish, as they are apt to do in handbooks and lecture courses, as new ones emerge; but continue on until the environment to which they are adapted is quite overwhelmed by a younger, expanding culture. Occasionally, however, a style is bypassed and isolated by the expansion of a new culture, either because it is provincial or because its government or religion opposes change; then its art may indeed decline through hardening of the arteries, as did Byzantine art, which the Eastern Orthodox churches have kept half alive for centuries after it ceased to be creative.

THE IMPACT OF ART ON THE ENVIRONMENT

The adaptation of art to the environment is not a one-way path: the environment also adjusts to art. As the introduction of new bacteria or germicides into a balanced ecology can cause far-reaching changes, so the introduction of a new art form (or the disappearance of an old one) may alter everyone's conceptual processes. Once one learns to interpret a radically new kind of visual communication, one looks at everything in a somewhat different way.

Modern Expressionism, for example, aided a re-evaluation of the past that brought Tintoretto and El Greco to the fore, to the disadvantage of Correggio and Murillo. But the impact of art is felt beyond its own sphere: fifteenth-century artists, Leonardo da Vinci in particular, in problems of illusion and of proportion promoted the progress of experimental science: Vesalius without the background of early Renaissance art might never have been known outside Padua.

Today, the potential effect of art on the cultural environment is enormously increased by photographs and the mass media. Books and magazines produced in a few urban centers are homogenizing the visual diet of the entire world, with the result that paintings and buildings in Japan are sometimes indistinguishable from those in Denmark and Brazil. The adaptation, in this case, is not primarily to a local culture, but to the world market, but it is certain that local cultures will be increasingly affected by this trend.

ADAPTATION TO THE PHYSICAL ENVIRONMENT

Climate, including climate change, and topography have not changed much since the era of cave art, but they do vary in different parts of the world, and are responsible for differences among local styles. Weather and geography affect architecture more than the figurative arts because architecture must be responsive to the natural environment. A sound building is structurally stable (defending against wind and snow loads, moisture, fire, etc.) and assures the comfort of inhabitants (through the control of light, heat and cold, air, noise, pollution, etc.). Even the design of roofs, windows, open and closed areas, and the choice of materials and colors is affected by a specific location. Modern building technology, however, has produced sufficient environmental defenses to make the same design viable in the most diverse climates, thus promoting the trend to global uniformity.

The more portable a work of art is, the less local conditions affect it. Variation in easel painting or graphic art is not usually attributable to the purely physical environment; also, most portable art in our culture is kept in buildings, isolated from natural conditions.

SPECULATION

Following the direction of our culture, architecture has become increasingly specialized in function. At one time, a community required only dwellings, a religious center, a marketplace, and perhaps recreational facilities, and a house was only a sheltered room with a hearth. Today a huge variety of structures is required, from hamburger stands to cyclotrons. The rate of specialization has not been uniform; at the height of the Roman Empire, architecture was more varied than in the Middle Ages and the Renaissance, when forensic basilicas, baths, amphitheaters, nymphaea, circuses, gymnasia, and other Roman types of buildings were not required, and a few types of domestic and ecclesiastical structures sufficed. By contrast, the figural arts have become less specialized since the late Renaissance, when they began to be produced for the market. Apart from rare ecclesiastical and civic commissions, modern painting and sculpture are done for no place and nobody in particular and function either in domestic spaces and work places or in museums, where art is held in suspension by the elimination of environment; in museums, every culture is on the same footing.

CONCLUSION

An evolutionary history of art explains changes in style through individual variations without implying a directing agent or a predetermined goal. It solves the dilemma of a discipline divided between those whose principles of historical change devaluate the uniqueness of the individual achievement, and those who appreciate the uniqueness but slight historical processes. The former attribute change in style to agencies outside the control of artists: determinism, expressed in terms either of cycles of growth and decline or of action and reaction, suggests inevitable patterns of development; social history ultimately makes the artist merely a chronicler of her or his times. The latter, connoisseurs and critics, discuss single works or single artists, but usually not the broader problems of style evolution.

In the evolutionary model the variations or innovations tend to be almost imperceptible in stable cultures and to be more abrupt and radical in fluid cultures. Some innovations are incorporated into traditional styles, and others become the root of new styles that often grow alongside the older ones. Poorly adapted innovations either are summarily rejected or, if they are potentially viable, lie dormant to be activated later, in a more congenial environment. So, while the individual imagination generates change, society, including artists, guides its rate and direction, but only by post-facto selectivity: the environment can prompt imaginative solutions by posing challenging problems, but cannot itself formulate the solutions.

To emphasize imaginative innovation is not to make a virtue of change, except in the limited sense that a total absence of variation ossifies an art. The measure that evolutionary theory offers to criticism is rather that of adaptation. The finest works of art are those whose message is sufficiently profound and universal to warrant and win respect not only at the place and time in which they were made, but also everywhere and at all times.

NOTES

I wish to acknowledge the assistance of Richard C. Lewontin, Alexander Agassiz Professor of Zoology in the Museum of Comparative Zoology Emeritus at Harvard University.

1 This essay owes much to Professor George Gaylord Simpson's extensive and imaginative criticism of an earlier draft, for which I am most grateful.

2 For example, the contribution of genetics, a science manifestly inapplicable to cultural history, finally justified Darwin and revealed the mechanics of natural selection; but genetics has refined, without altering, the basic principles of evolution that are useful to historians.

3 Professor Simpson reminded me that termination without issue is not the only form of extinction in the biological world. In life as in art, a line may be extinguished by being transformed into something new.

4 The change from cave culture to the present resembles an evolutionary process in which art is liberated progressively from a subordinate role: the magical significance of its early phase is followed by the religious, and ultimately, in recent times, by the autonomous. But such an image revives the fallacy of evolution as progress; it is not concerned with art itself, but with its function in society.

5 See George Gaylord Simpson, *Horses*, New York, 1951.

6 There are no revolutions in art. A work of art does not contain propositions and therefore cannot take a negative position. If it differs from earlier works, it may suggest an alternative path, but it does not diminish the powers of its predecessors.

7 The term "prevailing taste" is an oversimplification; there are often several tastes in a culture, each representing what biologists call an "ecological niche" that is likely to be filled by a different style the moment it is vacated by an abandoned one. A recent illustration is the niche created by American banking and industry, which in the 1920s and 1930s required eclectic architecture and after World War II demanded modern "International Style" buildings, generally without insisting on quality.

8 An intriguing example is the phenomenon of "industrial melanism" studied in peppered moths of the manufacturing areas of Great Britain. The progressive blackening of the landscape by smoke and soot selectively favored dark colored moths, since predators found light ones easier to spot. The light moths are no less vigorous than they were in the days of their ascendancy, and perhaps, if the age of solar power helps to brighten the industrial environment, they may again become the more fit. The role of environmental blight as the cause of unfitness and the promoter of variants suggests revealing parallels in cultural history.

9 Recent research on selection diverging from Darwin's *Origins* is provided by James T. Costa in *The Annotated Origin: A Facsmilile of the First Edition of On the Origin of Species* (London and Cambridge, 2009).

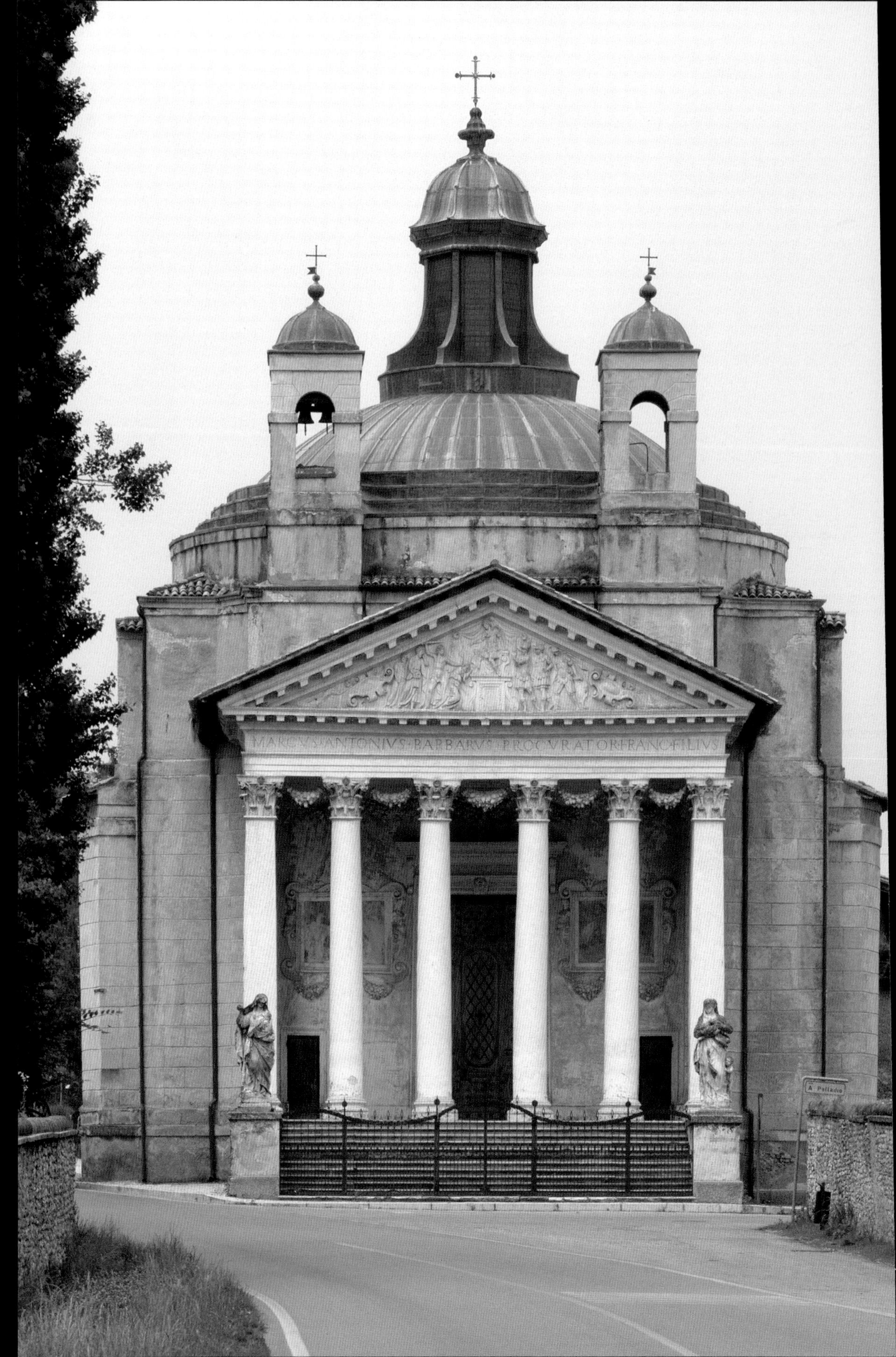
MARCVS ANTONIVS BARBARVS PROCVRATOR FRANC FILIVS

7

The *Magnificenza* of Palladio's Late Works and Its Legacy Abroad

A Study in Selection

I FIRST DISCUSSED THE RELEVANCE OF THE THEORY of selection to the study of the history of art in an essay of 1965, "Art and Evolution," included in this book. As I began to write this present study, I was reading, by chance, Michael Pollan's book *The Botany of Desire* (2001), which sparked my interpretation of how Palladio's ambition to realize a new vision of public *magnificenza* in designs for the Bolognese church of San Petronio, in two Venetian churches, and in his proposal for the Rialto bridge were rejected in Bologna and Venice but succeeded in Vicenza. The primary reason for this difference was that most of his clients in the first instance were republican men of affairs committed to the principle of moderation to which the sixteenth-century writer on ethics, Paolo Paruta, had given expression, while those in Vicenza were aristocrats who embraced the display of wealth and privilege. Pollan explains that selection does not occur solely as a result of changes in the environment. It requires a capacity to respond to the changes – in short, an interdependence. In Pollan's words,

> About a hundred million years ago plants stumbled on a way – actually a few thousand different ways – of getting animals to carry them, and their genes, here and there. This was the evolutionary watershed associated with

Detail of pl. 84

> the advent of the angiosperms, an extraordinary new class of plants that made showy flowers and formed large seeds that other species were induced to disseminate. Plants began evolving burrs that attach to animal fur like Velcro, flowers that seduce honeybees in order to powder their thighs with pollen, and acorns that squirrels obligingly taxi from one forest to another, bury, and then, just often enough, forget to eat.

The organism or plant is equivalent to an architect's design proposal, and the environment that accepts or rejects it is the system of beliefs, values, and opinions of the client or group of clients. The evolution of styles throughout the history of art has been controlled not only by the innovations – mutations – of artists, but also by the reception that these innovations have met in their social milieus.

The monumentality of Palladio's late work was a challenge – with ethical and political inferences – to the classicism of the earlier Renaissance. The ethical dimension has been revealed in recent studies of Renaissance texts, inspired by Aristotle's *Nichomachean Ethics*, that address the display of magnificence and, in particular, a fictional symposium published in Venice by Paolo Paruta in 1579, at the time when Palladio's church of the Redentore was under construction.

The Venetian understanding of magnificence in regard to public and private display of wealth and position, *magnificenza*, differed radically from that of the members of Vicentine aristocracy who held imperial and monarchical titles, whom Palladio served in the last years of his life. The latter were less concerned with observing restraint in the expression of magnificence, and incorporated a new vocabulary with echoes of ancient Roman grandeur into public and private buildings in Vicenza and in the villas of the surrounding territory. Palladio's response to his Vicentine patrons gave shape to an architecture that became a monumental affirmation of the ideology of imperial, regal, and papal autocrats of western Europe in the ensuing two centuries.

In 1570 Palladio published *I quattro libri dell'architettura*, the first treatise to include woodcut illustrations of his own designs for public buildings, palaces, and villas. Although it includes a "book" on *Tempii*, he discusses and depicts only Roman temples. At the time, he had built only one church façade, San Francesco della Vigna in Venice (see pl. 70), to complete the church designed by Jacopo Sansovino. Many of Venice's wealthiest families supported construction of the church by acquiring rights to the side chapels. In 1542 two brothers of the Grimani family, as executors of the will of Cardinal Domenico Grimani, had purchased the privilege to build the façade, and to place there the tomb of Doge Antonio Grimani. In addition, the interior wall of the façade was granted to Vettor, brother of the cardinal, and his sons for tombs and family arms. Two drawings for this project are preserved in the Museo Civico in Vicenza, but neither was carried out.

The temple section of *I quattro libri* (IV, I) opens by addressing the placement of the façade and its symbolic civic role:

> But we . . . should choose sites for temples in the most dignified and prestigious part of the city, far away from unsavory areas and on beautiful and ornate squares where many streets end, so that every part of the temple can be seen in all its majesty and arouse devotion and awe in whoever sees and admires it. And if there are hills in the city, one should choose the highest part, but if there are no elevated positions, one should raise the floor of the temple up from the rest of the city as much as is practical, and one will climb the steps of the temple, so that the ascent induces a greater sense of devotion and majesty. Temple fronts should be constructed overlooking the most impressive part of the city so that it may seem that religion has been placed there like a guard and protector of the citizens.

The church façade is a peculiar architectural form that, like San Francesco della Vigna, is not much influenced by liturgy; it relates to the interior only by providing a central entrance portal to the nave, often with a window above it. In most longitudinal Italian Renaissance churches the interior presents to the façade a basic form inherited from the Middle Ages – a tall central vessel flanked by lower aisles, and rows of lower chapels alongside them. Large basilicas, like the canonical church of the Gesù in Rome (pl. 69), most often were designed with portals on either side.

This made the basic problem of planning a façade one of successfully coordinating the high nave with lower side aisles and still lower chapels. Renaissance architects usually employed volutes or other curvilinear forms, which had no precedent in antiquity, to effect a transition between the dif-

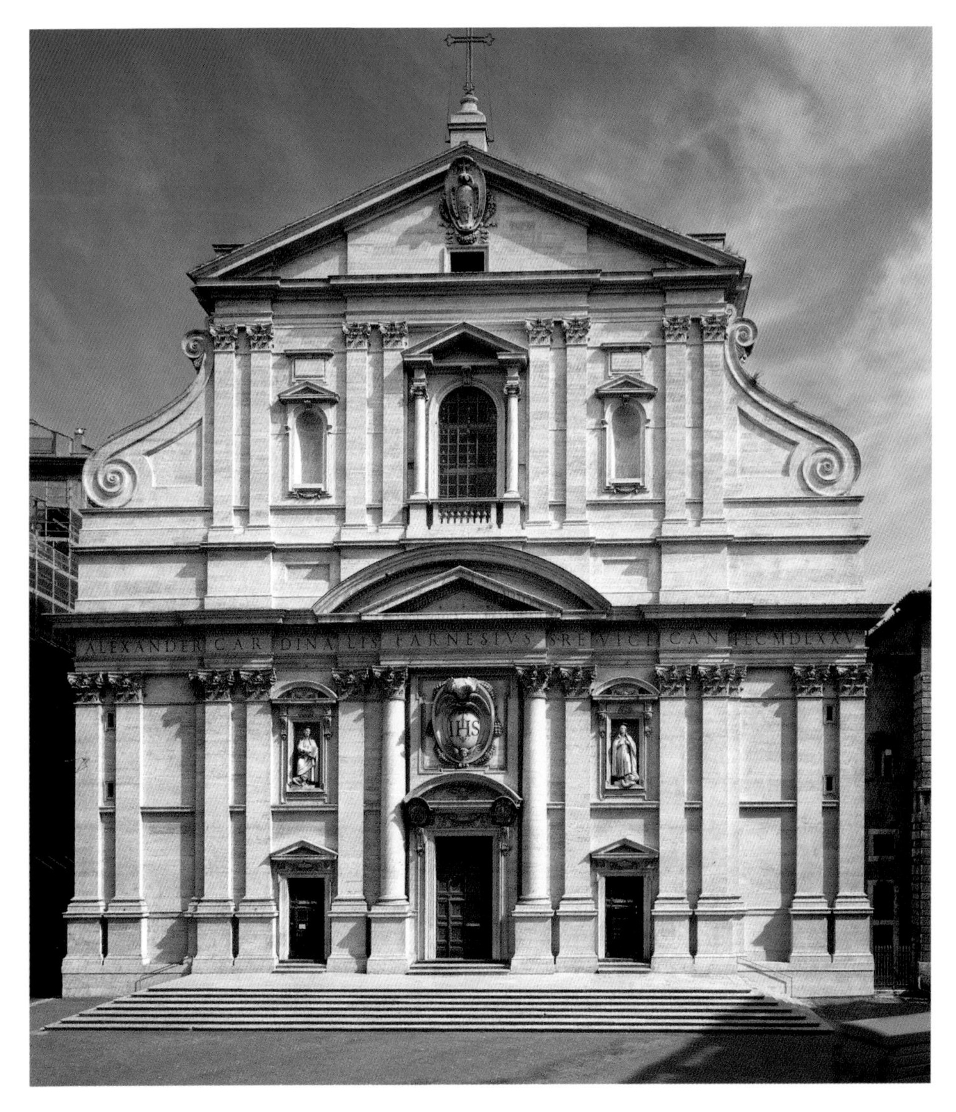

69 Il Gesù façade, Rome

ferent heights of the central and lateral elements. Palladio favored half-pediments echoing the full pediment crowning the center (pl. 70). In the classical tradition, the canon of the orders called for fixed proportions originally based on the human body, so that high elevations required wide columns and pilasters and lower elevations alongside called for thinner vertical elements. For

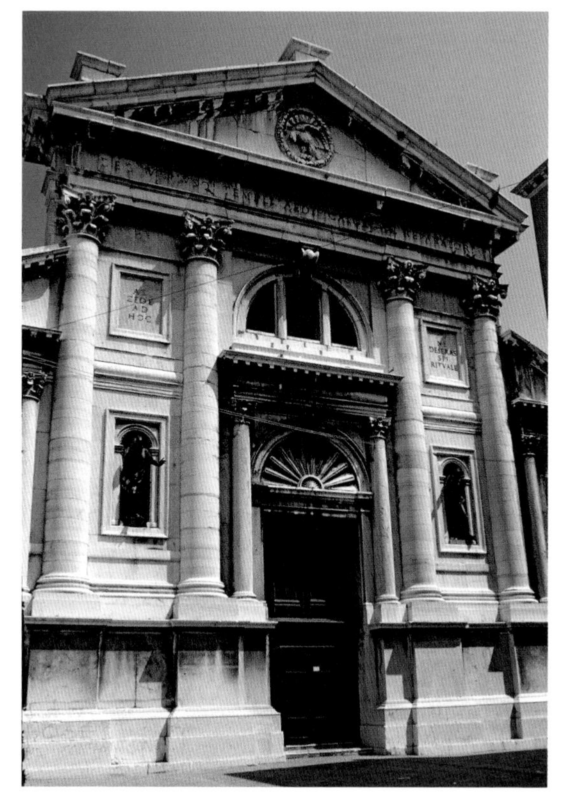

70 San Francesco della Vigna, Venice

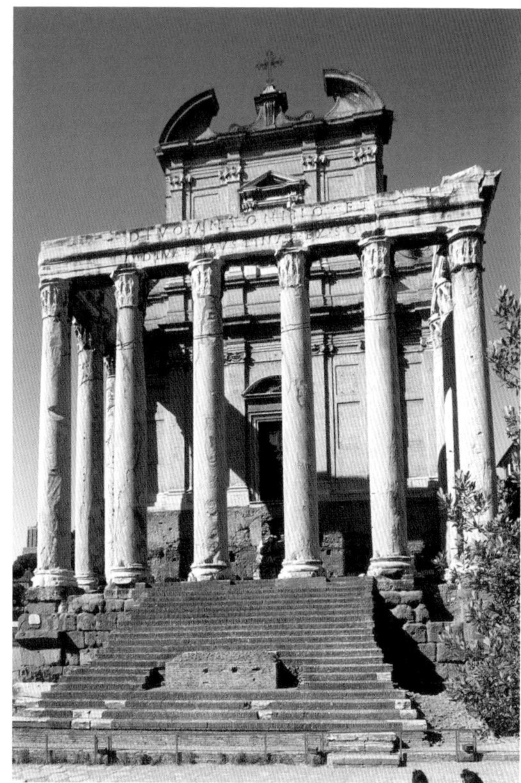

71 Temple of Antoninus and Faustina, Rome

example, the difference between the ancient Roman and Renaissance and Baroque façades is illustrated in plate 71, in which the tall columnar order of the second-century CE temple of Antoninus and Faustina in the Roman Forum reaches the incomplete frieze, while that of the San Lorenzo in Miranda behind (1602) requires two superimposed orders because of the height difference between the nave and the side aisles.

The ethical restraint on the magnificence of church façades did not become an issue until the 1570s. The church of the Gesù was financed by Cardinal Alessandro Farnese, the grandson of Pope Paul III, who commissioned the architect Giacomo Barozzi da Vignola in 1568, but in 1575 canceled Vignola's façade design (which is known from an engraving) and ordered a more imposing one from Giacomo della Porta.

When I was writing my book on Palladio in 1965, the following drawings for church façades that Palladio had proposed between 1565 and his death in 1580 either had not been discovered or had not yet been correctly identified; these now lead me to a reinterpretation of his late work:

Four in the Museo di San Petronio in Bologna, and a portico proposal for that basilica discovered in 1971 by John Harris in the Worcester College Library in Oxford, validating a workshop variant of the same in the Canadian Centre for Architecture in Montreal.

Two for San Giorgio Maggiore in Venice – a half-façade elevation with a columnar porch in the Royal Institute of British Architects in London first identified in 1949 by Rudolf Wittkower, and a plan of the entire monastery in the Venetian archives with a variant of the porch design.

Four for the church of the Redentore in Venice in the RIBA [Royal Institute of British Architecture] – a plan, section, and elevation with a portico and one façade elevation without – destined for a central-plan project previously believed to have been for a different Venetian church.

My desire to visualize these unrealized projects as they would have affected their urban settings prompted me to propose to my architect-collaborator Scott Schiamberg that he create computerized reconstructions from the drawings set into photographs of the sites as they are today.

The construction of the Gothic basilica of San Petronio in Bologna was halted in 1514 when only the ground level of the façade had been completed (pl. 72). In 1577 the director of the Fabbrica asked his predecessor to approach Palladio in Venice to collaborate with the chief architect in Bologna on a design to complete the upper two levels. While Palladio initially demanded that the early fifteenth-century work be removed, he ultimately agreed to retain it.

The solution (pl. 73) proposed a pair of pilasters without an entablature alongside the central portal that had to be stretched far beyond classical proportions and that covered the two upper levels with more canonical but uninspired orders. The design was approved, but for unknown reasons work was halted until 1577, at which time Palladio presented several unsolicited proposals for full classical façades that would have eliminated the existing lower level.

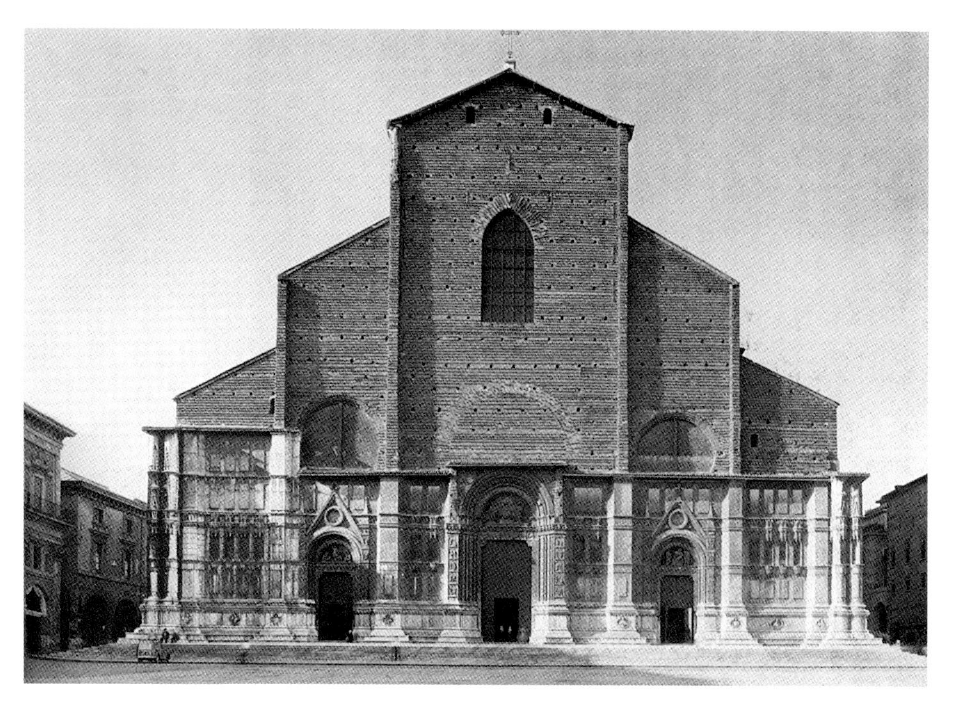

72 San Petronio, Bologna

73 Palladio, proposal for San Petronio (including existing façade), 1572

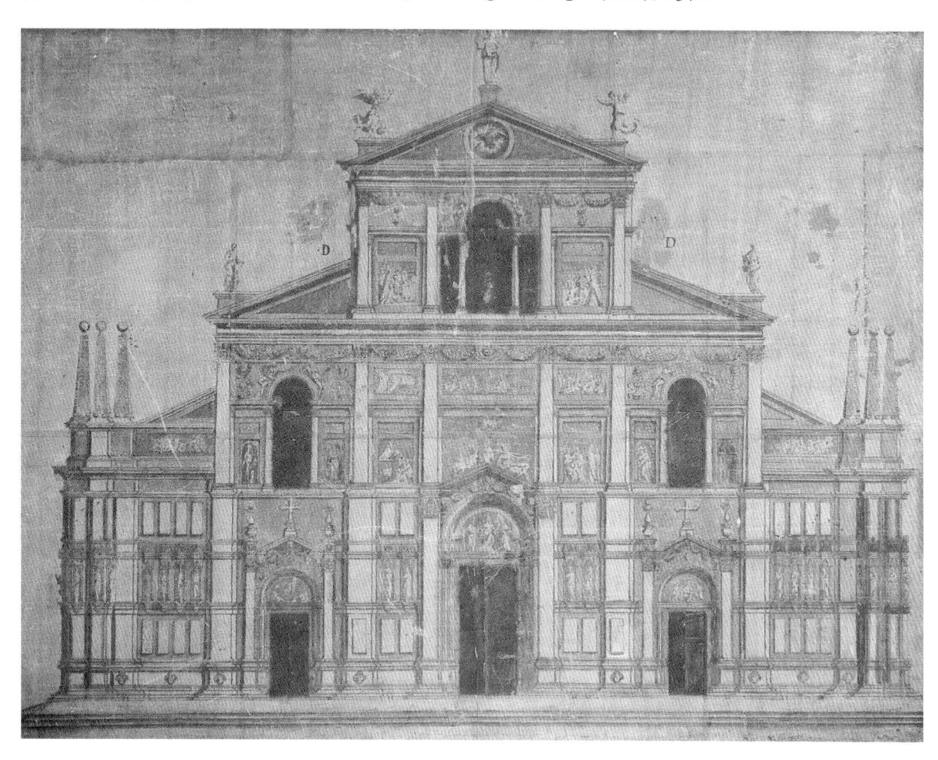

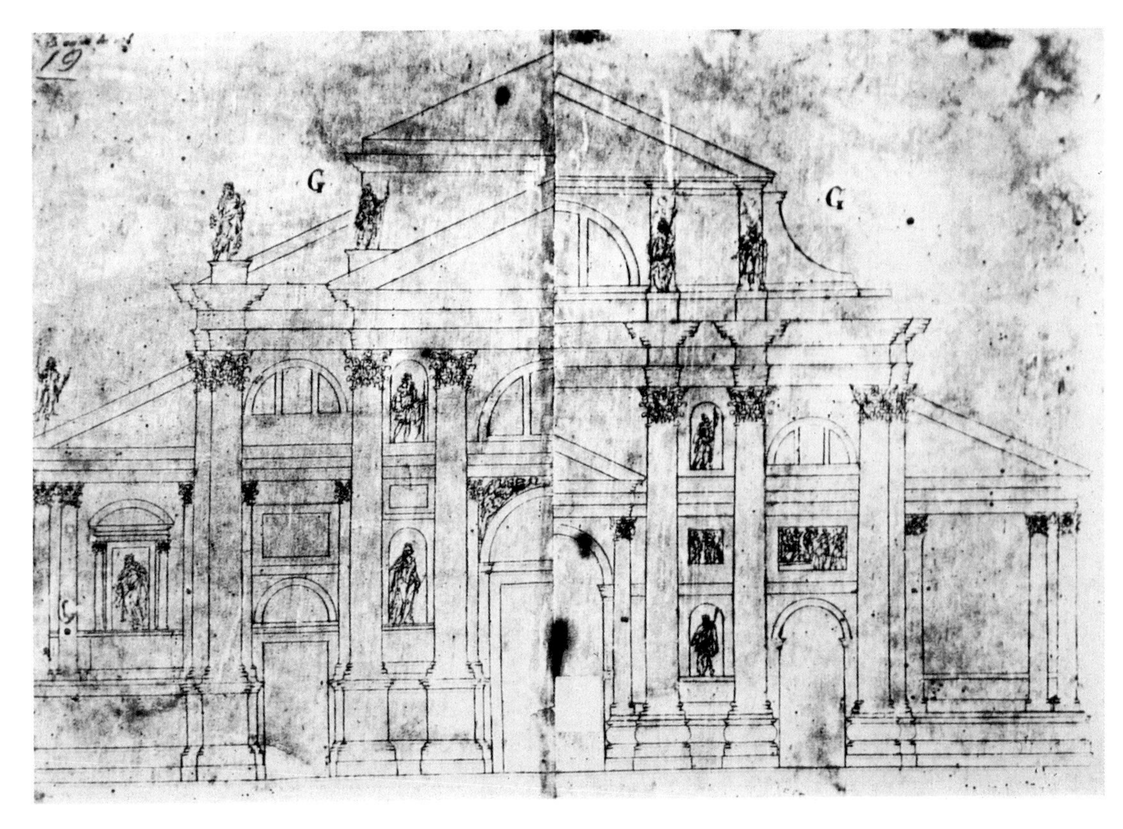

74 Palladio, two proposals for San Petronio (without existing façade), 1572

75 Digital representation of Palladio's proposal for San Petronio, Bologna

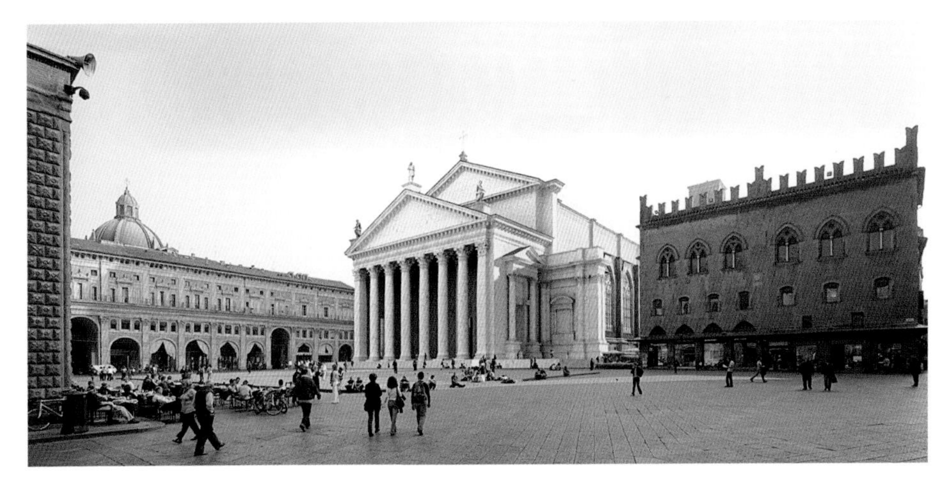

The most advanced of these (pl. 74) has two versions that sought to arrive at an *all'antica* integration of a high central nave and lower side aisles. It presents different solutions on either side of a central vertical line, both proposing a colossal order of half-columns rising from pedestals of customary height on the left while the base on the right is so low that it causes the entablature to be excessively high. The better-integrated solution on the left is close to that of the final façade solution of the Redentore in Venice (see pl. 81).

Probably in the same period, in the Oxford drawing (pl. 77), Palladio made a major departure, projecting a portico with freestanding columns modeled on the Pantheon that can be seen in several plates in his *Quattro libri dell'architettura* of 1570 (pl. 78). The San Petronio drawing was hastily made (the sides of the portico are ill proportioned and their portals collide with the side aisles), but Scott Schiamberg's computerized reconstruction (pl. 75) suggests that the effect would have been breathtaking. Palladio must have known the portico scheme, reflecting Michelangelo's unexecuted design for St. Peter in the Vatican, from the 1569 engravings of the plan, section, and elevation (restored in pl. 76). It was rejected by the Bolognese representative of the

76 Kenneth John Conant, *Michelangelo's Unexecuted Design for St. Peter's, Rome*, 1917

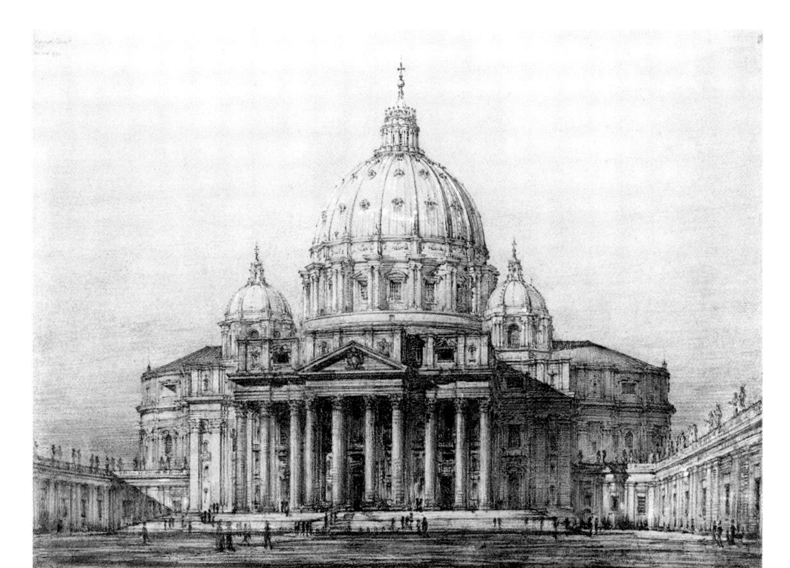

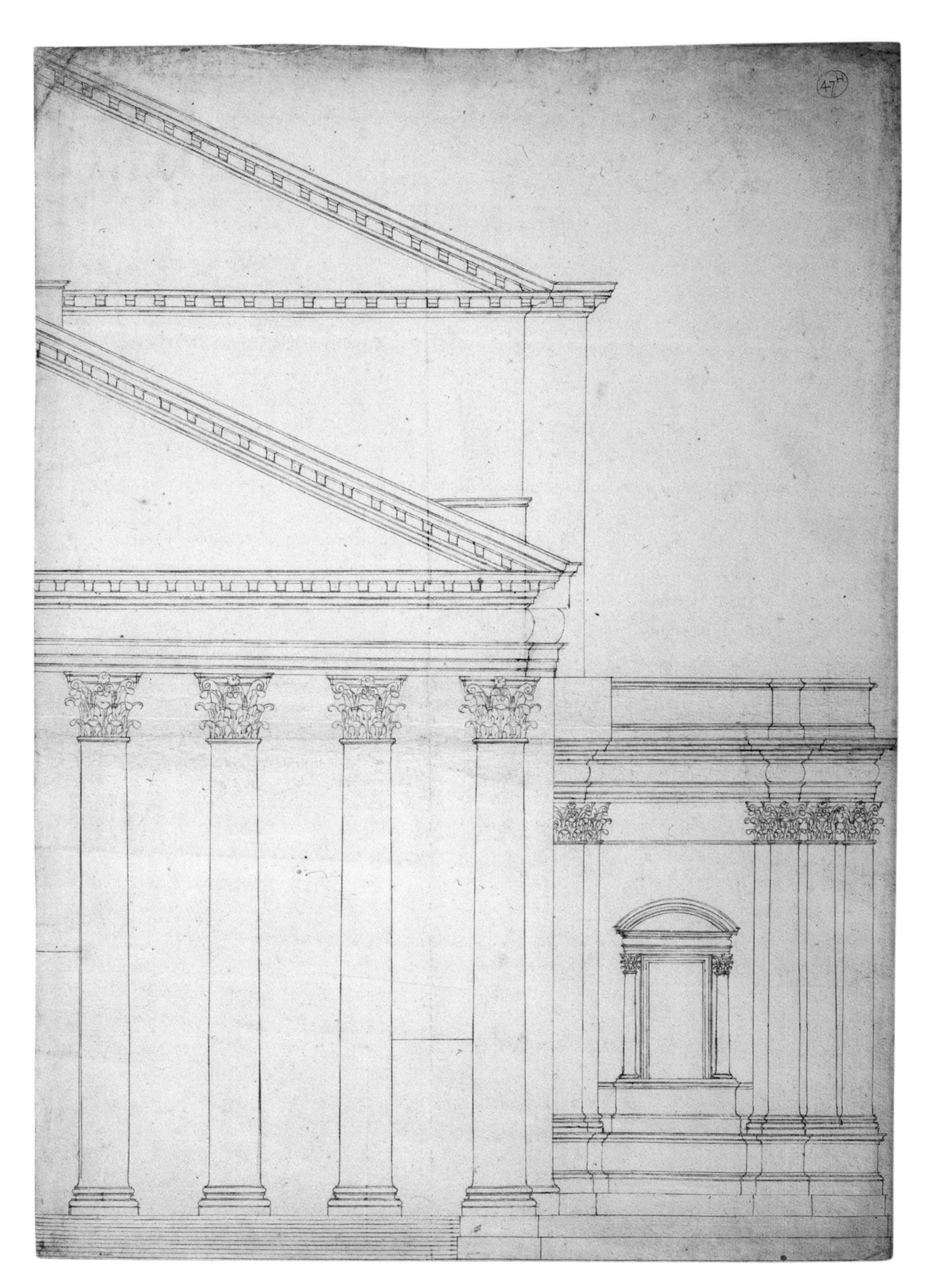

77 Palladio, drawing of the portico project for San Petronio, Bologna, 1578–9

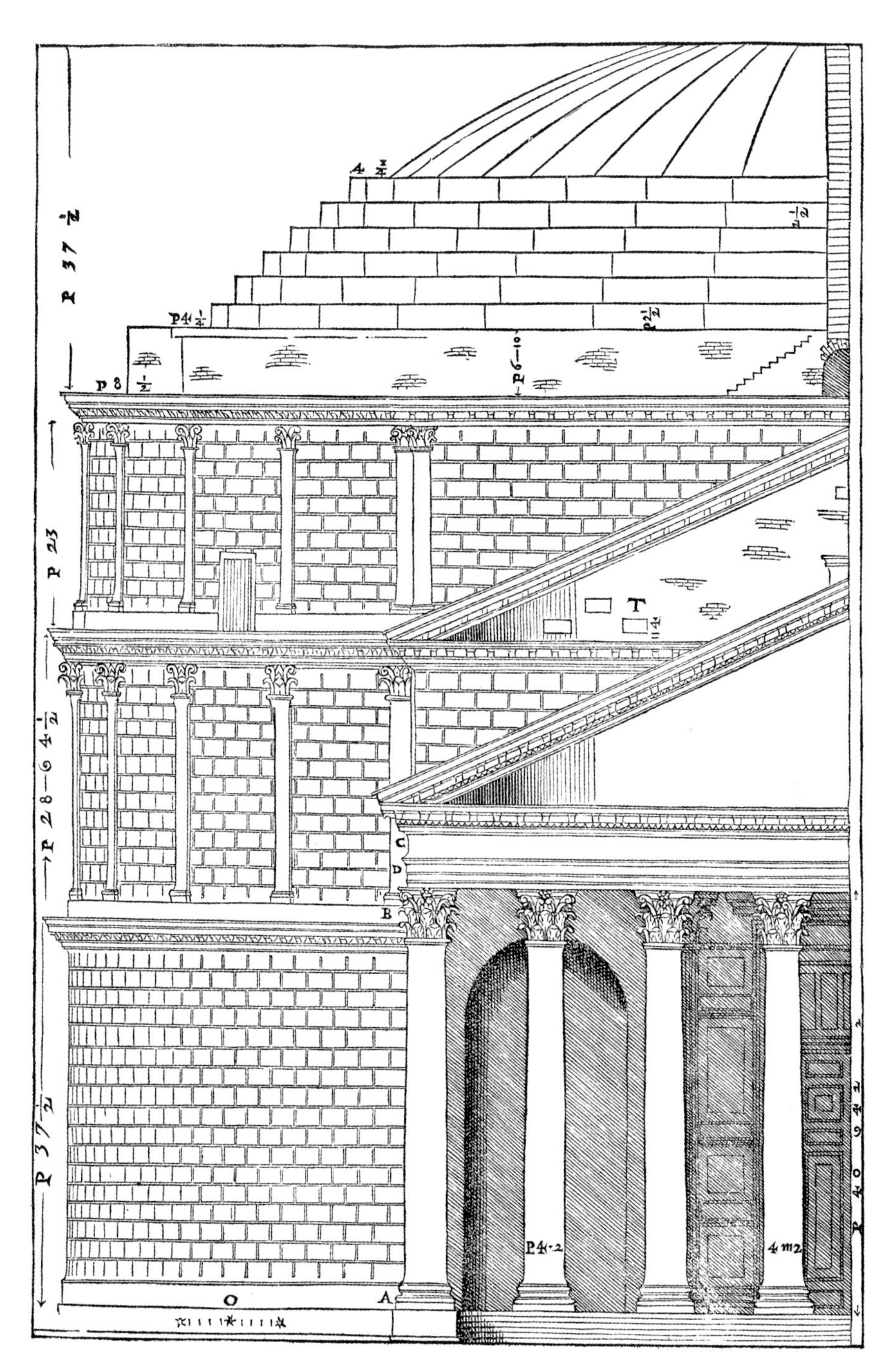

78 Palladio, elevation of the Pantheon, Rome, from *I Quattro Libri dell'Architettura*, 1570

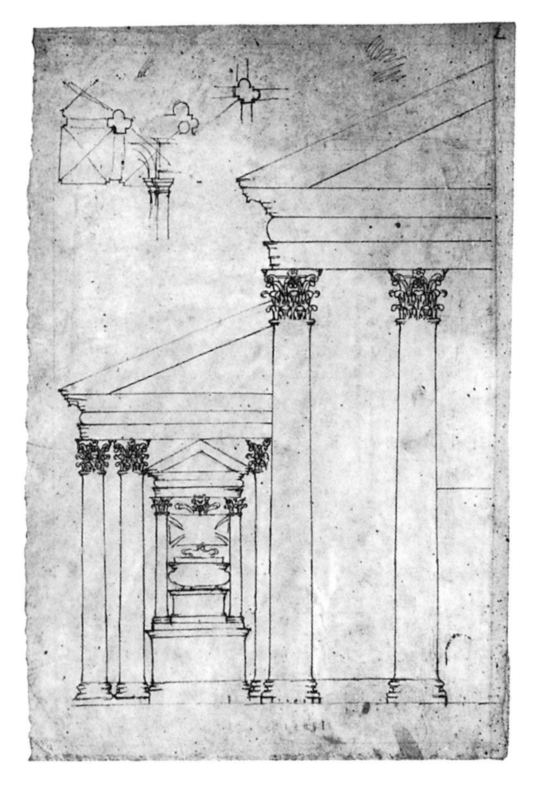

79 Palladio, elevation of San Giorgio, Venice, 1576

Vatican and by the pope himself because the reference to the pagan Pantheon was unacceptable, especially in the years following the Council of Trent.

Palladio's façade project for San Giorgio in Venice would have been the most prominent urban monument of his career by virtue of its majestic classicism and its site, which faces the Piazza San Marco and the Doge's Palace across the lagoon. The two surviving drawings propose a freestanding porch like that of San Petronio: an autograph elevation (pl. 79) and a plan of the entire monastery as it appeared at the end of Palladio's life in 1580 (Venice, Archivio di Stato, Mappe 857) showing the church with a portico somewhat different from the one in the RIBA. While the lateral bays of the façade on the RIBA elevation are not precisely aligned with the side aisles, they are so aligned in the Venice plan, which may have been drawn in the late 1570s. Our reconstruction based on the elevation (pl. 80) reveals the grandeur of the conception. Recent studies suggest that the existing façade constructed in the years 1597–1610 did not follow Palladio's lost wooden model of 1565 mentioned in documents from the period of the church construction. While I share this opinion, my reasons are different.

Two late sixteenth-century paintings with a view of the rough brick underlayer of the façade as it must have appeared at the time of Palladio's death show an oculus above the portal. Though the oculus was constructed under Palladio's supervision in the years between 1571 and 1574, presumably following the 1565 model, it was covered over by the existing façade, executed by Simone Sorella and his followers between 1597 and 1610 (the inner frame of the oculus is preserved on the interior wall of the façade).

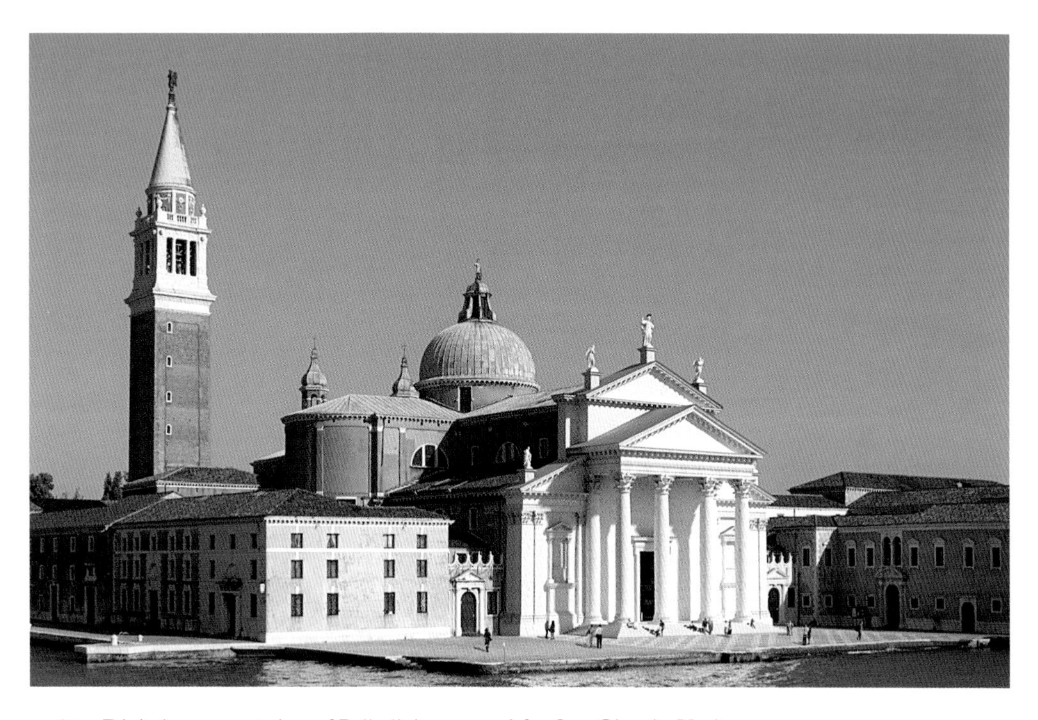

80 Digital representation of Palladio's proposal for San Giorgio, Venice

Although Antonio Guerra, in his intensive studies first published in 2001, and the majority of commentators following Rudolf Wittkower, who first identified the RIBA drawing, agreed that it was prepared for the 1565 model, there is no confirmed evidence for this conclusion. It seems more likely to have been executed after the construction of the oculus in the unfinished façade. Indeed, the portico would have negated the function of the oculus to illuminate the nave. Furthermore, such oculi were not consistent with the architect's approach to antiquity. Palladio's four projects involving porticoed façades were conceived in the last five years of the 1570s, whereas at the time of the 1565 model he was overseeing the construction of the façade of San Francesco della Vigna (see pl. 70), a quite different type of solution.

Guerra also discovered the surprising information that in 1595 the abbot, Alabardi, ordered twenty-four columns for a quadriportico before the church – apparently an atrium reflecting medieval pre-Gothic types. This constitutes a decisive rejection of the portico proposals, and of Palladio's

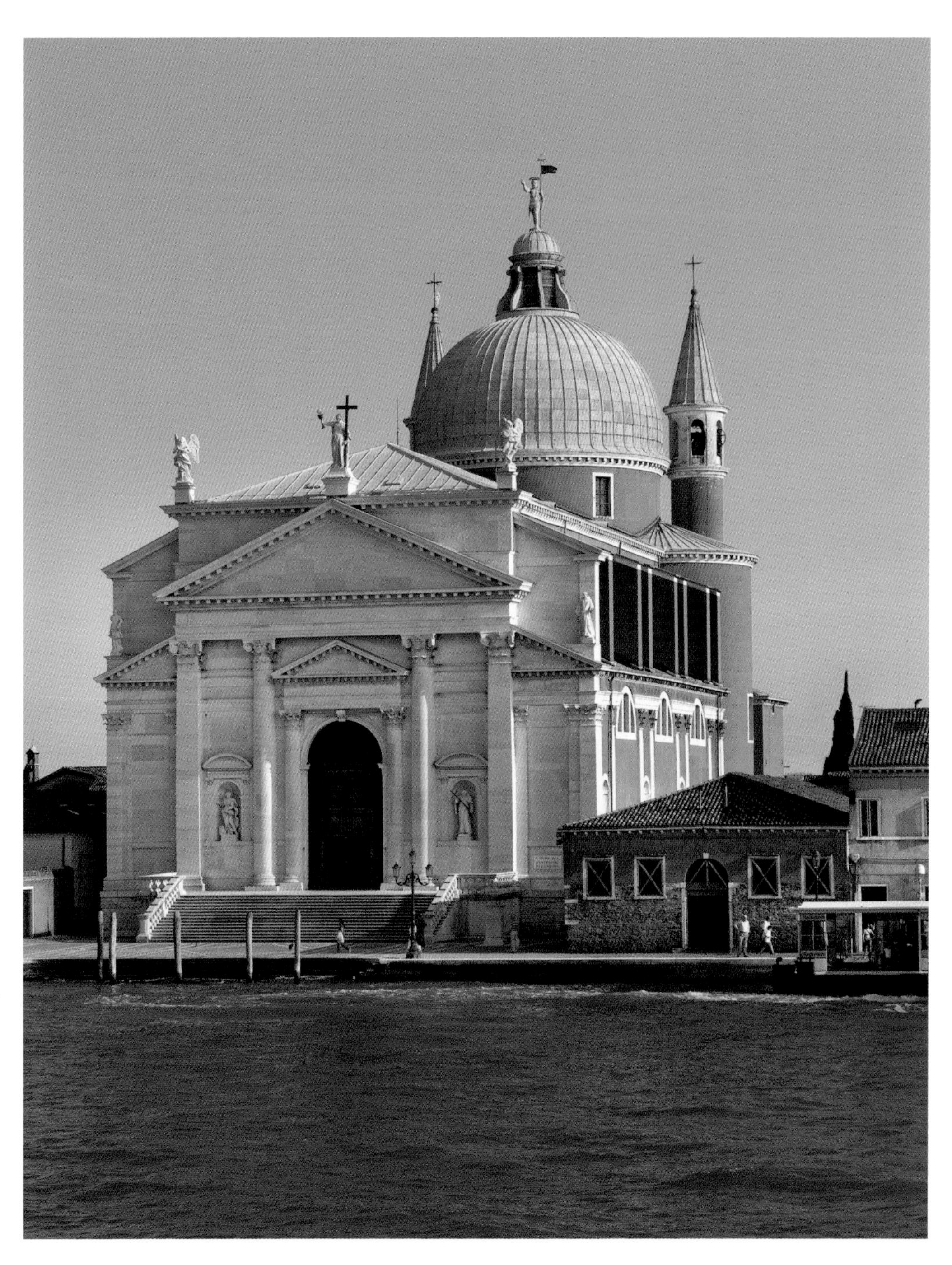

81 Church of the Redentore, Venice

principle that church façades be a prominent embellishment to the city. It probably would have closed off any view of the church from the canal.

The church of the Redentore (pl. 81), one of the most original and impressive ecclesiastical monuments of the Renaissance, is the best-documented example of the engagement of the Venetian Republic in architectural patronage. During the fall of 1575 a devastating plague hit the city, destroying a quarter of the population. It was seen as God's punishment for venality. As the plague diminished in the following year, survivors formed penitential processions and the Senate vowed to memorialize the city's salvation by founding a church dedicated to Christ the Redeemer. The committee of three senators set up to select an architect and to choose a site had members favorable toward Rome and toward the *all'antica* style – members of old patrician families, who had, a generation earlier, brought Jacopo Sansovino to the city, to design the Library on the Piazzetta of San Marco and other major Venetian buildings. Palladio was selected immediately, due no doubt to the support of Marcantonio Barbaro, brother of the patriarch-elect Daniele, the co-patrons of Palladio's villa at Maser. Daniele had employed Palladio to illustrate his edition of the treatise of Vitruvius.

The question of locus for the church was difficult; it had to be the property of a religious order with sufficient members to perform services and preferably owning property in a prominent location, visible from a distance. The Capuchin order prevailed, much to its distress, since it was the most committed to humility, and therefore insisted on the exclusion of private chapels and tomb monuments, in opposition to the senators' intention to express magnificence. Palladio's first design proposed a central plan – a square space supporting a very large dome and entered through a monumental portico – that is now identified with the four drawings preserved in the collection of the RIBA (pl. 82, reconstructed in pl. 83). It was rejected by a majority of the senators because of its style and its unsuitability (particularly in its lack of a secluded choir for the church of a religious order). The architect, required to produce a longitudinal section, brilliantly resolved the unique demands with a secluded and undecorated choir, an elevated tribune space under the dome large enough to hold the entire Senate on the occasion of the annual fulfillment of its original vow, and a façade design, approved in February 1577, that was the most successful of all of Palladio's façades without porches.

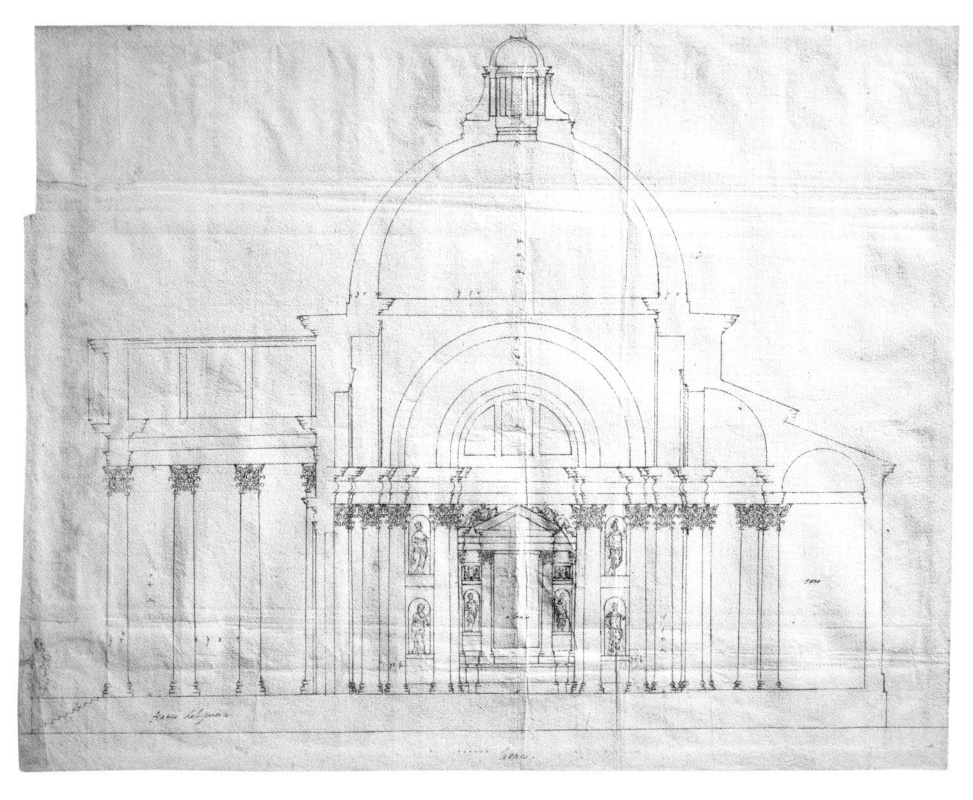

82 Palladio, proposal for the Redentore, Venice, 1577

83 Digital representation of the Redentore based on a section drawing that was rejected by the Senate

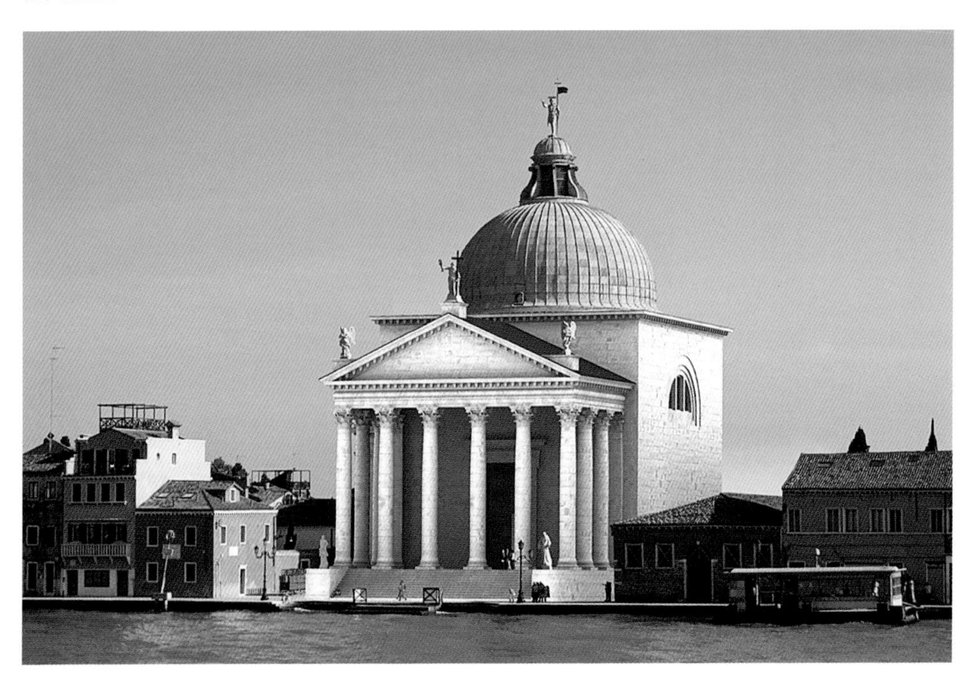

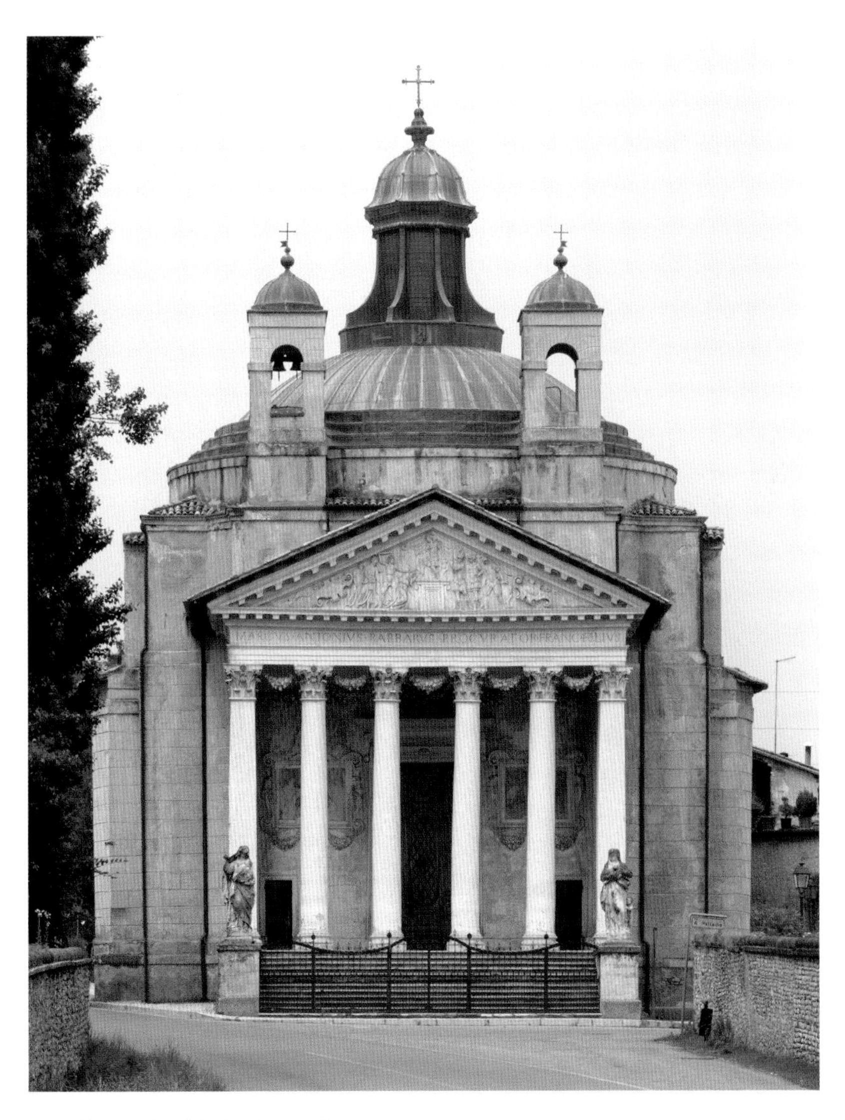

84 Chapel for Villa Barbaro, Maser

Ultimately, the only central-plan ecclesiastical building with a portico realized by Palladio was the small chapel for the Barbaro villa in Maser (pl. 84), an instance of private magnificence commissioned by Marcantonio Barbaro, who had been an active supporter of the rejected central-plan project for the Redentore.

Palladio's work in Venice was primarily ecclesiastical because he did not hold one of the government appointments as Proto (official city architect), although, following the death of Jacopo Sansovino in 1570, he was regarded as *de facto* successor to that position. Palladio's original construction displaying *magnificenza* was a distinctively Venetian manifestation. Venice was a republic that exercised control over most of northeast Italy, and the Venetian patriciate was entirely detached from the hereditary powers and variations of rank (counts, dukes, archdukes, princes, kings) of aristocrats within the structure of absolute monarchies. They were not nobles but members of a privileged class who acceded to the governing bodies by primogeniture; after the thirteenth century this membership was no longer open to other Venetians. They were all of equal rank, and they elected one – usually senior – leader, the doge, to a lifetime term in office; the doge could not pass on his position to descendants. The senators even appointed members of their group to the highest ecclesiastic office, patriarch of Aquilea, the equivalent of an archbishopric, much to the annoyance of the popes. Venetian nobles were industrious and successful merchants in the sixteenth century: many owned large and mostly profitable holdings on the Terraferma (mainland); some engaged Palladio to design villa residences – displaying *magnificenza*, often by employing porticoed entrances.

Magnificence was a subject that drew the attention of ancient writers on ethics; it relates to architecture in addressing limits to the display of extravagance. The fourth book of Aristotle's *Nichomachean Ethics* influenced all of the Renaissance works on the subject. Cicero wrote that "Romans hate private luxury but are delighted by public magnificence." In a penetrating study, Kornelia Imesch (*Magnificenza als architektonische Kategorie*, Oberhausen, 2003) discussed two treatises addressing the ethical implications of the privileges enjoyed by the Venetian patriarchy. One, published in 1498, was Giovanni Pontano's *I trattati delle virtù sociali: de liberalitate, de beneficentia, de magnificentia, de splendore, de conviventia.* The more valuable source for the interpretation of Palladio's late urban buildings, Paolo Paruta's *Della perfectione*, was published in Venice in 1579, precisely at the time when the architect was engaged in the construction of the Redentore. The text is in the form of a symposium involving living members of the Venetian patrician class, one of whom was Daniele Barbaro, Palladio's patron for the villa at

Maser. The Barbaro represented in the symposium explains the virtue of magnificence as follows:

> Magnificence calls for the making of grand things, as the name suggests . . . wherefore the world, which awards its greatest veneration for such extrinsic displays, and prizes most those virtues that are most widely known, is accustomed to use as the greatest honor the [patron with the] title of Magnificent, placing it, to tell the truth, in my estimation among those one applies to grand and difficult acts. Magnificence, as a noble virtue, cannot itself make just any activity worthy: indeed it does not show itself often, but only on those occasions which occur rarely, like feasts, weddings, and buildings, on which it is proper to spend without considering the cost, but only the grandeur and beauty of the work. But the occasion to spend on such things rarely comes to us.

Although Barbaro was greatly respected in Venice, not all the participants in Paruta's symposium accepted this definition of magnificence, despite this call for *decoro* (propriety) because it appeared to support the kind of *magnificentia pubblica* that Cicero had represented as offensive to the Roman public. Monsignor Michel della Torre, archbishop of Ceneda, spoke of the need for a greater restraint in the display of wealth:

> Signor Ambasciatore [Barbaro was also an ambassador], you are not taking into account a major problem, which regrettably has emerged in our time, and especially among Italian men, namely a way of life full of willfulness and pleasures which, when interpreted as works of magnificence, show that we would be better off not having such a virtue. And I certainly marvel that you [gentlemen], who are accustomed to denigrate all extremes in other aspects of behavior in which one seeks greater perfection, in this instance, which is for us a path to vice, can value such extremities.

The fictional Ceneda would have approved of the decision of the majority of the Venetian Senate to reject the central plan and pedimented portico of Palladio's first project for the church of the Redentore. Nonetheless, the construction of the existing longitudinal design, budgeted by the Senate at 10,000 ducats as recorded in its minutes, and "not made of marble," ultimately cost eight times that figure.

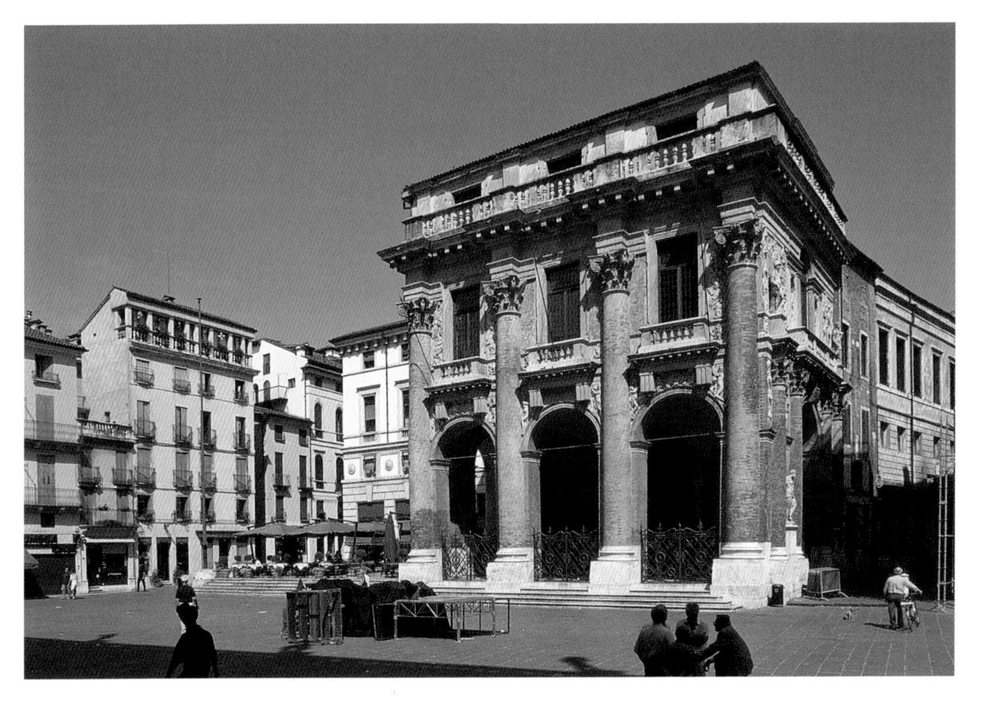

85 Loggia del Capitanio, Vicenza

In 1571 the city council of Vicenza called Palladio to design the Loggia del Capitaniato (pl. 85) – official chambers for the presiding representative of the Venetian Republic with a meeting hall above for the city council – directly across the Piazza dei Signori from the architect's first civic building, the Basilica (1549). The Venetians provided some funding, and the Vicentines doled out modest amounts of money at intervals – they regarded the Venetians as colonial oppressors – and probably Bollani, the Venetian captain during the building process, contributed more than the citizens. Its design was majestic and daring – departing in details from proper *all'antica* practice – but the brick columns and walls observed the modesty called for by Paruta. While early Palladio scholars assumed that Palladio had intended to extend the building to the west, the plan suggests that it was complete, except for the western façade, in its present form.

The *magnificenza* represented in the Valmarana and the unfinished Porto-Breganze palaces (pls. 86 and 87) was unlike any grand residence in Venice,

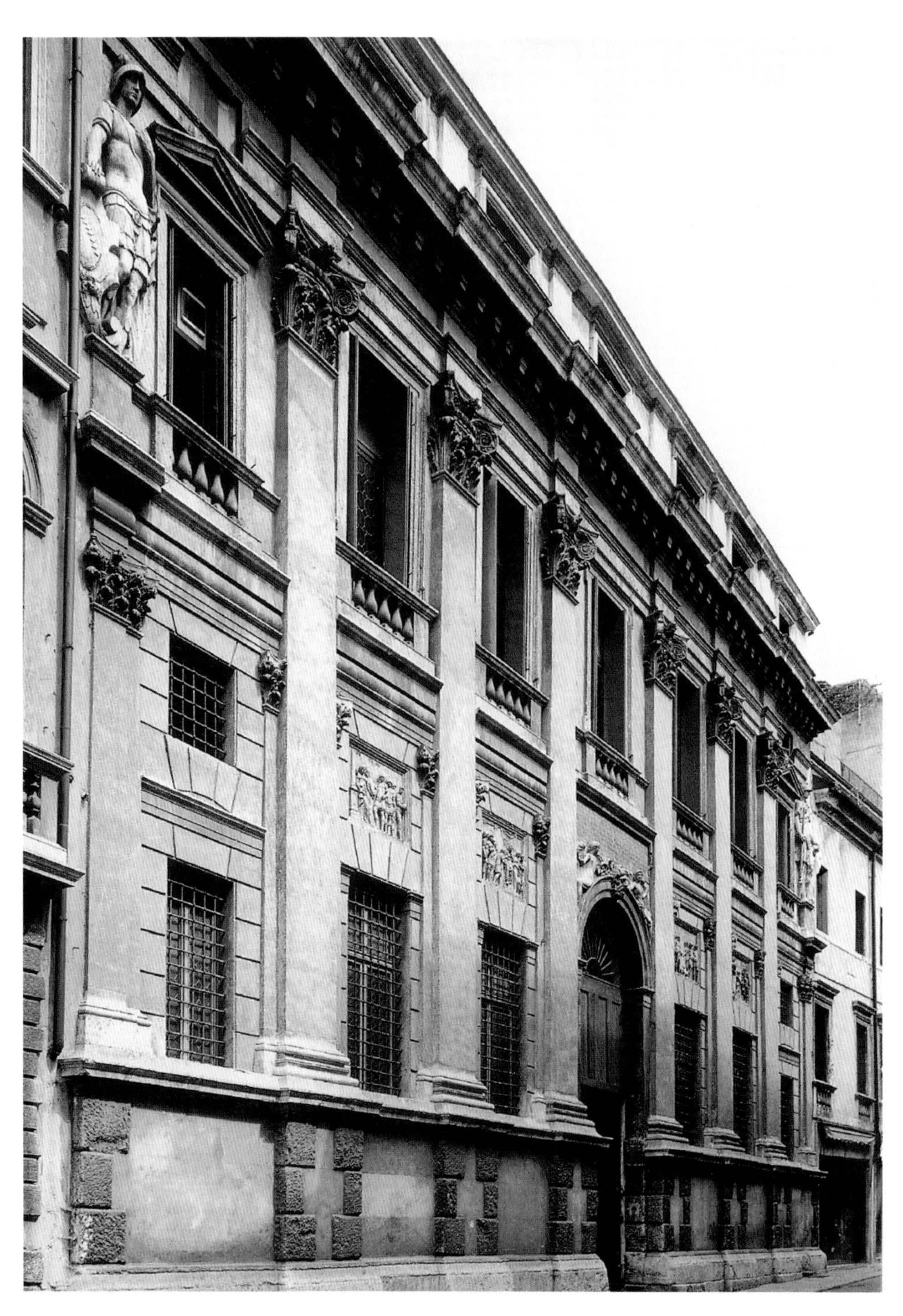

86 Palazzo Valmarana, Vicenza

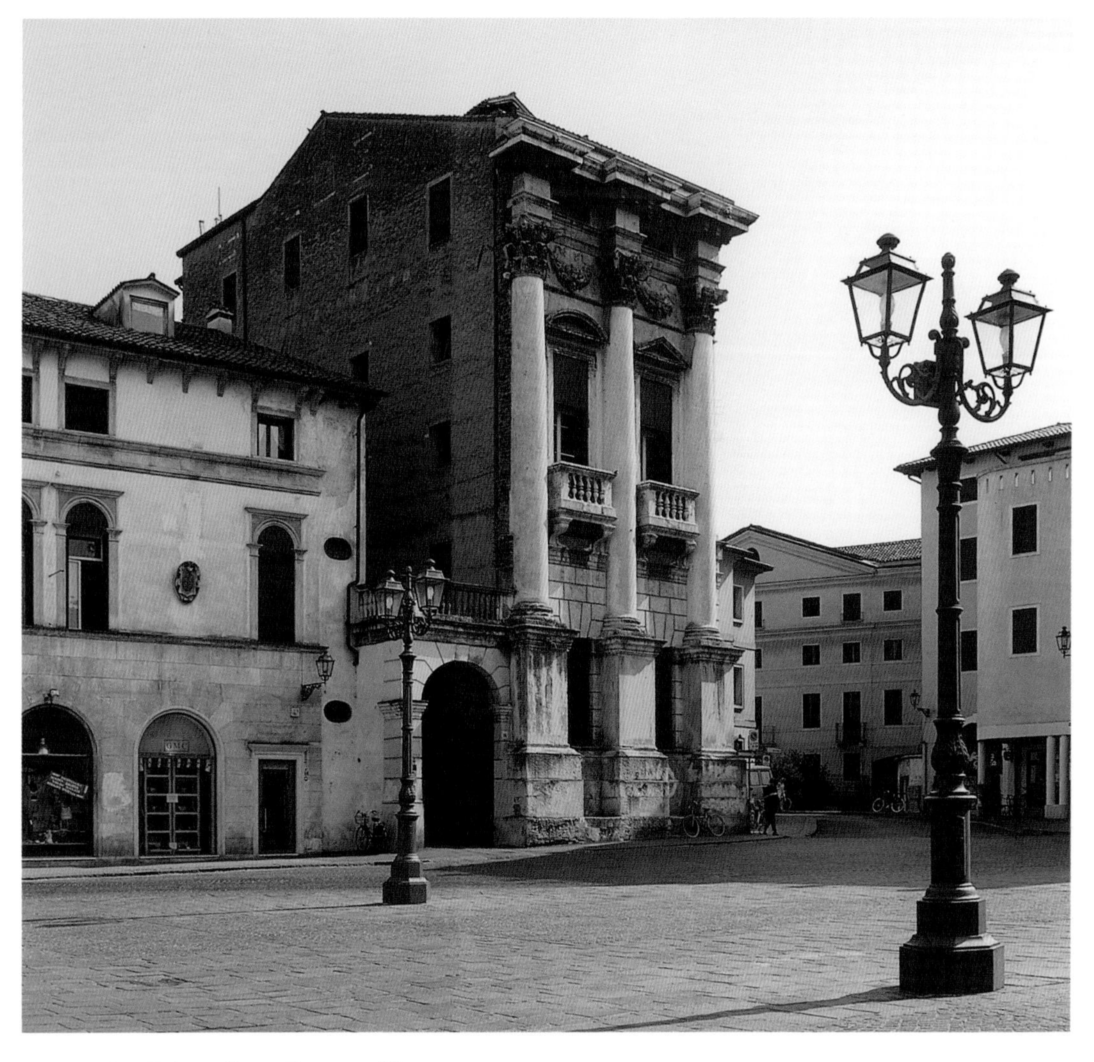

87 Palazzo Porto-Breganze, Vicenza

where, in the sixteenth century, the colossal order was never employed, and where even such imposing façades as those of the Cornaro Ca' Grande and the Palazzo Giustinian retained three superimposed orders and the late Gothic Venetian tripartite vertical division, which accentuates the central portion with a waterfront loggia on the lower floor below a clustered bank of windows illuminating a large reception hall on the *piano nobile*. The Vicen-

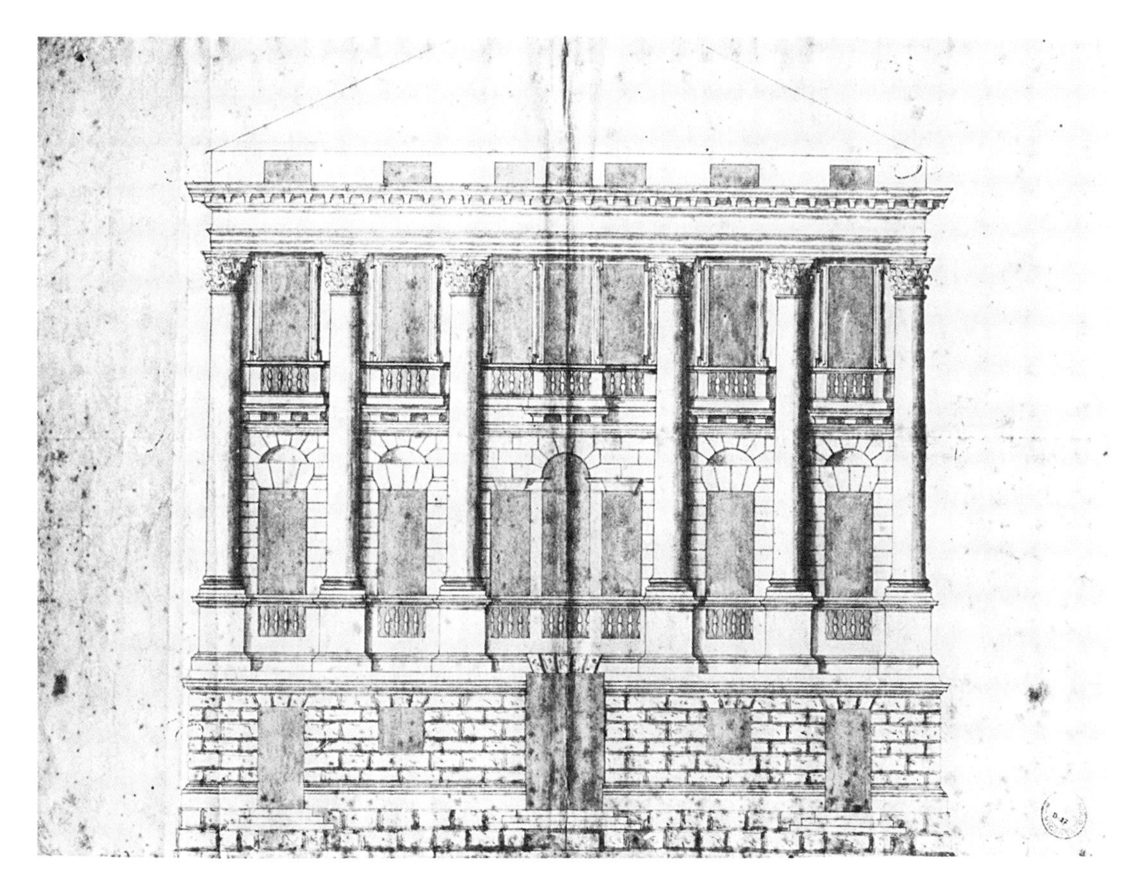

88 Palladio, design for a palace façade, 1570

tine palaces can be described as a preamble to a more triumphal, aristocratic, and imperial interpretation of *magnificenza*, one that advertised the rank of the clients and cast aside the demand for modesty and generosity toward the community and economy called for by Paruta.

Palladio's drawing for a waterfront palace façade, probably for the brothers Guido and Giovanni Piovene (pl. 88), though small, would have been as monumental as the more ambitious palaces of the Valmarana family and the unfinished Porto-Breganze.

Almost all commentators on Palladio's use of the colossal order refer to the influence of Michelangelo's employment of it on the elevations of St. Peter in the Vatican and the palaces on the Capitoline Hill in Rome. The order had

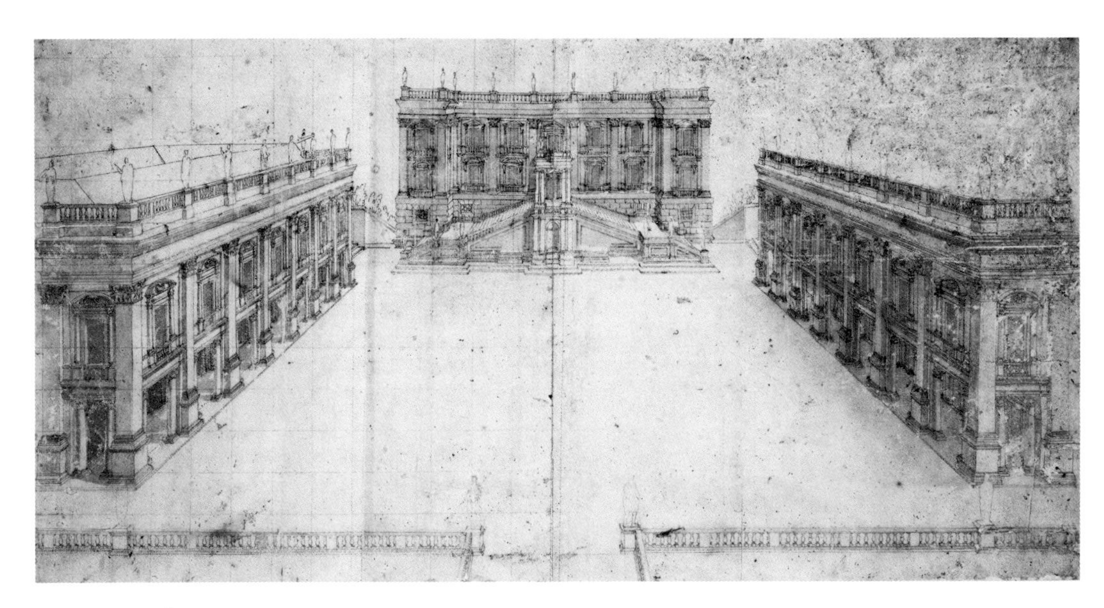

89 Étienne Dupérac, after Michelangelo, *Design for the Campidoglio in Rome*, 1569

been employed occasionally in the fifteenth century, and gained in expressiveness in studies by the collaborators and successors of Bramante in the Fabbrica of St. Peter, notably on the interior of the huge wooden model of the basilica by Antonio da Sangallo the Younger, which guided construction of the outer periphery of the south transept. Having been appointed to succeed Antonio after his death, Michelangelo demolished this portion and built exterior elevations that greatly increased the dramatic potential of the order.

Michelangelo began his reconstruction of the façade of the Palazzo del Senatore on the Capitoline, the civic center of Rome, in about 1546 or 1557. The design was recorded by Etienne Dupérac's drawing in Christ Church College, Oxford (pl. 89), made in preparation for a bird's-eye view of the entire piazza, which he engraved in 1569. Here the lowest of the three stories is faced with a robust rusticated stone while the two upper levels are drawn together by the colossal order, a formula repeated universally in western architecture of the following centuries. The actual façade of the Palazzo del Senatore, completed by later architects, is a feeble reflection of Michelangelo's intention as realized in the Palazzo dei Conservatori alongside. It may have been inspired by Bramante's design of the Palazzo di Giustizia in Rome

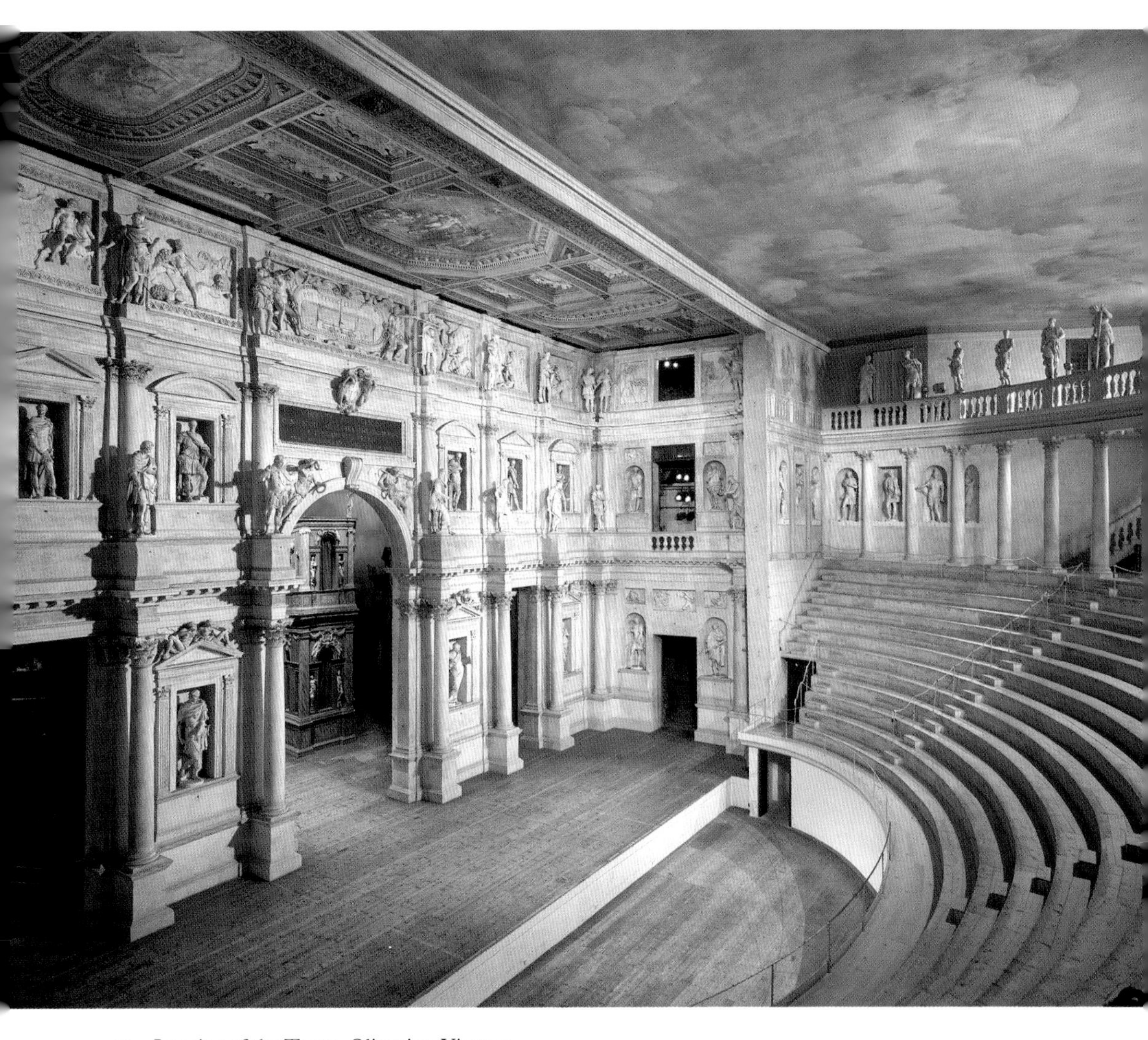

90 Interior of the Teatro Olimpico, Vicenza

to accommodate the law courts of Pope Julius II in 1505, which was abandoned after the construction of only a small portion of the rusticated base.

Palladio's design of the interior of the Teatro Olimpico in Vicenza (pl. 90) provides a key to the contrast of the principles that controlled the design of private palaces in the two cities. The theater was constructed by the wealthy members of the newly founded Accademia Olimpica as its central feature in

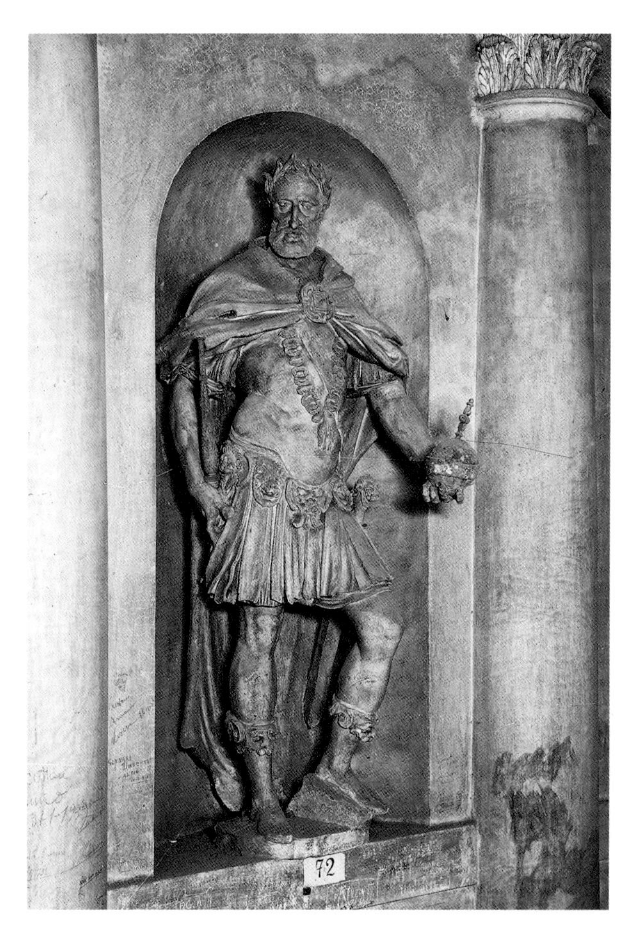

91 Statue of Leonardo Valmarana

1555. Membership was not restricted to the well born – Palladio himself, the son of a miller and almost impoverished, was elected at the end of his life in recognition of his mastery of ancient architecture. His design, based on the ancient Roman theater described by Vitruvius, was embellished by an ambitious array of sculpture celebrating military prowess, including the *Labors of Hercules* and full-length sculpted portraits of the noble sponsors in military dress in niches on three levels of the *scenae frons* and the walls enclosing the auditorium. The families of virtually all the patrons of Palladio's Vicentine palaces are represented. The statue of Leonardo Valmarana, son of the clients of Palladio's Palazzo Valmarana (see pl. 86), occupies the central niche of the rear circle directly facing the arch of the *scenae frons*, in recognition of his having provided the largest contribution to the building expenses and having been elected the *principe* of the Academy (pl. 91). Leonardo, who had been educated in Madrid at the court of the king of Spain, who was also the Habsburg emperor Charles V, is portrayed not as he actually looked, but with the features of (the much older) Charles himself, and with the emperor's attributes – a laurel crown, a scepter, the necklace of the Order of the Golden Fleece, and a globe in hand (indicating worldly dominion). Leonardo received a large annual sum as a hereditary Palatine count. His sponsorship of the theater represents one of the first steps toward providing Catholic European rulers of the seventeenth and eighteenth centuries with a suitable architectural expression of their power. Some of Palladio's Vicentine patrons, like members of the Thiene family, were vassals of the French monarchy and were antagonists – at times violent ones – of the imperial clique.

Private theaters in ancient Rome, though discouraged during the Republic, provided an original impetus for the concept of urban magnificence, initially in the Hellenistic East and then in the later years of Augustan Rome. The Elder Pliny cites the example of a luxurious theater of 58 BCE in the villa of M. Scaurus, which was even larger than those of the imperial period, and extravagant in its use of lavishly costly columns and decoration. Members of the Accademia Olimpica may well have been cautious about revealing the opulence of the theater to the Vicentine public, since the exterior of the building is totally devoid of decoration.

EPILOGUE

By the close of the sixteenth century the ethical concept of magnificence had been forgotten, and the formal innovations of Palladio had come to serve the unfettered manifestation of wealth and power, particularly in later Baroque architecture, and eventually were adopted throughout Europe by emperors, kings, and popes as symbols of their absolute power. The Superga in Turin by Filippo Juvarra (pl. 92), finished in 1731, commanding the city from a high cliff, exploited the dramatic symbolism of the pedimented portico and the commanding dome. The Karlskirche in Vienna (pl. 93), designed by Johann Fischer von Erlach (1739), is equally emphatic, adding a pair of triumphal

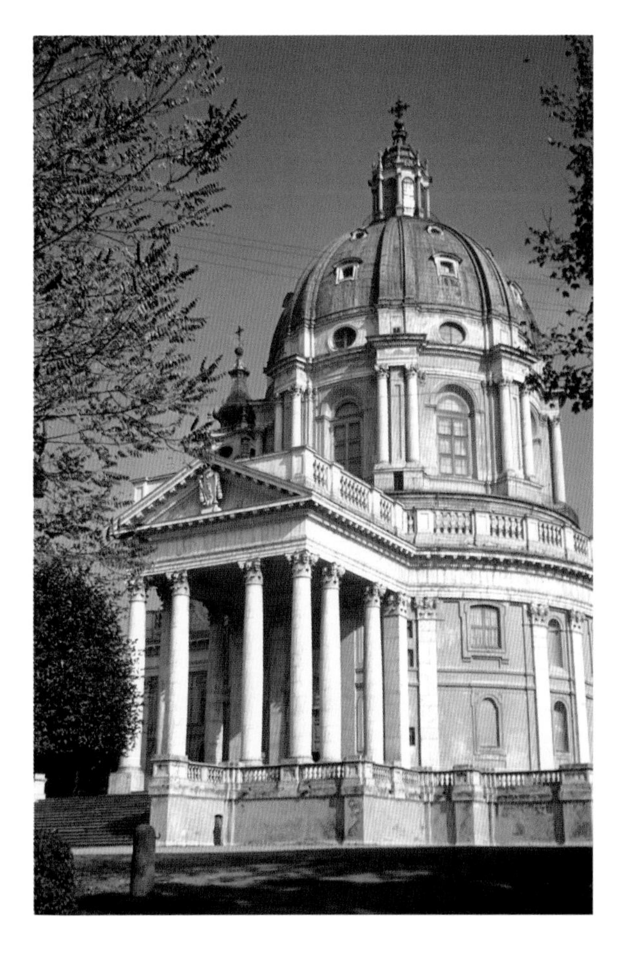

92 Basilica di Superga, Turin

columns ornamented with scenes from the life of St. Charles Borromeo that echo the column of the emperor Trajan in his Forum in Rome, which celebrates a military triumph. Paradoxically, the church was dedicated to St. Charles Borromeo, whose architectural treatise and patronage emphasized modesty.

The Place de la Concorde in Paris (pl. 94) was designed by Jacques-Ange Gabriel in 1754 for Louis XV, whose equestrian statue was placed at its center. It became Place de la Revolution after the overthrow of the monarchy, but later returned to its royal designation. Ultimately, it acquired its present name in an overt attempt to overcome its absolutist symbolism. The colossal order of its public buildings and the Roman portico of the church of the Madeleine behind it are indebted to the inventions of Michelangelo and Palladio.

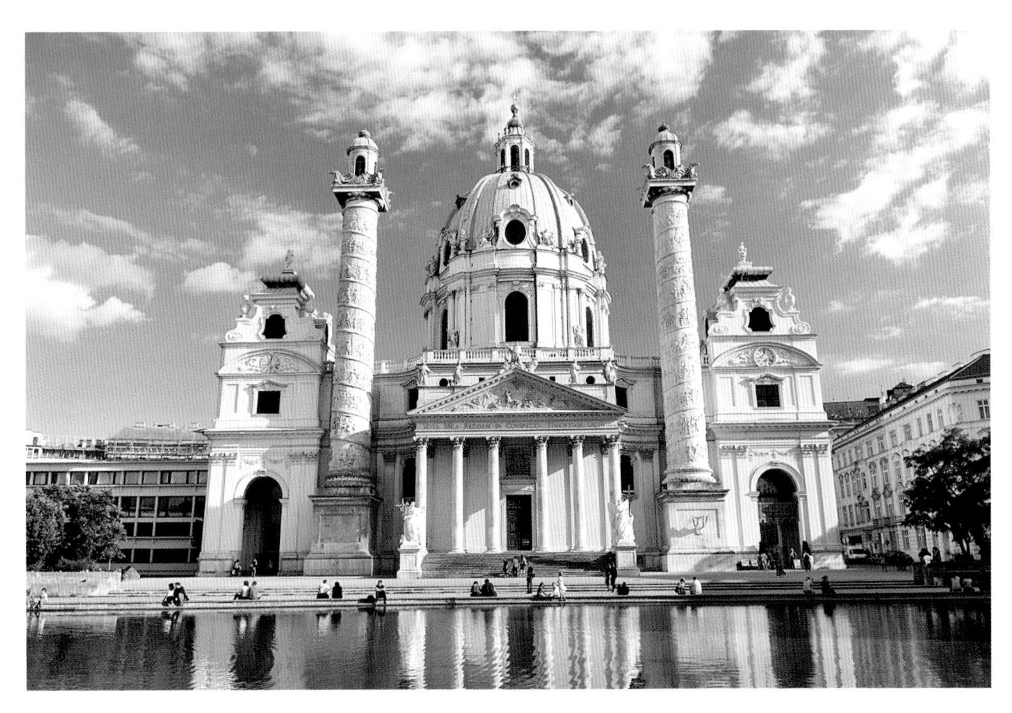

93 Karlskirche, Vienna

94 Place de la Concorde, Paris

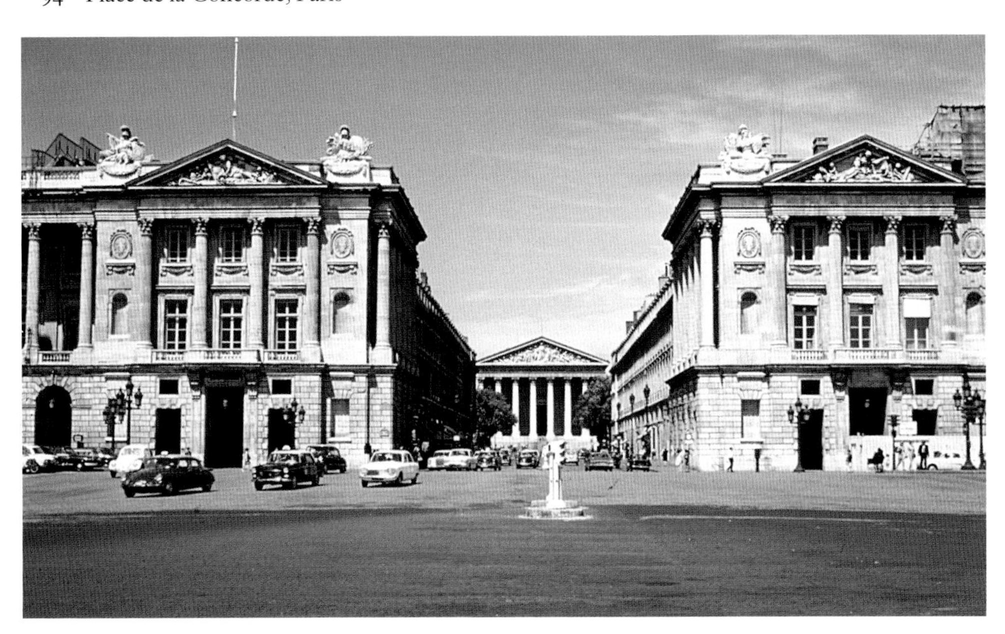

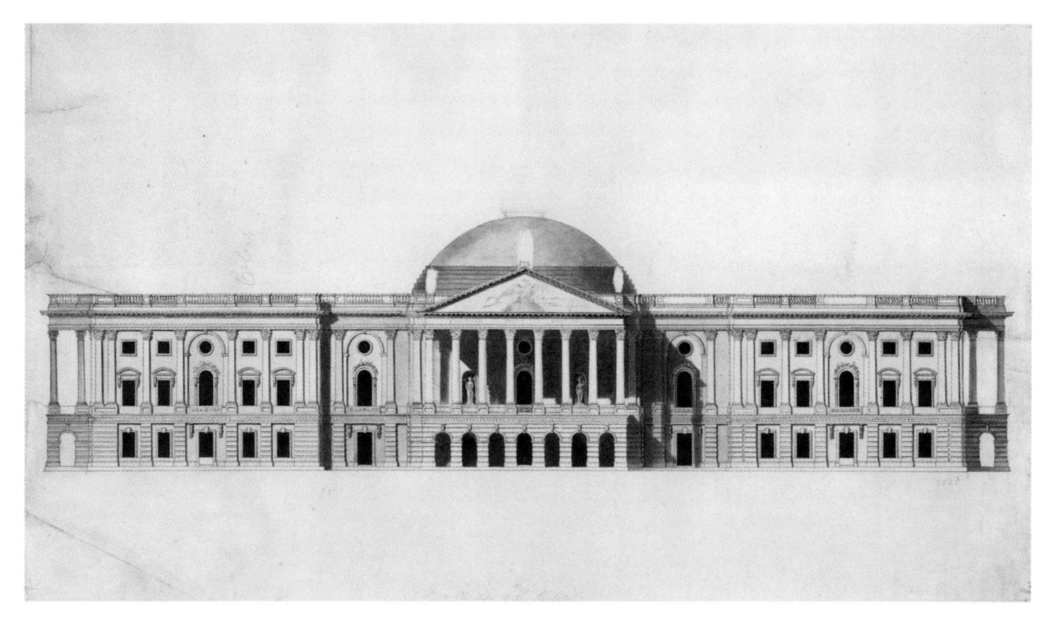

95 William Thornton, first design for the Capitol Building, east elevation, *c.*1793–1800

However, the vocabulary of magnificence survived long after the fall of emperors and kings – paradoxically in the first democratic republic of modern times, the United States of America (pls. 95–99). Established in an almost unpopulated continent, rich with vast plains, rugged mountains and virgin forests, the new nation was impelled to borrow its symbols from others with more ancient traditions, and chose to express pride in its institutions through the vocabulary of aristocracy. Most of the earliest American architects were trained abroad; the first design for the US Capitol by the Englishman William Thornton (1794) was later revised by his countryman Benjamin Latrobe (pl. 95). Thomas Jefferson learned architectural design from European books; his initial work was inspired by a luxurious (but not consistently faithful) version of Palladio's *Four Books of Architecture* published by Giacomo Leoni in London in 1715. The dominant feature of Jefferson's design of the University of Virginia (1817–26; pl. 96), of which he was the major founder, was the porticoed library, called the Rotonda, based on Palladio's illustrations of the Pantheon as represented by Leoni. Jefferson visited Italy while he was ambassador to France but, like most other Palladianists, he never saw a building by Palladio.

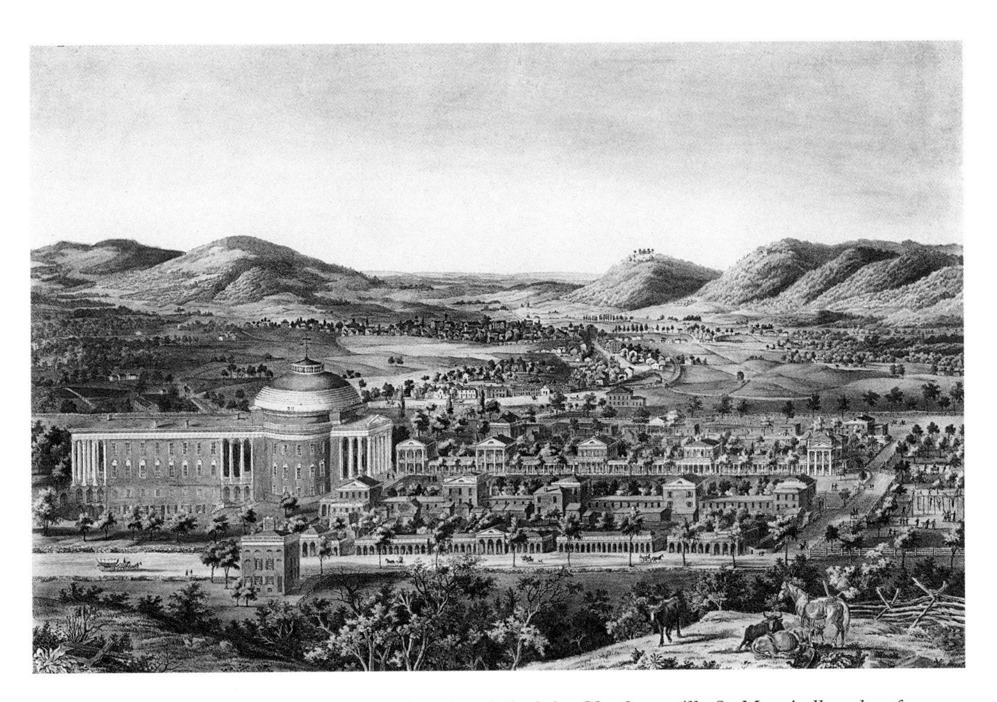

96 Thomas Jefferson, *View of the University of Virginia, Charlottesville & Monticello, taken from Lewis Mountain*, 1856

American architects, initially H. H. Richardson, Louis Sullivan and Frank Lloyd Wright, ultimately conceived versions of *magnificenza* more appropriate to a democracy, but at the same time the classical tradition was glorified in the Chicago World's Columbian Exhibition of 1893 and survived into the twentieth century. The City Hall of my birthplace, San Francisco (pl. 97), completed in 1915, only four years before I was born, perpetuates the message of autocratic power: the portico, the colossal order over a rusticated ground floor, and the cupola derived from St. Peter.

During the nineteenth century, classicism in architecture was sustained by a culture in which ancient Greece and Rome played a major role in higher education; but this is no longer the case. Yet it has enjoyed a resurrection prompted by a reaction against the harsher aspects of modernism and by clients' demands for buildings, especially domestic, that exhibit nostalgia for the magnificence and implications of superiority and grandeur of an earlier era.

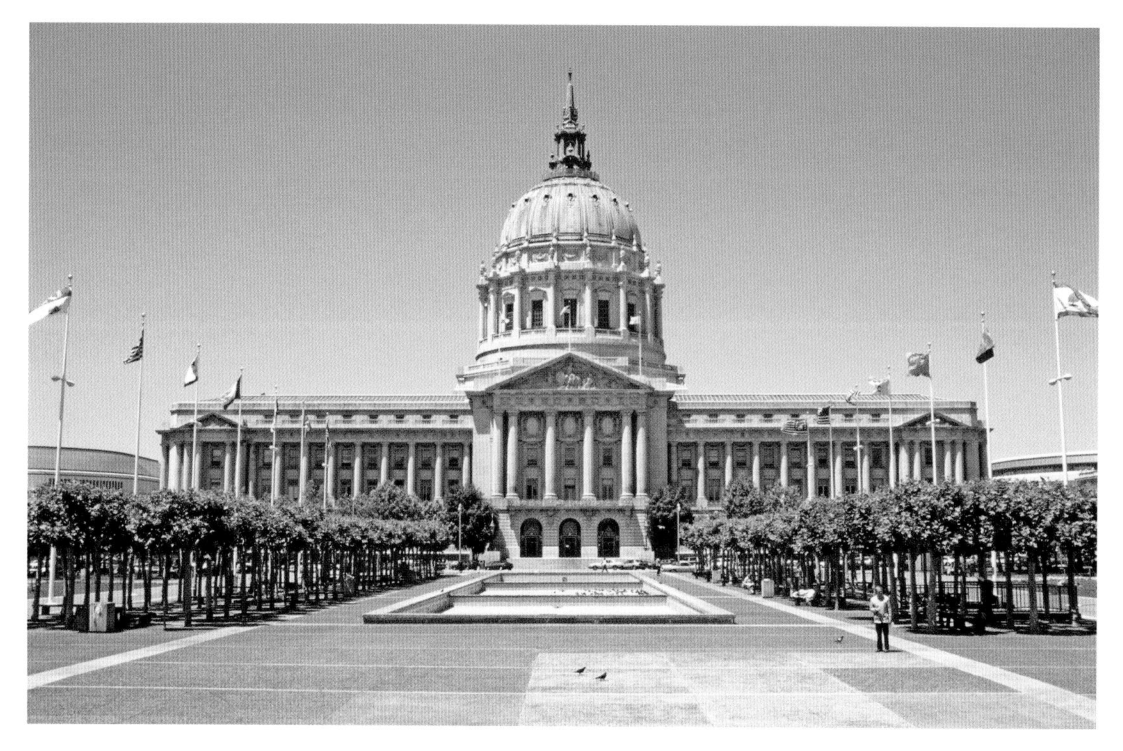

97 San Francisco City Hall

Today's most accomplished classicists, predominantly in the Palladian tradition, can design such elegant residences and public buildings as Allan Greenberg's Beechwoods in Greenwich, Connecticut, of 1992 (pl. 98) and Quinlan Terry's Abercrombie House in Kentucky of 1998 (pl. 99). But these works raise the question of whether it is the architect's responsibility to emulate the best of the past, despite its adherence to the symbols of predemocratic societies – or is it, as I believe, to seek expression for contemporary functions and ideals, as Palladio did?

The answer suggests an analogy to the conflict over the US Constitution within today's Federal judiciary between those who believe that the interpretation of that document must give priority to the views expressed by Jefferson and his contemporaries, and those who believe, again as I do, that its interpretation must incorporate the evolving ideals, needs, and even foibles of a far more diverse society than those of its distant antecedents.

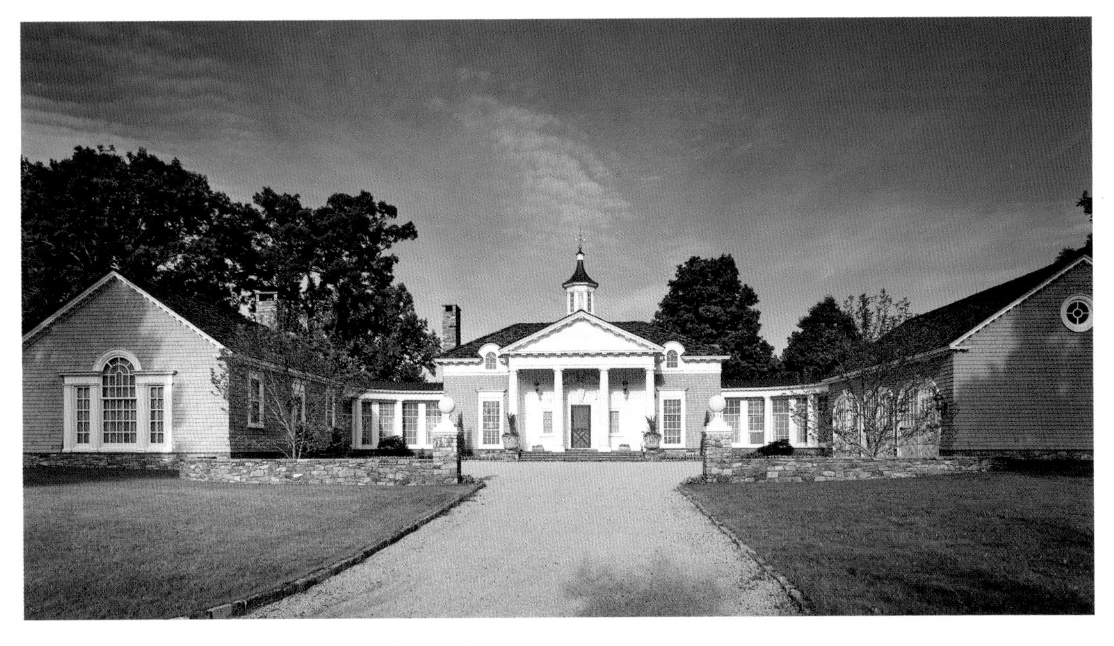

98 Beechwoods, Greenwich, Connecticut

99 Abercrombie House, Kentucky

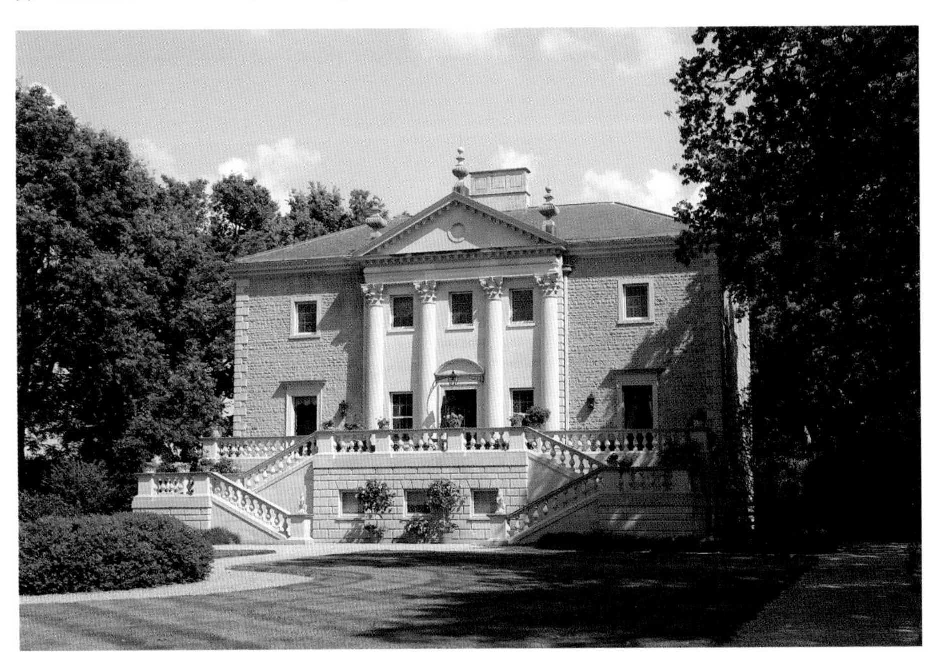

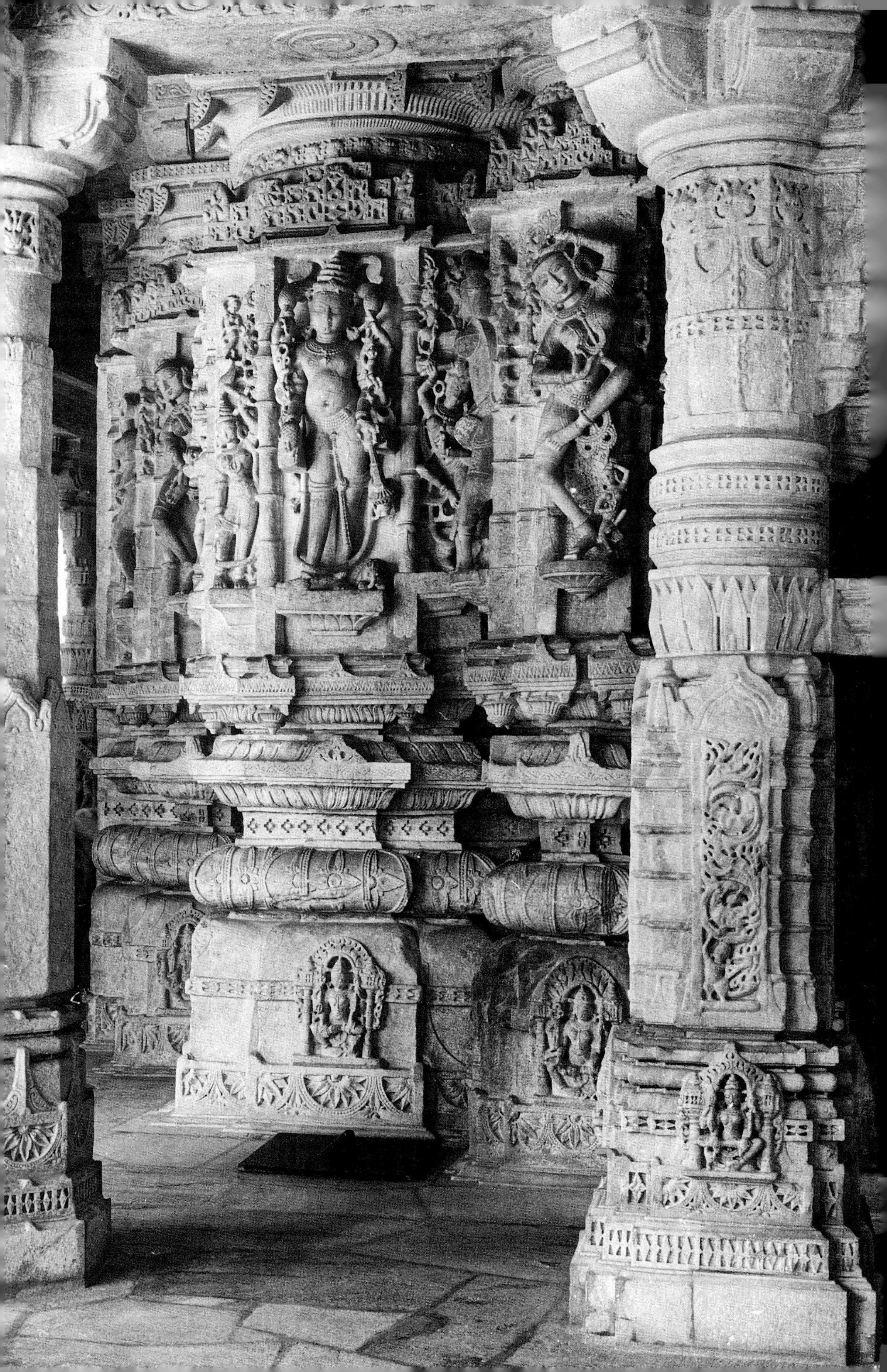

8

My Passage to India

IN 2006, SIXTEEN YEARS AFTER MY RETIREMENT, I went with my wife, Jill, to India for a tour of Rajasthan in the northwest. Soon after arrival, we visited three temples, and my perspective on western architecture was transformed. The interiors of these temples devote virtually every visible surface save their pavements to the stories of the deities and beings recorded in the mythic narratives of their sects. Every other architectural element – pier, column, lintel, ceiling slab, stele, saucer dome – is carved with symbols and with fantastic and realistic human or animal figures.

The Adinatha Temple of Ranakpur (1452 CE; pl. 100) is a major monument of the Jain faith (Jainism is an ancient ascetic faith with similarities to Buddhism, independent of Hinduism). The plan (pl. 101) is a blunted regular cruciform.

I was intrigued on entering, to be introduced, not to a great nave extending to the opposite end of the building as in mosques and Christian basilicas, but to an amplitude of connected spaces on slightly different levels, spaces uniquely imaginative in their varying sizes and structures, some open to the sky, some with fountains, and some with ancient trees growing out of the roof, many amply illuminated by clerestory elements.[1] Part of my delight in this interior was the sense of being enveloped in it rather than directed to a particular destination. This proliferation of intimate spaces is called for by Jain theology, which has no single deity; the worshiper's primary forms of practice are prayer

Detail of pl. 103

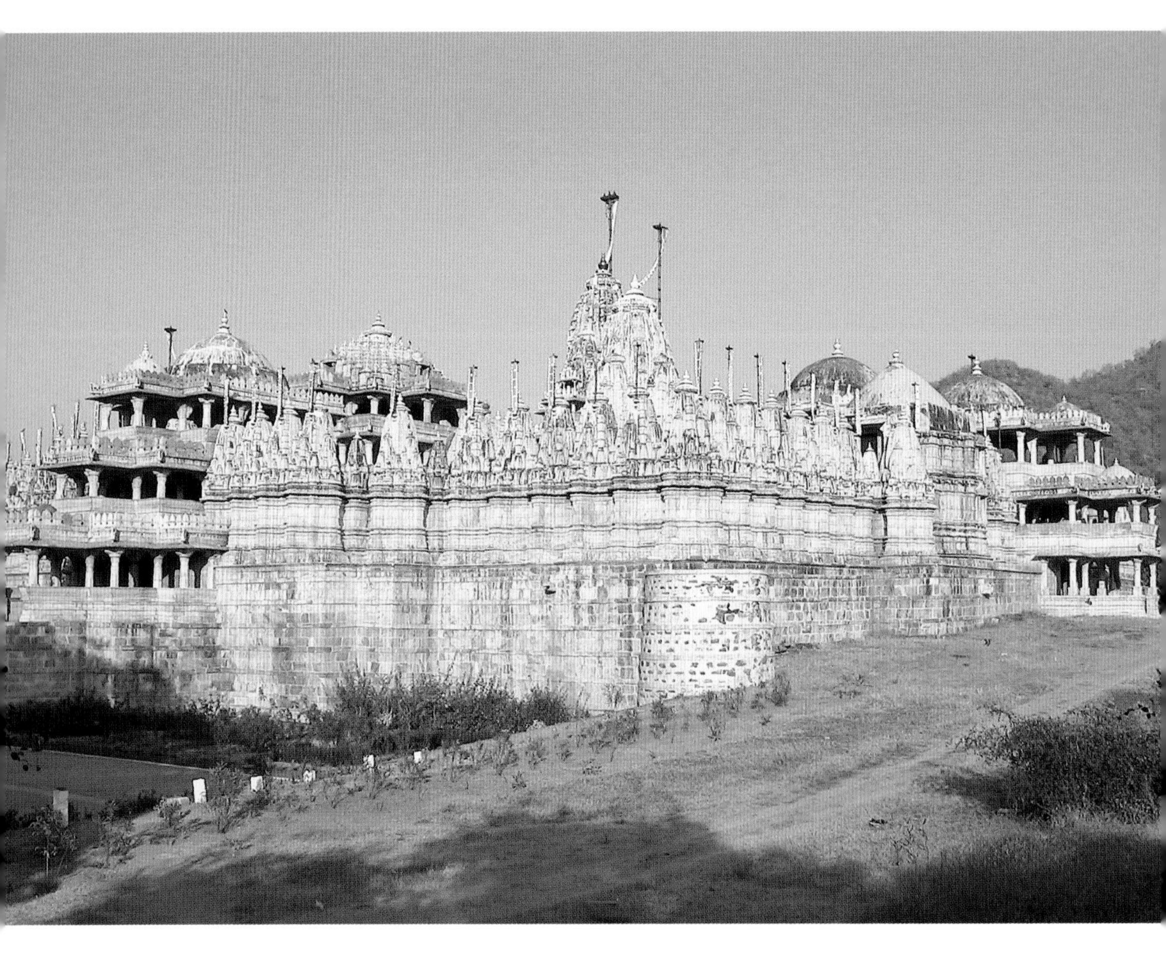

100 Adinatha temple of Ranakpur

and meditation in a space containing a statue of one of the twenty-four original teachers of the faith, the *tirthankara*. There are also countless lesser deities who, though living in heaven, are mortal and exhibit all the virtues and vices of humans, providing rich material for the sculptors' narratives.

Within the temple there are about 200 supporting columns and piers. These were carved by a very large team of artisans who, as in other castes of the society, had descended from centuries of practitioners of their crafts. The master builder, no doubt of a higher caste, would have determined the overall design, and architectural treatises would have dictated general prin-ciples such

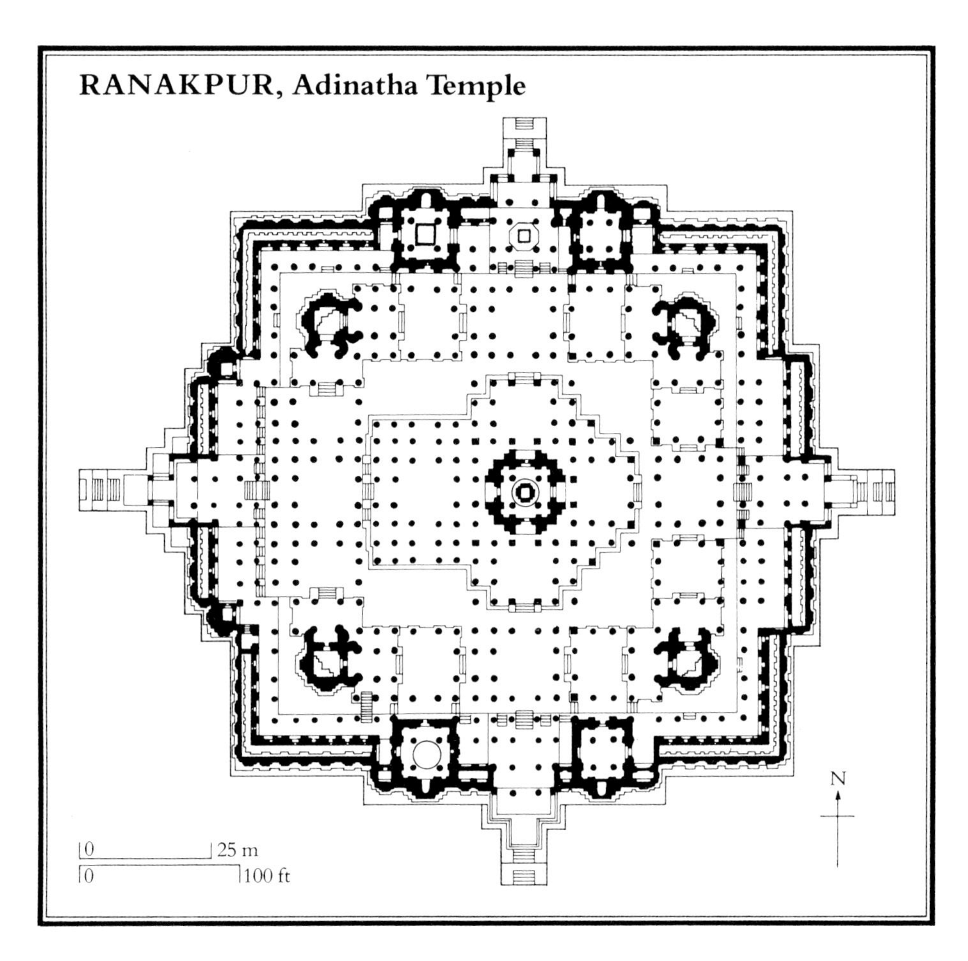

101 Temple of Ranakpur, plan

as the proportions of the supporting elements, along with roofing techniques, such as the forming of domes by corbeling.[2] The scale is particularly congenial; in contrast to western temple and church monuments, the courts and passages are small and intimate – open areas can contain only a few worshipers or visitors. Figural and symbolic reliefs are not high overhead as in the Parthenon and Chartres cathedral, but at one's own level, making it possible to experience each sculptor's individuality (pls. 102 and 103). An example of this detail used on the exterior is found at a neighboring temple (pl. 104). Most of the piers are a little over twice my height, and the figuration begins

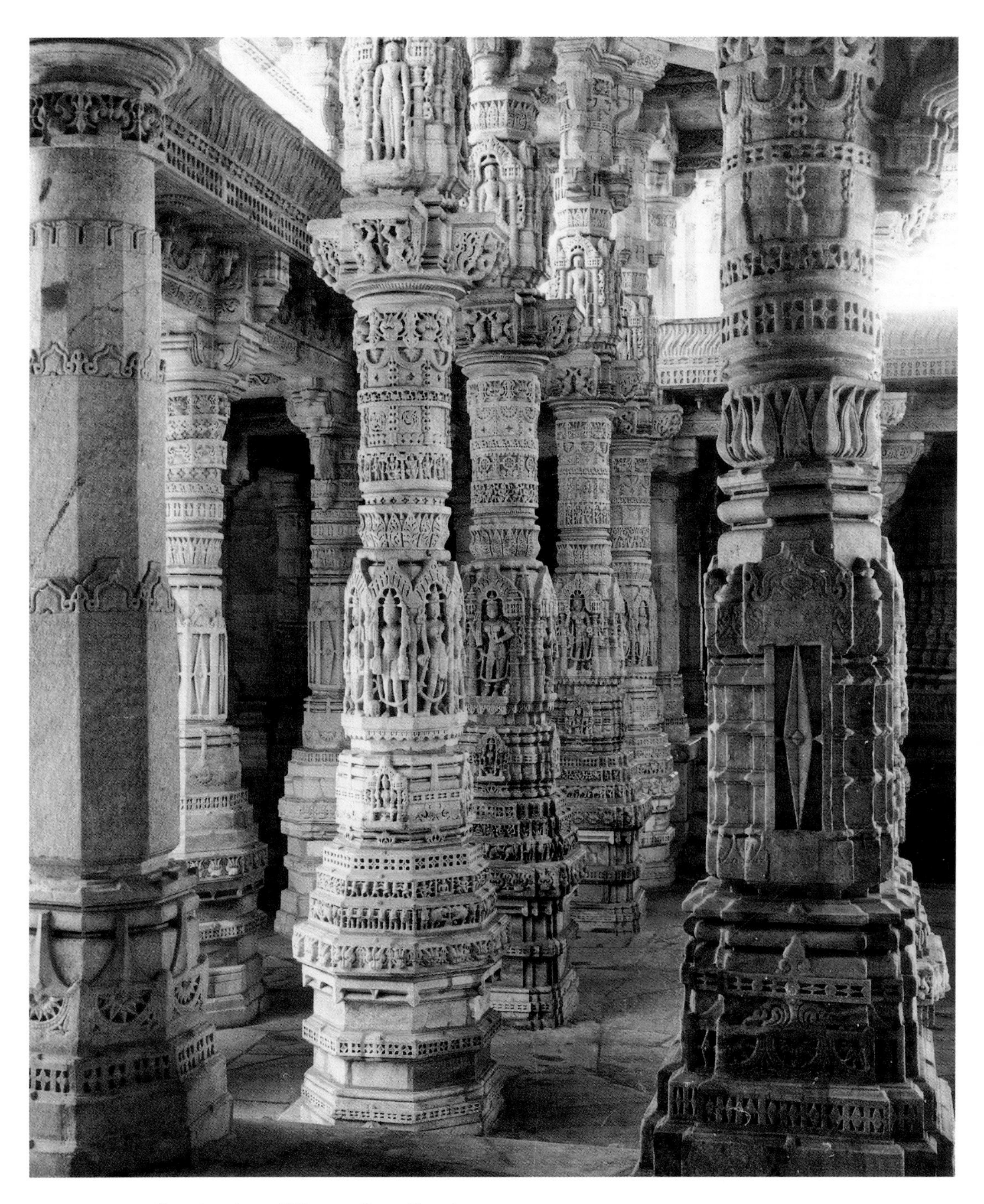

102 Interior view of Dharanvihara, Ranakpur

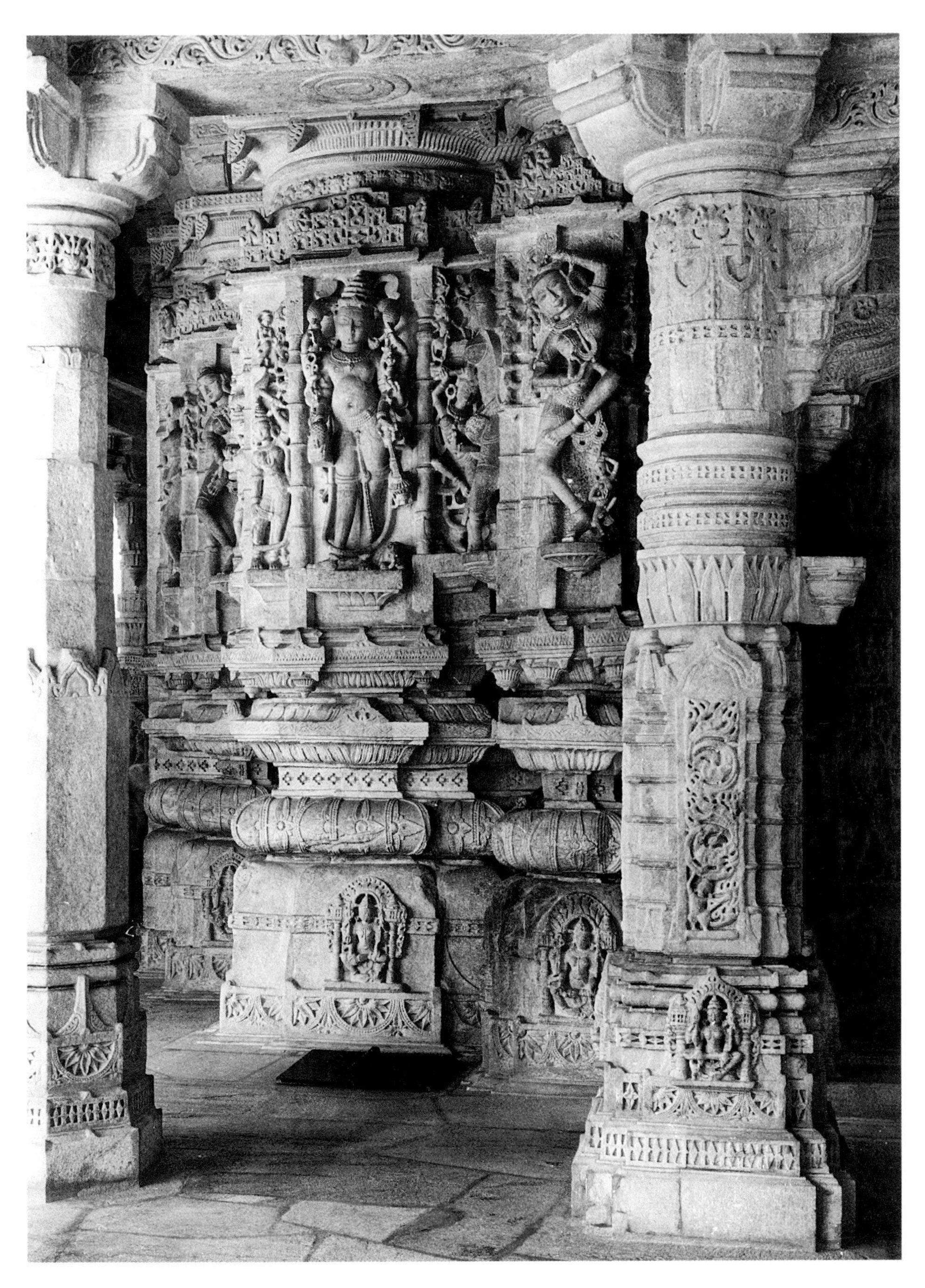

103 Interior view of Dharanvihara, Ranakpur

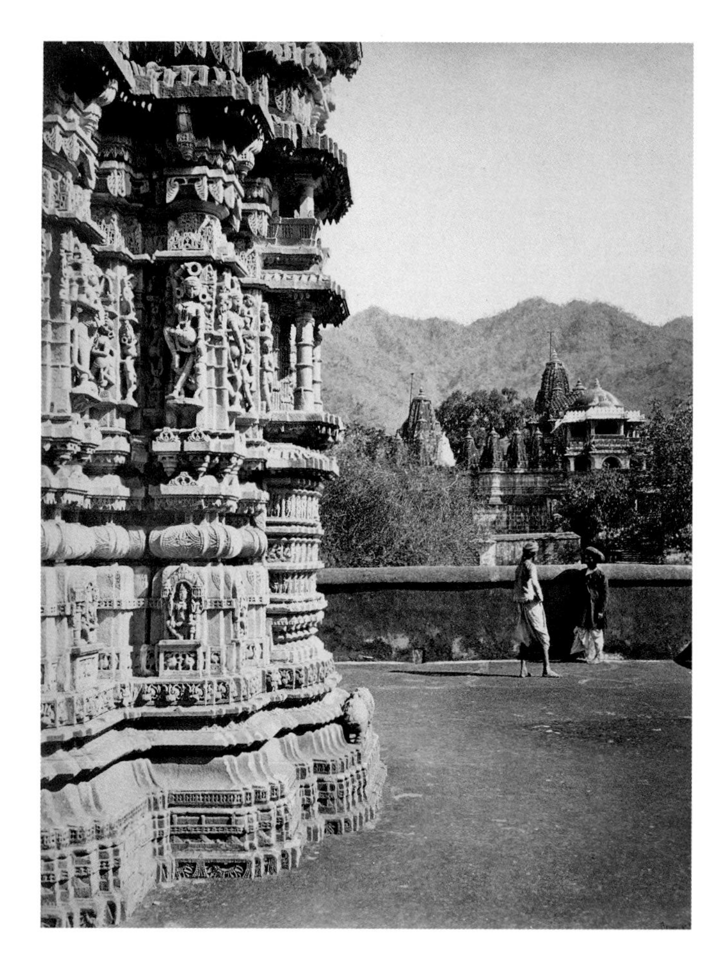

104 Jain temple, Ranakpur, 1872

105 (*facing page*) James Ackerman in the Jain temple at Ranakpur, India

immediately above the socle (base). In the center of a couple of the courts quasi-naturalistic freestanding elephants of roughly half life size – a major feature of Hindu as well as Jain temples – step forward on platforms (pl. 105).

I vividly recall one shrine, probably the repository of the temple's most sacred objects, a closed structure near the temple's center about the size of a family mausoleum in modern cemeteries. A large metal door framed by densely figured carvings provides the only entrance (see pl. 103). As in other Jain temples, there are no steps and instead a central socle, like those of neighboring columns, helps priests to enter. In front of it is a columnar porch with octagonal columns, in one bay of which is a broad stele with a peaked top like a gable (pl. 106) – I keep a photograph of it over my desk. Rectan-

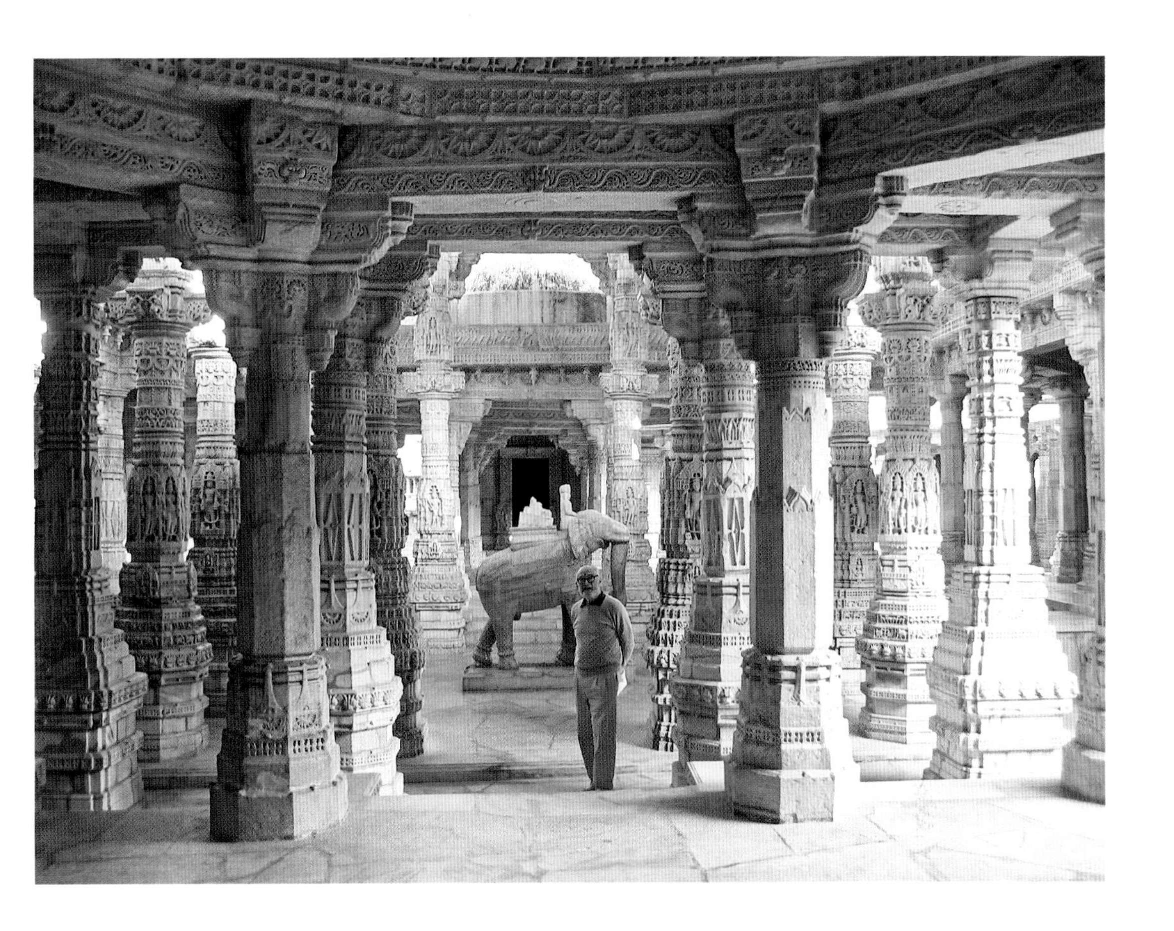

gular niches of varying sizes carved into the surface contain ritual objects, sages in meditative postures, deities, human and animal figures, and conic architectural shapes that may represent other temples (possibly the stele is a stone version of the painted maps depicting Jain sites). While order is imposed by the box grid, it is challenged by the size and proportion of the niches and by the asymmetry of the dominant horizontals and verticals. I find the figurative stone an embodiment of the vitality of every aspect of the building in its fusion of individual invention guided by established rules within a community with a common purpose.

This experience was somewhat like that of listening to the performance of a choral group, producing sound with many voices. The analogy occurred to me when I visited the artist Janet Cardiff's installation *The Forty Part Motet*

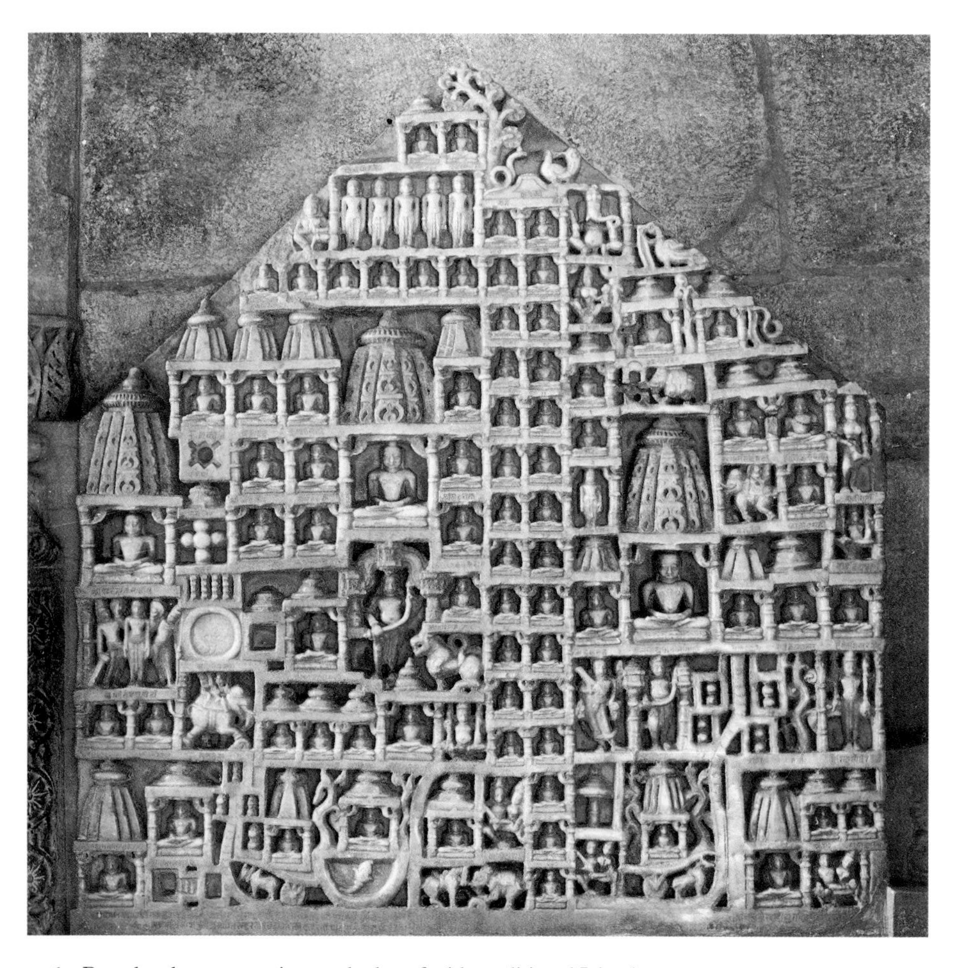

106 Broad stele representing peaked roof with traditional Jain shape

in 2004 at the Power Plant gallery in Toronto. Cardiff had recorded the performance of a Tallis motet by giving each of the forty members of the Salisbury Cathedral Choir a microphone capable of recording him in isolation from the others. In the installation, forty speakers were set around the periphery of a square hall to reproduce a performance far from Salisbury, a performance that, when I stood in the center, was more profound than any I had experienced in a live concert, since I was enveloped by the music, rather than getting it from one direction. Obviously, the choral performance does not have the same impact as the temple because it is wholly controlled by

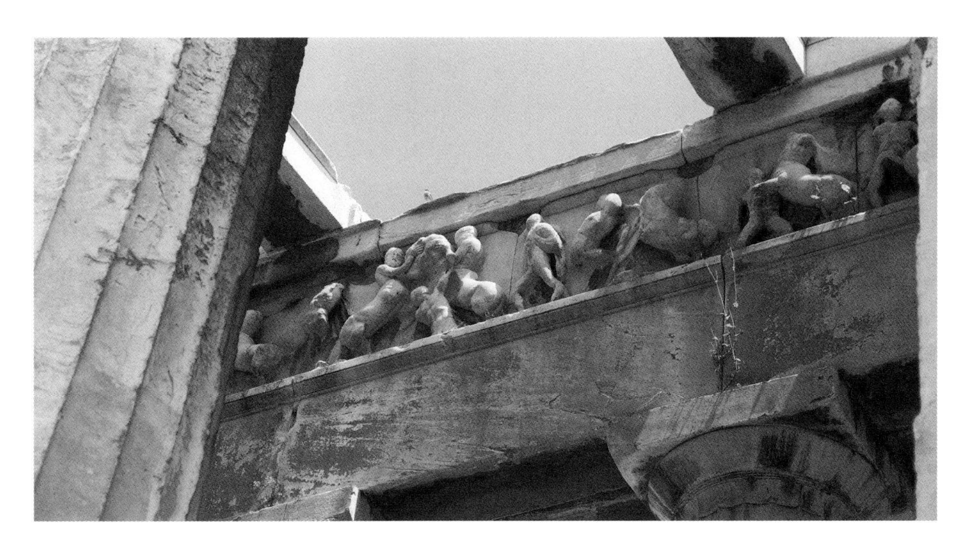

107 Detail of the Temple of Hephaestus / Theseion, Athens

the composer and modulated by the conductor, and is the product of a top-down hierarchy. That hierarchy has operated in various degrees throughout the history of western architecture.

The visit to Ranakpur led me to examine the limitations of my approach to architecture and, for the first time, the history of the role of narrative in religious architecture in the west. The telling of stories has also been a function of western architecture since antiquity. The Greeks portrayed their gods and their primeval battles in the pediments and friezes of temples (pl. 107); these were often colored, though it is still not known how and to what extent. The potential effectiveness of coloration can be grasped in the lively terracotta architectural reliefs of Etruscan artists. But since the Renaissance, the adherents to the classical tradition have preferred to think of and to emulate ancient buildings as being monochrome.

In Early Christian basilicas, narration moved inside (as in Santa Maria Maggiore in Rome, pl. 108). Architects assigned spaces above the nave arcades and in the apse for brilliantly colored mosaics of Bible stories and supernatural manifestations, such as the Epiphany of the Trinity, Christ and the Apostles, and the Last Judgment, a tradition preserved in Byzantine churches. The mosaic tradition continued into early Byzantine art but became more hierarchical and abstract (pl. 109), the figures being brought to the

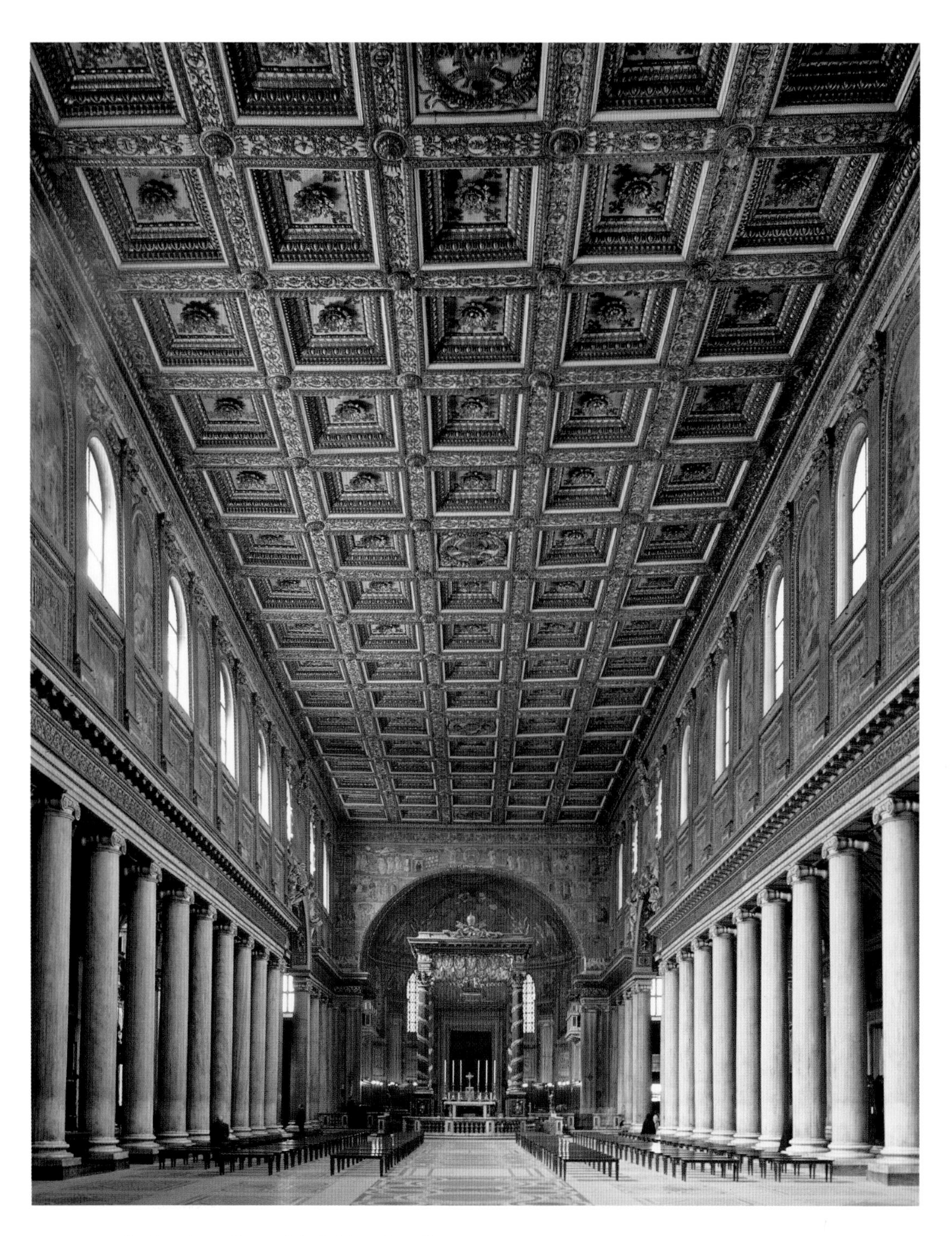

108 Interior of Santa Maria Maggiore, Rome

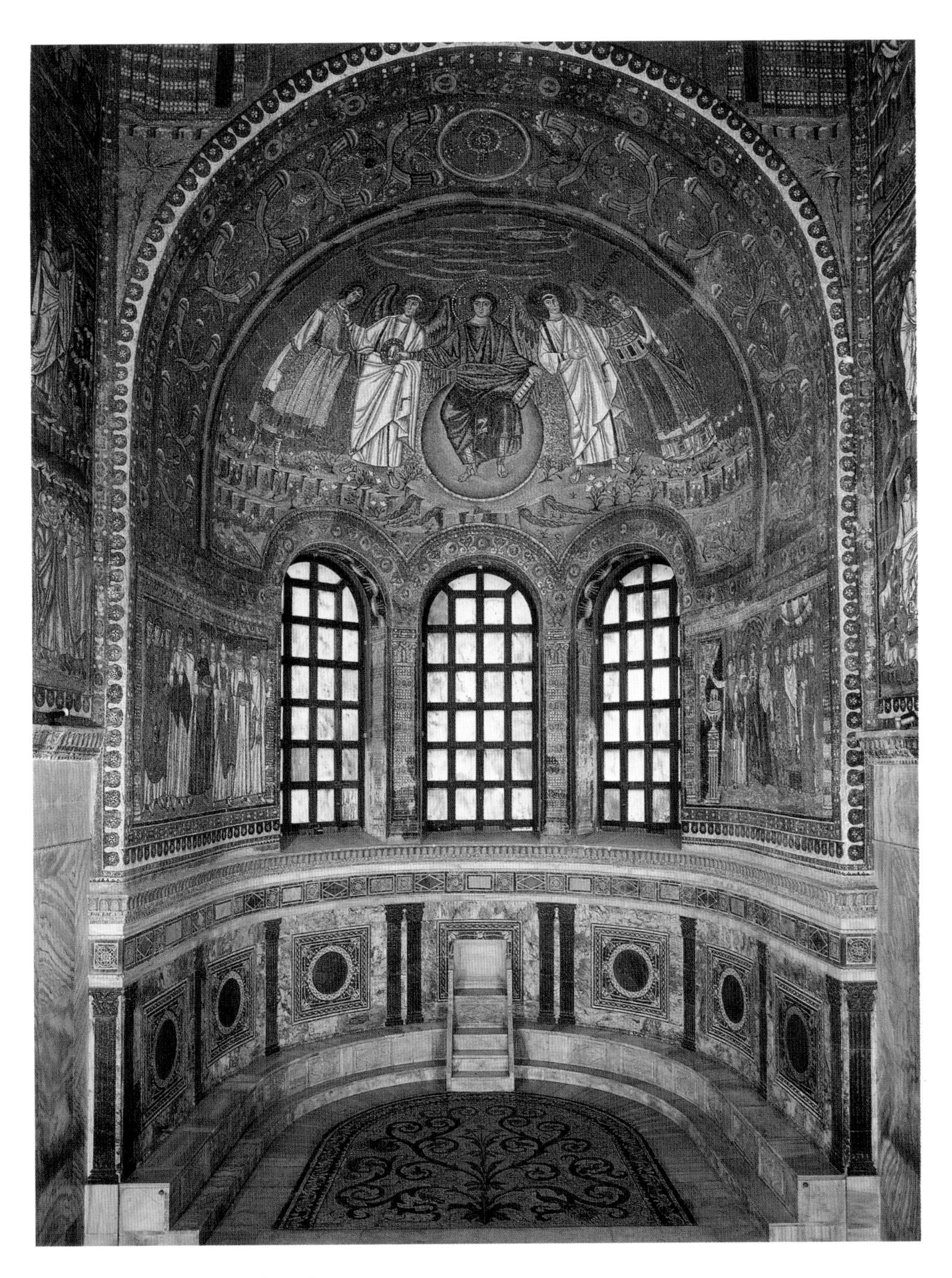

109 Interior of San Vitale, Ravenna

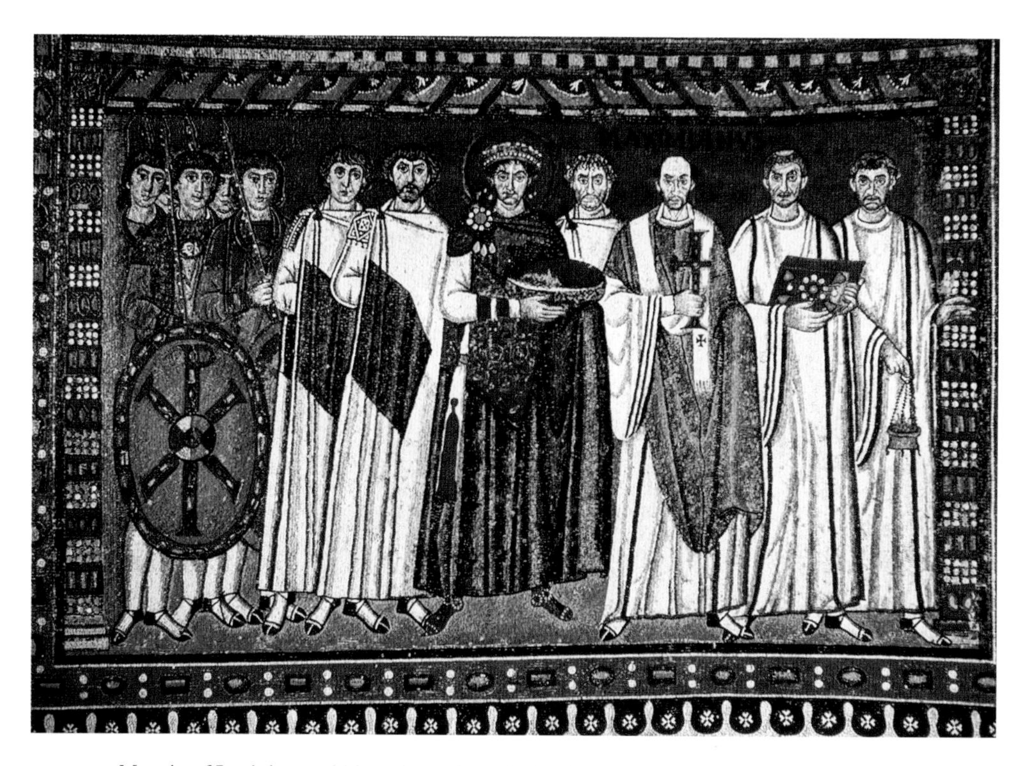

110 Mosaic of Justinian and his retinue, San Vitale, Ravenna

front plane and the backgrounds flattened. Portraits of imperial family members and court dignitaries were also depicted (pl. 110).

The Iconoclastic period in the Eastern Church in the eighth and ninth centuries sharply restricted imagery. Iconoclasm was a permanent rule in Muslim (pl. 111) and Jewish ecclesiastical architecture and in Protestant churches of the Reformation and after (pl. 112). Western Europe enjoyed a burst in church building in the Romanesque style during the eleventh century, when narrative in relief sculpture, employing the same material as the structural members, was restricted to portals and their flanking embrasures (pls. 113 and 114) and to the capitals of columns or piers supporting the arches and shafts of the nave and side aisles (pl. 115). This is in contrast to the Jain and Hindu temple, where narrative and structure are fused, and every surface is devoted to storytelling. In neither case, I suppose, did the architect know precisely what the story would be.

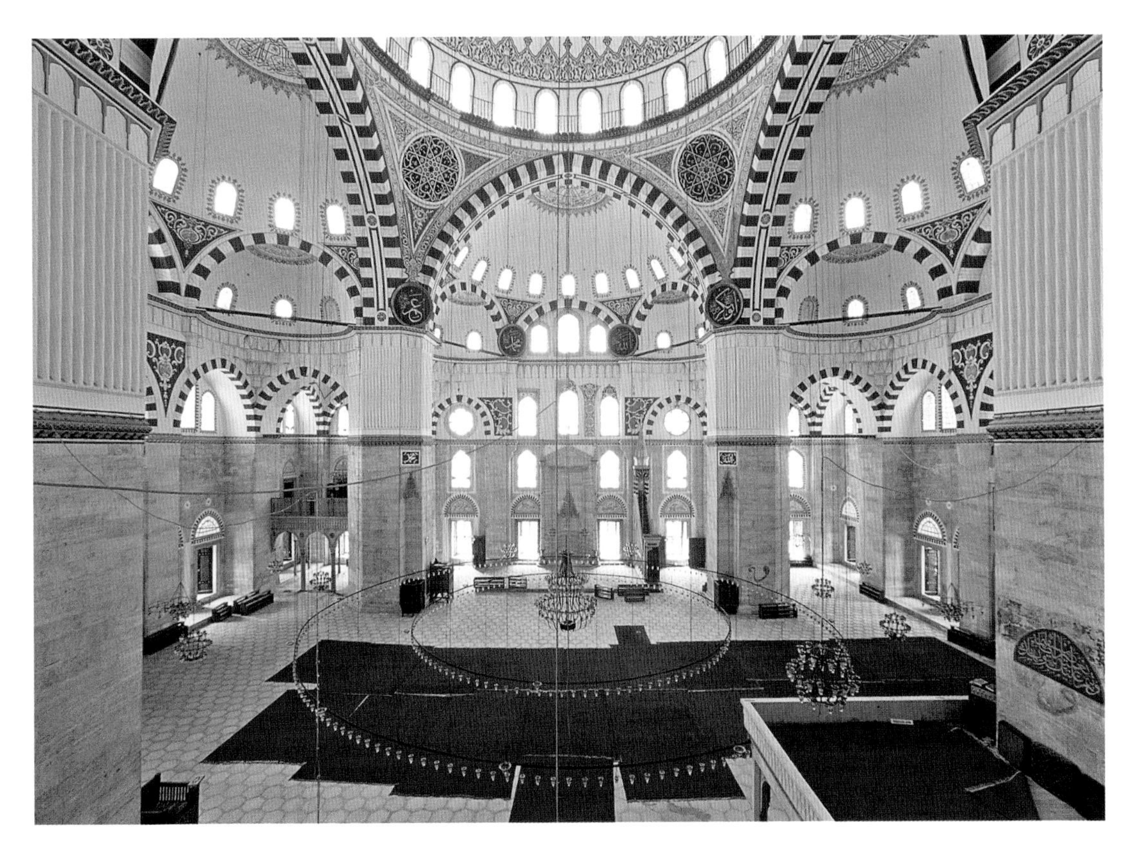

111 Interior of the Sehzade Mehmet mosque, Istanbul

The hierarchal interpretation of the Bible that characterized Byzantine figuration changed into a more socio-political one in Romanesque and Gothic architecture, when the development of urban life led to a great expansion of church building. The favorite Romanesque themes in the portal tympana of churches included the *Majesty of Christ*, in which Christ appears crowned and seated on a throne like contemporary kings and emperors, and the Last Judgment, depicted as a terrifying event in a court of justice admitting no appeal. Other awesome subjects were chosen for the nave and cloister capitals. The Gothic church added narratives in colored stained glass to the repertory, and frescos by the close of the Middle Ages. The divorce of narration from western structure was sealed in the beginning of the fifteenth century, at the origins of the classical Renaissance.

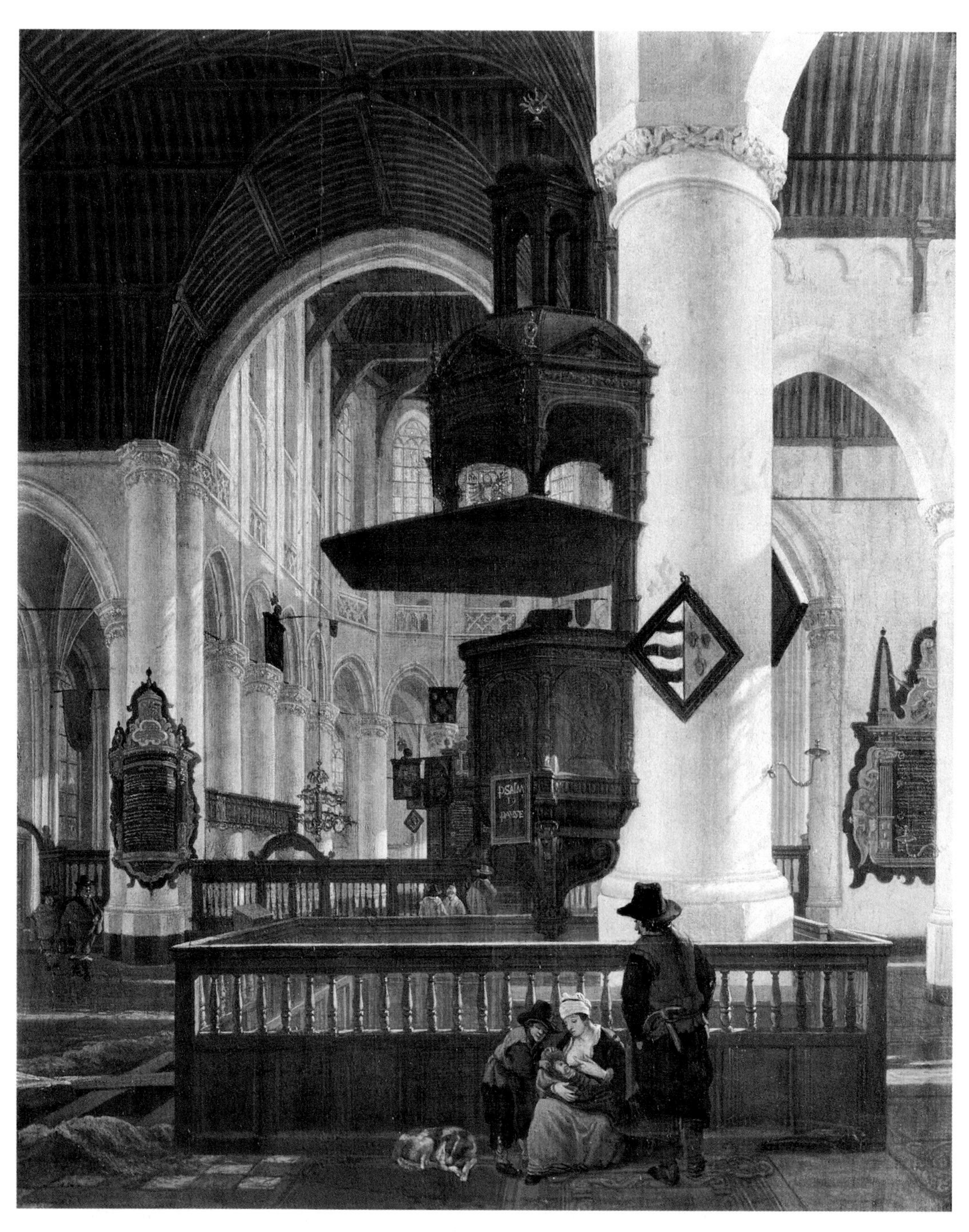

112 Gerard Houckgeest, *Interior of a Church*, c.1650s

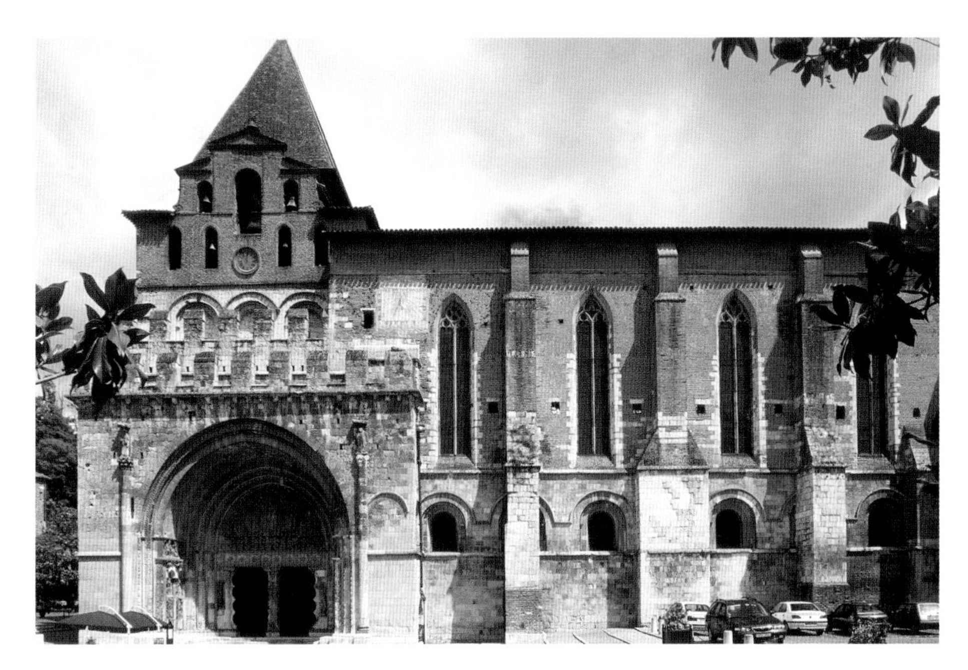

113 Saint Pierre, Tarn-et-Garonne

114 South portal tympanum, Saint Pierre, Tarn-et-Garonne

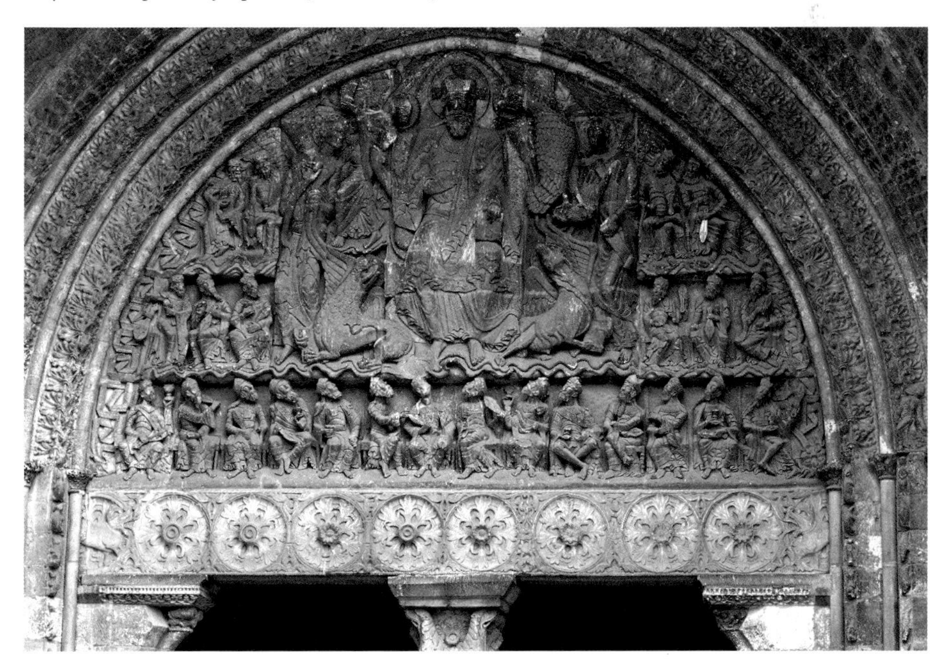

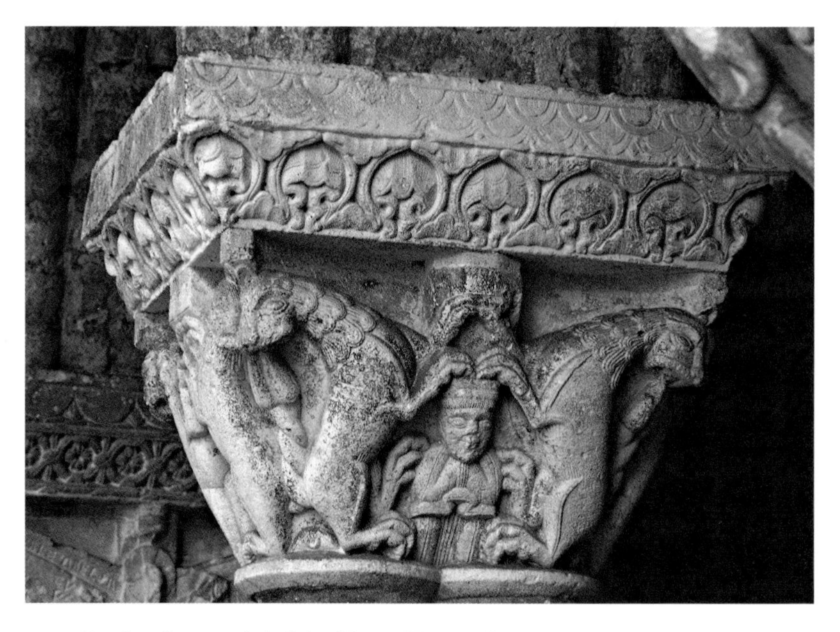

115 South gallery capital, Saint Pierre, Tarn-et-Garonne

This dominance over the worshiper was reversed in the culture of Renaissance humanist thought. The Last Judgment was still represented as horrific, but images of Christ evolved. The harsh monarch became the compassionate healer, often to the point of being feminized, and the Virgin frequently replaced him in the altarpieces of chapels and high altars.

At the end of the fourteenth century the relationship of the master builder to the craftsman was evolving toward the Renaissance elevation of the role of the former and the diminution of the latter. The phenomenon is documented in the archives of Milan cathedral of around 1390 (the subject of my first published article).[3] The project of the guild of Comacene masons sparked criticism of its structural stability, and this led the Visconti duke to invite a number of celebrated Gothic masters from northern Europe to give their opinions. They were firmly negative, but nonetheless the Comacene project continued to rise and the cathedral still stands.

In the late Middle Ages, wall frescos extended the territory of narrative, but representation in western architecture still was confined to those spaces provided in the architect's or builder's plan.

The exclusion of narration from the structural core of western church architecture was realized by the beginning of the fifteenth century in Italy. The cultural manifestation that is called Humanism brought about a *rinascenza* of classical art, science, and literature (the term "Renaissance" was not used until the early nineteenth century). Humanists worked feverishly to bring to light the surviving relics of the ancient world, especially the manuscripts preserved and mostly untouched for centuries in monastic libraries (an enterprise vividly depicted in Stephen Greenblatt's recent book, *The Swerve*, 2011). Among these was the sole treatise on architecture to survive from antiquity, written by the Roman architect Vitruvius, active in the first century BCE, which exerted a huge influence on architects of ensuing centuries.

Humanists sought to elevate the status of practitioners of the arts. In the case of architecture, this implied the control of every element of a structure.[4] Establishing an auteur dominance modeled on that in literature, it was no more acceptable for changes to be made in the project of an architect than it would be for anyone but the author to alter the text of a poem. In the preface of his astonishingly encyclopedic treatise on architecture, *De re aedificatoria*, completed in 1452, Leon Battista Alberti (1404–1472) explicitly denies craftsmen the license for independent invention:

> But, before going further, I believe it would be useful to clarify what I believe we should understand to be an architect. . . . I would not consider a carpenter [Alberti, whose buildings were of brick and stone, must have used the words "*Tignarius*" and "*Fabri*" to stand for "craftsman"] comparable to the most qualified practitioners of other disciplines: the work of the carpenter indeed is only instrumental with respect to that of the architect . . .

This dictum, which became fixed in the early Renaissance, blinded architects committed to a classical revival to what little had survived of narrative sculpture on Roman temples.

Moreover, the fourteenth-century importation from Asia of the technology of paper-making enabled architects to use drawings to fix every detail of a design – the plan, elevation, and section and even the profiles of moldings or the curvature of the volutes of an Ionic or Composite capital. Only a few of the many thousands of drawings of ancient temples represent the reliefs that survived in the friezes and pediments.

Besides the *De re aedificatoria*, Alberti wrote an influential treatise on painting in which he codified the invention, shared with his contemporary Filippo Brunelleschi, of one-point linear perspective. The construction favored the choice of rectangular surfaces; Alberti likened a painting to a window through which one could see the events or objects beyond. As a window it called for a frame, which in his time ceased to be constructed by the painter as integral to the work. This made painting independent of its setting, though it could be accommodated in churches as an altarpiece, and it became movable – in churches from one chapel to another, or even to a different church. The tapestries depicting the *Life of Christ* designed by Raphael for the Sistine Chapel in the Vatican have been removed to the safety of the Vatican Museum.

Some Baroque painters eventually achieved a bit of revenge on the dominance of architecture by devising frescoes that appear to demolish nave vaults and domes by giving the illusion of opening to a sunlit heaven and its divine occupants who sit on or float around clouds (Andrea Pozzo and Giovanni Battista Gaulli, in the seventeenth-century Jesuit Roman churches of Sant'Ignazio and the Gesù, Giovanni Battista Tiepolo in the eighteenth-century Santa Maria del Rosario in Venice, pl. 116).

When I first planned this essay I called it "Architecture Hot and Cold," to characterize the contrast of religious interior space in India and the west. But my focus soon changed to investigating the evolution of western narrative solutions and of the gradual restriction of the role of the craftsman. That title also called attention to the differing approaches of Indian and western historians. The former favor descriptions and interpretations of carved narratives, focusing on their responses to the exuberance and mastery of the craftsmen rather than the contribution of the architect.

In the twentieth century church interiors became an opportunity for architects to celebrate their own imaginations. Of his early work, including the Unitarian Unity Temple in Oak Park, Illinois (1905; pl. 117), Frank Lloyd Wright wrote:

> There is a certain aesthetic joy in letting the thing alone which has for centuries been tortured, distorted, and dickered with in the name of Art, letting its native dignity show forth once more. I confess to a love for the clean arris; the cube I find comforting; the sphere, inspiring.

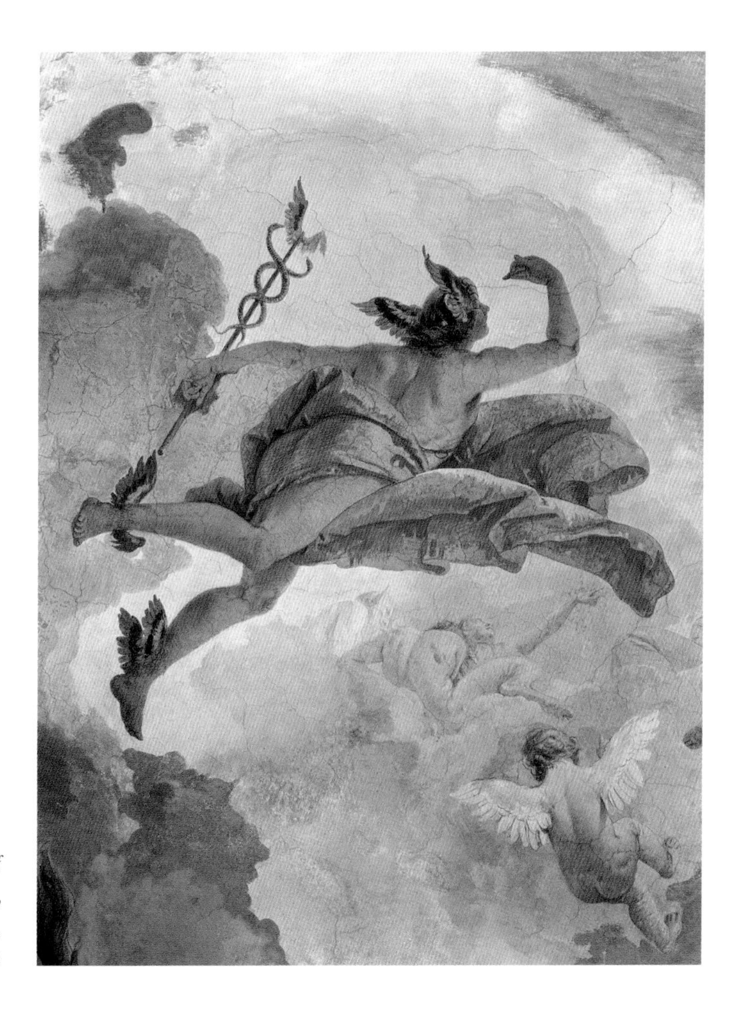

116 Tiepolo, *The Course of the Chariot of the Sun,* detail showing Mercury, 1726

In the chapel of Notre Dame du Haut at Ronchamp (1950–54; pl. 118), Le Corbusier created sculpted curvilinear walls that open to the exterior through many small rectangular windows of varied sizes. In the place of narrative he sought a sublimity of his own invention

Western architectural historians, myself included, have devoted most of our studies to monographs on individual architects or buildings, focusing on the development of particular styles of architects and periods, as Alberti would have approved – seven centuries of Pritzger prizewinners, so to speak!

The title "My Passage to India" pays homage to E. M. Forster's novel *A Passage to India* (1924). Two of the characters, Aziz, a young Indian physi-

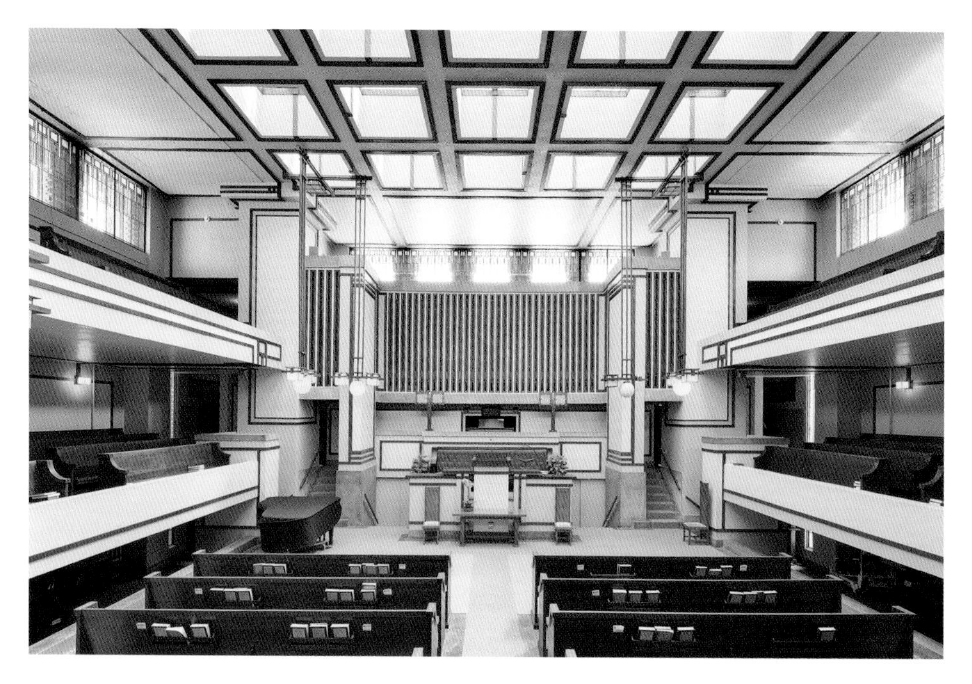

117 Interior of the Unitarian Unity Temple, Oak Park, Illinois

118 Interior of Notre-Dame du Haut, Ronchamp

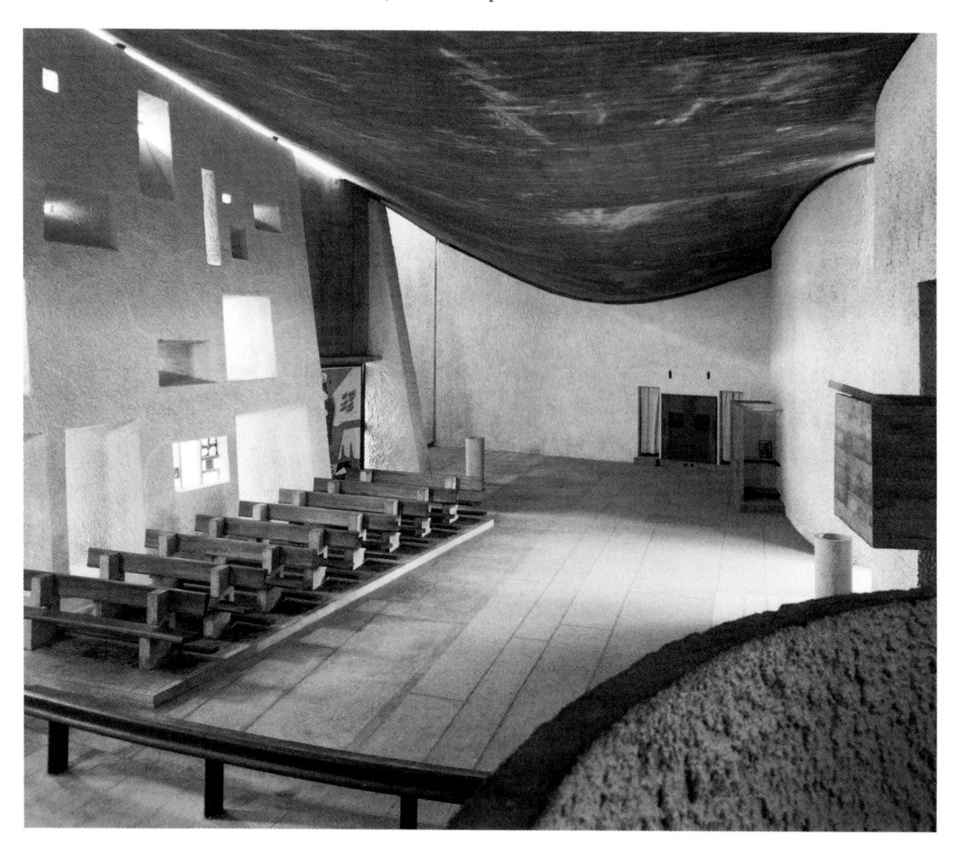

cian, and Fielding, a British teacher, acknowledge the great cultural and political divide that prevents them from becoming true friends. My experience of sacred architecture in India led me to an awareness of the nature of the divide between eastern and western architecture that I had not considered before. "Hot and Cold" was my immediate response to contrasts, but "My Passage" became a more measured study of how some of those contrasts evolved.

NOTES

1 For a three-dimensional tour of the interior of the temple, see http://www.360cities.net/image/ranakpur-temple-with-stone-elephant#733.03,-90.00,70.0 (accessed September 2015).

2 A corbeled dome is one in which the curvature is achieved by laying horizontal slabs, each of which is laid slightly more toward the center than the one below to form a uniform curve from base to apex. I do not know if the figures and symbols were carved before or after installation.

3 James S. Ackerman, "*Ars Sine Scientia Nihil Est*: Gothic Theory of Architecture at the Cathedral of Milan," *Art Bulletin*, 31 (1949), pp. 84–111.

4 A major account of this change is Marvin Trachtenberg's *Building-in-Time: From Giotto to Alberti and Modern Oblivion*, New Haven and London, 2010.